The economics of
the financial system

JB

The economics of
the financial system

A. D. Bain

BLACKWELL
Oxford UK & Cambridge USA

First published 1981 by Martin Robertson & Company Ltd

Reprinted 1983, 1988 and 1991 by Basil Blackwell Ltd.

Second edition published 1992

Basil Blackwell Ltd
108 Cowley Road,
Oxford, OX4 1JF,
UK

Three Cambridge Center
Cambridge, Massachusetts 02142,
USA

British Library Cataloguing in Publication Data

A CIP catalogue record for this book is available from the British Library.

Library of Congress Cataloging-in-Publication Data
Bain, A. D. (Andrew David)
The economics of the Financial System / A. D. Bain. – 2nd ed.
p.   cm.
Includes bibliographical references and index.
ISBN 0–631–18196–2 (alk. paper). – ISBN 0–631–18197–0 (pbk. :
alk. paper)
1. Finance – Great Britain.   I. Title.
HG186.G7B28   1991
332'.0941–dc20   91–42972 CIP

Typeset in 11 on 12pt Times
by Hope Services Ltd., (Abingdon) Oxon
Printed in Great Britain by T. J. Press Ltd., Padstow, Cornwall

This book is printed on acid-free paper

Contents

List of tables   vii
Preface to the Second Edition   xi
Preface to the First Edition   xv
Part I   Introduction   1
 1   The financial system   3
 2   Finance in Britain   16
Part II   Theory of the financial system   35
 3   Mobilizing saving   37
 4   Asset transformation   51
 5   Interest rates   72
 6   Interest rates: further development   87
Part III   The users of the system   103
 7   Personal saving and investment   105
 8   Company financial behaviour   124
 9   Public sector investment and financing   152
10   The overseas sector and the UK financial system   170
Part IV   Financial institutions and markets   177
11   Banks and building societies   179
12   Investing institutions   203
13   Specialized financial institutions   227
14   Financial markets   239
Part V   The control and efficiency of the system   267
15   Regulation and control   269
16   The efficiency of the financial system   286
Select bibliography and further reading   307
Index   310

Tables

2.1 Banks and building societies: domestic sterling deposits and lending, end-1989   18

2.2 Investing institutions: assets, end-1989   19

2.3 Sterling securities and money markets, end-1990   20

2.4 Saving and investment in the UK, 1978–89   21

2.5 Saving in major industrial countries, 1980–89   22

2.6 Saving and investment by sector, 1978–89   23

2.7 Sectoral financial surpluses and deficits in the UK, 1978–89   26

2.8 Saving, investment and transactions in financial assets and liabilities   28

2.9 Flows of funds, 1985–89   29

4.1 Loan losses where $p = 0.01$ 55

7.1 Balance sheet of the personal sector, end-1989   107

7.2 Personal sector balance sheet trends, 1979–89   108

7.3 Personal saving as a percentage of personal disposable income, 1970–89   111

7.4 Personal sector liquid assets as a percentage of personal disposable income, 1979–89   114

7.5 Sources and uses of funds of the personal sector, 1985–89   121

8.1 Balance sheet of the industrial and commercial companies sector, 1987 and 1989 (end-years)   125

8.2   The effect of primary gearing on the equity return   130
       ($i = 10$ per cent)

8.3   Primary gearing and income gearing: the effects of   130
       varying the rate of interest ($p = 15$ per cent)

8.4   The effect of primary gearing on the equity return   131
       when profits (p) fall from 15 to 5 per cent and the
       cost of borrowing (i) rises from 10 to 15 per cent

8.5   Sources and uses of funds of industrial and   141
       commercial companies, 1958–89

9.1   Balance sheet of the public sector, 1987 and 1989   155
       (end-years)

9.2   Public sector debt to GDP ratio   156

9.3   Capital spending and borrowing by local authorities,   157
       1978–89

9.4   Capital spending and borrowing by public   159
       corporations, 1978–89

9.5   Capital spending and borrowing by the central   161
       government, 1978–89

9.6   Financing of the central government borrowing   163
       requirement, 1985–89

9.7   Public sector borrowing, 1978–89   165

9.8   General government financial deficit, 1958–89   166

10.1   Financial transactions with other countries, 1978–89   171

11.1   Sector distribution of bank and building society   191
       deposits and lending, end-1989

11.2   Banks in the UK: sterling assets and liabilities,   193
       December 1989

11.3   Bank sterling lending to UK residents, November   195
       1989

11.4   Banks and building societies: balance sheets,   196
       end-1989

11.5   Building societies: selected liabilities, level end-1989   199
       and increase 1985–89

11.6   Building societies: commercial assets, level end-1989   200
       and increase 1985–89

12.1 Investing institutions: assets and net inflows, 1989   204

12.2 Life assurance and pension funds: composition of   211
asset portfolios, end-1989

12.3 Life assurance and pension funds: investment,   213
1985–89

12.4 Saving through life assurance and pension funds,   218
1980–89

12.5 General insurance funds: assets, end-1989 and   220
investment, 1985–89

13.1 Leasing and non-leasing business, 1989   230

13.2 Finance houses: personal lending, 1990   231

14.1 Capital issues by UK companies, 1989   243

14.2 Securities listed on the ISE, end-1990   245

14.3 Turnover on the ISE, 1990   245

14.4 Capital issues of listed securities in the UK, 1989   249

14.5 Money-market instruments, September 1990   257

14.6 Discount houses: balance sheets, end-1989   259

Preface to the second edition

For the British financial system the 1980s were a decade of change and development. In 1981, when the first edition of this book was written, the financial institutions knew their business, and by and large they kept to it. The banks did not compete for mortgage business – that was the preserve of the building societies. Building societies relied on retail deposits, leaving the wholesale deposit markets to the banks. Life assurance companies sold insurance with a savings element, not retail savings products with a dash of insurance. Stockbrokers were independent partnerships carrying on business as agents, not well-capitalized market-making subsidiaries of major financial businesses.

Now all this has changed, and the boundaries have become blurred under the pressures of competition and technological development. Competition has come from all sides – domestic and international, spontaneous from within the industries and external, fostered by competition policy and deregulation. The new system has required a new legislative framework – for banks, for building societies, and above all, in the form of the Financial Services Act, for financial services businesses generally.

The 1980s were also a decade of increasing international economic and financial integration, enhancing the influence of international factors on domestic financial behaviour. Large firms now raise their funds in the international capital markets, and international capital flows have a dominant influence on exchange rates and equity yields – the stock market crash of October 1987 was a worldwide phenomenon. In 1981, when analysing financial conditions in the UK, it still (just) made sense to focus on domestic factors whilst noting the importance also of international influences. Ten years later it has to be international conditions which form the core of the analysis, with UK domestic factors explaining local deviations.

The consequence is that very little of the institutional material in the first edition has survived. But the object remains the same: to enable students to understand the forces governing financial behaviour and, within that context, to learn how the British financial system works. The book aims to complement courses on macro and monetary economics, the intention being that it should be intelligible to higher education students with only one year of economics behind them.

The structure of the book is still based upon the flow-of-funds table, which shows in a consistent form the interrelationships between the sectors, institutions and markets. It also provides a guide at the outset to what is relatively important – which are the *big* numbers? – and what is not. The flow of funds is introduced in Part I, along with a thumbnail sketch of the economic context of the eighties and a brief description of the financial institutions and markets in the UK.

Part II deals with the theory of financial systems and is the most technical part of the book. Readers who are prepared to take on trust the important part played by financial institutions and markets in mobilizing saving and stimulating productive investment may choose to skip the indifference curve analysis in chapter 3. Chapter 4 deals with asset transformation, and chapter 5 brings together monetary and real factors in a loanable funds version of interest rate theory. A clear distinction is now drawn between the yield on long-term assets, which is determined in the markets, and short-term interest rates, on which the monetary authorities have more say. The theory is developed further and put in an international context in chapter 6. Students with only the minimum formal training in economics may find this chapter difficult. My reason for including it is that, while the relationships between international yields on equity, bond yields, short-term interest rates, inflation and exchange rate regimes genuinely are complex, they need to be understood by anyone working with financial matters in business, or even simply managing their own money.

Part III is concerned with the users of the financial system, taking the personal, company, public and overseas sectors in turn in chapters 7–10. The principles governing financial decisions in each sector are discussed first, after which the actual behaviour in the UK is examined. As the financial flows at the end of the 1980s were by no means typical and cannot be expected to persist – the personal and company sectors had financial deficits, the public sector a surplus, and there was an unsustainable deficit in the balance of payments – more attention has been given to medium-term levels and trends than to the precise conditions at that time.

The financial institutions and markets are dealt with in Part IV. In discussing banks and building societies in chapter 11, I have stressed capital rather than liquidity as a constraint on behaviour – it was excess capital which led to the credit boom in the second half of the eighties and a shortage of capital which threatened to cause a credit crunch subsequently. The common feature of the investing institutions in chapter 12 is their involvement in fund management, with all its implications for the securities markets, but their main importance in the saving/investment process now derives from pension and home mortgage business. These are very dependent on the current arrangements for pension provision in Britain and on the tax treatment of mortgage interest respectively. Leasing and venture capital companies are prominent amongst the specialized financial institutions in chapter 13, and the markets discussed in chapter 14 now include the international securities, foreign exchange and financial derivatives markets as well as the domestic securities and sterling money markets treated previously.

Chapters 15 and 16 in Part V deal with regulation and control and the efficiency of the financial system respectively. Issues connected with deposit insurance and the marketing of retail savings products are considered in the former, while the latter includes a section on the system of corporate governance in the UK as a possible source of weakness in the financial system.

I am indebted to my former colleagues in Midland Bank, who taught me so much about many of the issues touched on in the book, and to Dr Stephen Diacon of the University of Nottingham for helping to bring me up to date on the insurance industry. My greatest debt, however, is to my wife, who has not only put up with my preoccupation with the book during the last year, but also advised on word processing and produced the final copy herself. None is responsible for the views expressed – the prejudices displayed and any remaining errors are entirely mine.

A. D. B.

Postscript

Revised estimates (January 1992) of pension funds' assets give end-1989 total assets as £340 billion, compared with £250 billion previously (see pp. 203–4). The composition (pp. 211–12) has not changed materially.

Preface to the first edition

Students of economics often reach the end of their courses with only the most basic knowledge of the financial system. The macro-economic models they meet concentrate on saving, investment, money and 'the' rate of interest. The entire range of non-monetary financial instruments is represented by long-term securities. The only financial institutions worthy of detailed attention are banks, some of whose liabilities happen to be money, with other institutions considered only in so far as their activities complicate the tasks of the monetary authorities. While bond-holders' attitudes have a crucial influence in the Keynesian model, the financial system itself is down-graded – it is the level of income, rather than the interest rate, which brings saving and investment into balance, and the rate of interest depends only on the demand and supply of money.

This comparative neglect of the internal workings of the financial system contrasts with a high level of public concern. Financial institutions have always been in the public eye and frequently attract politicians' attention. The availability of finance, the terms which lenders demand before parting with their funds, and the economic power wielded by large financial institutions are matters for controversy. Public debate, however, is seldom founded on a deep understanding of how the financial system works, partly due to the complex nature of the system itself and partly to the reticence of its practitioners.

The evidence submitted to the Wilson Committee (Committee to Review the Functioning of Financial Institutions) did much to overcome this reticence, and the committee's report contained an authoritative account of many important aspects of the UK financial system in 1980. While some people will disagree with the committee's recommendations, there is now less excuse for ignorance and misunderstanding. Nevertheless the report does not pretend to go into the theory of the system in any detail, and the treatment is selective, linked to the questions the committee was asked to consider, rather than comprehensive.

My object in this book has been to provide a complete account of the working of the financial system in the UK at a level which is suitable both for students with only a basic course in economics behind them and for informed laymen or people embarking on a career in the financial sector. I have tried to put the emphasis on *behaviour* – what motivates the actors in the financial system, why they behave as they do, what constraints influence the decisions they take – rather than on detailed descriptions; these can be found elsewhere, as for example in Jack Revell's excellent book, *The British Financial System* (Macmillan Press 1973). I have also attempted to provide an evaluation of the efficiency of the financial system in Britain, and to consider some issues of current interest.

The framework around which the book is organized is the flow-of-funds table. This is introduced in Part I in the context of a brief overall view of finance in the UK. The sectors are discussed in Part III and the institutions and markets in Part IV.

Part II, which precedes the institutional material, deals with the theory of financial systems. It is the most technical section of the book; readers who are prepared to take on trust the important part played by financial institutions and markets in mobilizing saving and stimulating productive investment may choose to skip the indifference curve analysis in chapter 3. Chapter 4 deals with asset transformation in a non-technical fashion and chapter 5 contains a loanable funds model of interest rate determination. I have not entered into the debate concerning stocks and flows, nor attempted to reconcile loanable funds with Keynesian interest theory – though the possibility that interest rates may fail to balance saving and investment at a high level of income is discussed later.

Parts III and IV draw upon this theory to explain the behaviour of the participants in the financial system. The importance of structural and legislative factors is emphasized, as well as the market considerations, which are usually more central to economic models. Some issues concerning the needs of particular sectors or the facilities provided by the financial institutions are discussed in the relevant chapters.

Part V contains three chapters on broader issues: first, the efficiency of the system as a whole and its success in meeting the demands which fall upon it; secondly, the effects of inflation and possible remedies for the difficulties it causes; thirdly, the thorny questions of whether, and if so what, changes in the financial system are needed in order to promote industrial investment in the UK.

Some, but not all, of these issues were considered in the report of the Wilson Committee. My work on the book has arisen naturally out of my service on that committee, and I acknowledge my debt to my colleagues – not least to those with whom I frequently disagreed. I am also indebted to colleagues at the University of Strathclyde, particularly John Harvey for the many helpful suggestions he made, and Dick Davies who cast an informed eye over a key chapter. Neither is responsible for any heresies or errors that remain. My greatest debt, however, is to my secretary, Jean Paterson, who worked tirelessly at successive drafts and without whose dedication the book could not have been completed at this time.

A. D. B.
May 1981

Part I

Introduction

This Part is intended to provide the reader with the background knowledge required for the more detailed discussion which follows in the rest of the book. The first chapter is an introduction to the functions of financial systems, their importance, and the ways in which they perform their tasks. The second provides a bird's-eye view of the UK financial system, focusing on the salient features and seen against the background of developments in the UK economy in the second half of the 1980s. Attention is drawn to the levels of saving and investment in the economy as a whole and in individual sectors, the size and importance of the major categories of financial institutions and financial markets, and the channels through which savings flow on their way to investors. The flow-of-funds framework is introduced as a means of providing a coherent description of financial activity and as the organizing framework for later chapters.

1

The financial system

Everyone has some contact with the financial system. We are all aware of financial institutions like banks, building societies, and insurance companies, each providing in its own way for some of our everyday needs – for example, payments facilities through banks, convenient savings and access to home loans from building societies, and car, house, or life insurance. Other financial institutions, such as investment trusts, venture capital companies, and discount houses – to name only a few – are less well-known and carry out more specialized functions. Most people also know something about financial markets, like the Stock Exchange where securities are bought and sold, though comparatively few are directly concerned with their activities. Again, there are other important but less familiar financial markets, like the money market in which large sums are borrowed and lent for very short periods, and the foreign exchange market in which dealings in foreign currencies take place. All these financial institutions and markets fit together into a network which comprises the financial system.

The quality of the services provided by the financial system affects the performance of the economy as a whole. The most basic function of any financial system is to facilitate payments in the economy. Normally the responsibility for providing the necessary facilities falls on the note-issuing authority – the government or the central bank – and the commercial banking system. Satisfactory payments facilities are something which we are inclined nowadays to take for granted, but productive economic activity is dependent on their existence, and indeed on traders having reasonable access to short-term credit facilities.

Important as payments facilities are, they will receive relatively slight consideration here, because a properly developed and smooth-running financial system can do much more for the economy. It raises the levels of saving and investment and provides incentives for the allocation of the available resources to those uses where they are likely to give the highest returns. The financial system thus facilitates effective capital accumulation, one of the major engines of economic growth, and it is the saving/investment aspect which will be the focus of our attention.

How well a country's financial system satisfies users' needs is a matter for public concern. By their very nature financial institutions attract criticism: bankers would not be doing their jobs if they did not turn down some requests for loans, and those who are denied funds sometimes feel hard done by and are vociferous in their complaints. The control which financial institutions wield over very substantial sums of money also attracts the attention of governments, partly because they may see irresistible opportunities to secure cheap finance for favoured borrowers (notably governments themselves), and partly in view of the economic power attached to control of finance. Official enquiries into the financial system are therefore not uncommon, the most recent British enquiry being the Wilson Committee (1980).[1]

Any evaluation of the financial system should be founded on an understanding of its functions within the economic system as a whole, and the means by which these can be carried out. This must be complemented by a knowledge of users' requirements, of the behaviour of institutions, and of market practices. Moreover, institutions and markets cannot be viewed in isolation, for it may not be important that one category of financial institution makes no provision for certain needs if these can be satisfied elsewhere in the system. What matters is not the shapes of the individual pieces, but how well the jigsaw fits together and the quality of the picture that emerges.

The participants in the system

The participants in the financial system can be classified into five broad groups: savers; investors and other borrowers; financial intermediaries; brokers and advisers; and regulators. The end-users of the financial system are the *savers*, whose current spending is less than their income and who have money available to lend to others; and the *investors*, who want to borrow money in order to buy capital goods or increase the scale of their business, as well as other borrowers who want to spend more than their incomes. In between lie the financial institutions and markets. Ensuring that money flows smoothly from savers through institutions and/or markets to investors is an important function of the financial system. It is the ultimate savers and ultimate borrowers who are, as it were, on the periphery of the financial system, whose needs it serves and who provide the rationale for its existence.

Nevertheless, a good deal of the business of financial institutions and activity in financial markets is generated, not by new saving and investment, but by rearrangements of existing savings or changes in the form of existing borrowings. People shift money from bank accounts to building societies or vice versa, and firms raise new long-term capital in order to pay off short-term debts. Moreover, investors do not always need to borrow in order to finance expenditure; they may choose instead to run down savings accumulated from earnings previously, or they may use balances obtained by borrowing on other occasions. By permitting economic agents to organize their financing in a flexible manner, the financial system helps to make all this possible.

Financial intermediaries are institutions which attempt to serve the needs of both lenders and borrowers. As we shall see later the forms in which savers wish to hold their savings – for example bank deposits – frequently differ from the ways in which borrowers would like to obtain their funds – for example long-term loans. Financial intermediaries are often able to reconcile these divergent requirements. In addition they provide a variety of specific services which savers and borrowers value in their own right. Examples are money transmission facilities and advice on corporate finance in the case of banks, life assurance cover in the case of insurance companies. Moreover, while there is nothing to prevent savers and investors from dealing directly with each other if they wish, the existence of financial institutions makes direct contact unnecessary, since both groups can deal with the intermediating institutions.

In a competitive financial system (like that in Britain) institutions compete for business in broadly construed 'markets' for saving and lending business; they seek to attract funds from savers and supply funds to borrowers. But there are also *organized* markets which provide facilities for economic agents to borrow and lend or to buy or sell securities. The main role of brokers and advisers is to help these organized markets to function properly. Brokers and advisers provide information to participants in the markets, and attempt to ensure that lenders and borrowers, buyers and sellers, have the facts they need to strike a fair bargain. They also perform the vital task of putting actual lenders and borrowers in touch with each other – for example, the money-market broker brings together the lender who has money to spare with the borrower who wants it temporarily. By obviating the need for individual borrowers or lenders to search out counterparts themselves the brokers substantially reduce transactions costs. In most organized markets there are also *market makers*, professional dealers whose function is to ensure that lenders and borrowers are always able to find a counterpart for their deals.

Historical experience in many countries has shown that where large sums of money are involved in financial markets there is a considerable danger of fraud or other malpractices. Most countries therefore need *regulators*, who control their financial institutions and regulate dealings in securities markets with the objects of ensuring that the financial institutions are able to honour their commitments, that people have access to relevant information before they enter into contracts, and that dealing in securities is fair. These rules come under the general heading of *prudential* regulations. But more general *economic* controls are also needed. Sharp expansions or contractions of activity in financial markets are often associated with booms and slumps in the economy at large, and the intimate connection between money, credit and economic stability compels countries to curb the expansion of credit in some periods and to stimulate it in others. Economic controls may also be required to guard against monopolistic structures or practices in the financial system.

Financial instruments

The financial system deals in financial instruments. These are mostly more or less sophisticated forms of IOUs or claims – they are an asset of one party and a liability of another. In most instances the former party is entitled to repayment at a specified time, and receives a promise of some interest, share of profits, or other service as compensation for the loan. For example, deposits are liabilities of banks or other institutions, are generally repayable on demand or in the fairly near future, and usually bear interest. Loans are often liabilities of ultimate borrowers, are usually repayable by the end of some predetermined period, and carry an obligation to pay interest. And ordinary shares are liabilities of firms, which confer on their owners the right to a share of the profits earned but, in contrast with loans, do not have to be repaid. As well as claims there are also *derivative* instruments – contracts relating to the prices of securities, interest rates or foreign exchange rates at some date in the future.

Although a wide variety of financial instruments exists, differing significantly in detail, the major distinctions rest on three character-istics – risk, liquidity, and real-value certainty (that is, their susceptibility to loss of value due to inflation). A distinction can be drawn between on the one hand deposits and loans, which are generally made only if repayment of capital and interest is confidently expected, and on the other company shares, which are claims to a share of the surplus income after prior claims have been met. People think of their deposits with financial institutions as safe,[2] and loans are usually secured on assets or made conditional on the borrower's financial performance, to give the lender added confidence in the safety of the funds, though there is usually some small chance of partial or total loss. The *risk* of loss, and conversely the possibility of gain, is heavily concentrated on equity assets, mainly the ordinary shares of companies. The shareholder is entitled to a share of the company's profits but must also accept the chance of experiencing some loss. Indeed, for reasons discussed in chapter 8, the effects on the shareholders of success or failure of a company are magnified if the company has loans outstanding as well as ordinary shares.

Liquidity refers to the ease and speed with which savings in non-monetary form can be turned into cash, and reflects both the *maturity* of financial instruments and their *marketability*. By maturity we mean the time which elapses before a deposit or loan is due to be repaid. Deposits which are repayable on demand have a short maturity, mortgage loans due for repayment after 25 years a long one. Thus maturity covers a very wide range, and the shorter is the maturity of a deposit or loan the greater is its liquidity. But assets which are marketable may also be liquid, even if they are not automatically repayable in the near future. For example, ordinary shares in many companies can be sold at short notice and their value turned into cash, though at a price which is uncertain. Not all assets are marketable – fixed-term deposits are an example – and in other cases the ease of selling and ability to obtain a reasonable price may be in doubt. A house may hang fire for many months and the price received will be a matter for negotiation. The existence of an organized market for an asset and the ability to deal at short notice therefore adds to an asset's liquidity.

The third distinguishing characteristic of financial instruments is their *real-value certainty*. Neither deposits nor loans, whose values are fixed in money (or *nominal*) terms, provide their holders with protection against price level changes.[3] Ordinary shares stand a good chance of doing better on this score, because profits can be expected in the end to rise roughly in line with the general price level, though there may be prolonged periods when this does not hold good. The same goes for property, where rents can be expected to mirror general price changes over long periods – though as with ordinary shares there may be considerable fluctuations in prices around any long-term trends.

Savers and investors

In developed economies decisions to invest are often taken separately from decisions to save. The investor may be a company manager who wishes to expand the activities of the firm by which he or she is employed, while the saver may be a private individual who wishes to put some money aside for retirement. Even when saving and investment are carried out by the same economic agent, the timing is usually different, with saving either preceding the investment which is to take place, or occurring afterwards as debts are gradually repaid. Moreover, the acts of saving and investment are also often far apart in space. British savings in the nineteenth century helped to finance the construction of the US railroads, just as in more recent times US saving helped to pay for the development of North Sea oil and saving by oil-rich countries in the Middle East was used to finance investment in many other countries.

There are of course important exceptions. The small firm that ploughs its profits back into the business is saving and investing simultaneously, and the same is true of the large company which holds down its dividends in order to retain profits for investment. A substantial part of company investment is in fact financed in this way, with funds put aside for depreciation being used to replace capital equipment as it wears out or to finance new investment. Nevertheless, a high proportion of saving is not employed directly or immediately by the saver, and is made available to investors elsewhere.

Savers' objectives are varied. Some people save for short periods merely as a means of levelling out their income and consumption patterns, or they save up for some especially heavy expenditures, such as presents at Christmas or a holiday. Others have motives directed to longer-term needs, of which the most important is saving for retirement. Firms save to finance future investment or to provide a cushion against the possibility of adverse business conditions. Governments may add to saving through the tax system if they anticipate that there will be a shortage of saving in the economy as a whole and decide to compel people to save more (through the fiscal system) rather than curtail investment.

Their motives for saving have a bearing on the characteristics of the financial instruments which people wish to hold. First and foremost people look for *safety*: they wish to be sure that their savings will not be lost. Security of money value is important for many asset holders and it is comparatively easy to ensure that savings will not lose their value in this sense; but the objective of securing the real value of saving is difficult to attain in periods of inflation, when the real value of monetary savings is eroded by rising prices.

Secondly, most firms and many individuals want a large part of their savings to be readily available. This means that *liquidity* is vitally important – the maturity of the assets which they hold must be short, or good markets must exist in which assets can be sold so that cash can be raised if necessary. In consequence, savers have a strong demand for deposits and short-term loans. There are, however, very important exceptions to this preference for liquidity: savings built up for retirement, for example, will often not be required until many years have elapsed, and do not need to be held in a liquid form. Long-term loans, and assets which provide some protection against inflation, may be suitable for this purpose.

Thirdly, savers seek a *yield* (income) on their assets. For most, this ranks well behind safety and liquidity. But in choosing between financial claims which are similar in other respects savers can generally be expected to select that which offers the higher yield. Some savers are also prepared to hold risky financial assets, like ordinary shares, if the return[4] they hope to earn is sufficient to compensate them for the risk of loss.

Investors' needs are very different. The bulk of physical investment is durable, generating a flow of earnings which permits its value to be recovered gradually and over a long period. Most of it is specialized and could be sold only at a considerable loss. Moreover investment is an inherently risky activity, and the investor can never be certain about the income which an investment is likely to produce. The rents on commercial properties may not rise as has been anticipated, the market for a new product may be misjudged, or the costs involved in production may turn out higher than expected.

The characteristics which investors seek in the liabilities they issue reflect these features of physical investment. Ideally, they prefer to issue long-term liabilities, like long-term loans, reflecting the extended period over which many investments pay for themselves.

Since the profitability of investment is uncertain it is essential for part of their liabilities to have the form of equity capital, to be remunerated in a way which reflects their profitability. Finally, other things equal, investors wish to pay as little as possible for the funds they obtain.

Financial intermediaries and markets

The separation of saving from investment and the differing and often conflicting requirements of savers and borrowers create opportunities for financial institutions. They perform a variety of functions, including mobilizing saving, encouraging investment, transforming maturities, averaging and transforming risks, and reducing information and transaction costs.

Financial intermediaries *mobilize* saving. They draw attention to the benefits of saving, stressing for example security in the case of life insurance and safety combined with income in the case of building society deposits; in so doing they change peoples' attitudes, and raise the level of saving in the economy. Moreover they encourage people to save, and to do so through the financial system, rather than by buying land, jewellery, or some other more tangible assets; pension funds, for example, enable people to convert present into future income without becoming directly involved in productive investment themselves. Many financial institutions also collect the comparatively small savings of individuals and make them available in large sums to borrowers: the savings of many individual building society depositors are required to make up each single mortgage loan; the liquid funds of a large number of firms and individuals are needed to supply a bank loan sufficient to finance a large industrial investment project; and the pension contributions of many working people are put together by a pension fund to provide money to a property development company. Investment, which is on a comparatively large scale, requires access to funds gathered together from many sources.

While many of the financial institutions set out actively to stimulate saving they often take a more passive stance on the lending side of their business. They *facilitate investment*, rather than directly *encourage* it. This is certainly the case for long-term investment institutions like insurance and pension funds, which buy and sell securities in the financial markets. It is less true of banks, some of which put a considerable effort into marketing their loan facilities and, particularly with corporate customers, encouraging clients to go ahead with developments which create a need for finance. However, as a general rule institutions respond to the demand for funds and influence demand by varying the price at which they are prepared to supply funds or the terms attached to loans, rather than attempt to persuade customers to take on additional spending commitments. Their role in encouraging investment is therefore mainly indirect – by providing funds at a price that is lower and on other terms which are more favourable than borrowers could negotiate if they had to seek funds directly from savers themselves.

One way in which financial institutions improve the terms facing borrowers is by *transforming maturities* – they provide liquid liabilities which meet the needs of savers whilst employing their funds in the longer-term financial instruments which are more convenient for borrowers. Deposit-taking institutions like banks and building societies are able to do this because, although some individual depositors may be reducing their deposits, others will simultaneously be adding to theirs, and the institutions can rely on a considerable degree of stability in their deposit-base as a whole. It is therefore legitimate for them to regard at least a proportion of their deposits as available for long-term loans. Moreover, the existence of organized markets in which they can bid for large deposits provides banks with the assurance they need to make loan commitments.

Most financial institutions issue liabilities which are comparatively safe, but hold amongst their assets instruments on at least some of which there is a possibility of loss. To do this they *average risk* and *transform risk* by taking the residual risk of loss on their own equity capital. For example, by making a large number of loans, and spreading them over a wide range of activities, banks try to ensure that their overall loss experience is small. They attempt to allow for losses in the charge they make for loans, and if this allowance is insufficient their own capital is available to absorb any further losses before the funds supplied to them by depositors are at risk. Life insurance companies hold a much greater proportion of risky assets than banks, and the possibility of capital gain or loss on individual assets is also higher. But they too are able to offer life insurance policies with a guaranteed minimum value and to protect their policyholders from undue risk. Indeed, by holding different types of assets in their portfolios – bonds, ordinary shares and property – and by diversifying their holdings within each category they are able to eliminate much of the risk involved in financial investment.

For the private individual, personally holding the liabilities of ultimate borrowers involves substantial costs. These *information and transaction costs* are much lower for financial institutions. For example, the individual with funds to lend is not usually in a position to assess accurately the value of a house on which a mortgage loan is secured, but the bank or building society specializing in this type of lending can do so easily. Moreover the legal documentation which is required can be prepared with much less effort by the specialist for whom it is an everyday occurrence. Through their network of branches and agencies building societies are also in a position to make contact with depositors and borrowers, whereas the private individual might have considerable difficulty in finding a suitable mortgagee. Turning to stock-market investments, unless the private investor has a really substantial amount of money to invest, he or she faces proportionately high transactions costs when buying or selling ordinary shares. It makes sense, therefore, for the individual to invest through an intermediary like a unit or investment trust, which, by dealing in large amounts, incurs proportionately lower costs.

While financial intermediaries usually perform one or more of these functions, they also provide a variety of other services, which may indeed be their *raison d'etre*. For example, insurane companies provide insurance against the risk of early death (life policies) or prolonged life (annuities and pension policies); banks provide money transmission services which allow people to make payments easily; and investment and unit trusts seek to offer expert investment management, which removes from the individual the need to monitor continuously the progress of the companies whose shares he or she holds. All these services are important in their own right.

The organized markets provide alternative and complementary mechanisms to financial intermediaries for meeting the needs of savers and borrowers. Organized markets *provide liquidity*, because they make it easy for the saver to sell a financial instrument before it reaches maturity. Thus what is a long-term liability for a borrower becomes liquid in the hands of the holder. Organized markets *mobilize saving* and allow large sums to be borrowed. Through the new-issue market, firms or the government can raise very large sums of money, drawing at the same time on the savings of a host of individuals and financial institutions, each of whom can provide only a small proportion of the total that is required. Organized markets help to *disseminate information* and ensure that those who participate in the markets as buyers or sellers are well-informed. This means, for example, that share prices will reflect an up-to-date assessment of the performance of the companies concerned, and that even the less well-informed investor may therefore expect to be able to deal at a fair price. Finally, organized markets *reduce transactions costs*, because a mechanism for bringing buyers and sellers together is created. Examples of organized markets are the new-issue market, which helps companies or the government to raise new capital, the stock market where trading in existing securities takes place, and the money market which facilitates short-term deposit-taking and borrowing in large amounts.

It is important to observe that markets do not just happen – they need some form of organization. Thus issuing houses and stock-brokers help to organize the new-issue market; the Stock Exchange includes agency brokers, through whom clients deal, and market makers who carry out the additional functions of providing the counterpart of buying and selling orders and who quote prices continuously; and the money market has money brokers who bring borrowers and lenders together and institutions such as the discount houses which act as dealers in a variety of short-term securities. Without these specialists savers would be likely to experience difficulty both in finding buyers for securities they wished to sell and in ensuring that they received a fair price for their assets, which would therefore lose liquidity. Borrowers would find equal difficulty in gaining access on reasonable terms to the funds they required.

Rates of interest and other terms

The prices prevailing in financial markets and the rates of return on financial instruments have important economic functions. They help to allocate resources in the economy and they play a significant part in achieving macroeconomic balance – balance between saving and investment overall at a satisfactory level of economic activity.

At this point it may be helpful to digress briefly to draw attention to the relationship between the prices of assets and their *rates of interest*. A financial asset is a claim to a stream of income in the future, the interest on the asset. The rate of interest, or yield, on a security is simply the income per period expressed as a percentage of the price of the asset. Thus, if Y is the income in some period, P is the price of the asset and r is the rate of interest for the period, we have

$$r = \frac{100Y}{P} \text{ per cent.}$$

It is clear that there is an inverse relationship between P and r; for any given income, Y, the higher is P the lower is r.

This connection is reflected in the behaviour of asset prices and interest rates in the financial system. People can choose between holding securities directly and lending to institutions, firms can choose between issuing securities in the financial markets and borrowing from institutions, and the rates of interest and asset prices affect their decisions. If deposit interest rates rise people will be less inclined to hold securities unless security prices fall to offer an equivalent yield. If companies are actively seeking funds, this will tend simultaneously to increase the supply of securities in the markets, so lowering security prices, and to raise the rate of interest charged for bank loans. Interest rates and asset prices therefore tend to change together (though in opposite directions).

In a market economy prices are at the centre of the process of resource allocation. People with resources are persuaded by a high price to make them available to others; and the limited supply of resources goes to those who are willing to pay the prevailing price for them. Economic agents, whether sellers or purchasers, respond to impersonal market incentives. This applies to capital markets, where securities are bought and sold, and to a lesser degree to financial institutions, which have to compete for funds and vary their own charges for loans in line with what they themselves have to pay. The rates of interest charged by lenders also normally reflect the risk of loss, so that when risk is high borrowers pay more.

Nevertheless there is a sense in which the financial system allocates funds more directly and in a less impersonal fashion. Lenders and financial investors do not automatically provide funds to all potential borrowers who claim to be able to pay the going rate. Lenders make their own assessment of the probability of loss, and refuse funds in those cases where they think the risk is too high. Moreover, in the past when credit was particularly tight, lenders often chose to ration funds – to lend to some customers, but decline requests from others who satisfied all the appropriate risk criteria – though increasing competition within the financial system has now made this kind of behaviour unusual in Britain.

Non-competitive features of the financial system such as these affect the efficiency of resource allocation. When allocation of funds amongst those borrowers who satisfy the appropriate risk criteria is by price, there is a presumption that funds will go to those who are able to pay most for them and that resources will be channelled into those areas where they are likely to prove most productive. In this sense allocation through the price system is 'efficient' and rationing by institutions detracts from efficiency. But this concept of efficiency does presuppose that the value of an investment is reflected in ability to pay for funds, and it can be argued that the ability to pay the going rate and meet the risk standards set by the institutions may not always be appropriate criteria for deciding who should get funds.[5]

The prices of financial assets and rates of interest also act to equate the supply of saving with the demand for investment in the economy as a whole. Just as the price of the shares of some company will rise if demand is greater than supply, so the prices of securities generally rise when there is excess demand in securities markets. The same principle applies to institutions. If a bank or building society fails to attract sufficient deposits to meet the demand for loans, it is likely to react by raising both its deposit and lending interest rates. By paying more for deposits it attracts a higher proportion of the available savings, and by raising its lending rates it curtails the demand for funds. Thus supply and demand come into balance.

The role of interest rates in achieving a balance between saving and investment in the economy as a whole is complex. Discrepancies between the desired levels of saving and investment have repercussions for economic activity and inflation, and conditions in financial markets are influenced by monetary as well as real factors. These issues, which are bound up with the conduct of monetary policy as well as with the operations of financial institutions and markets, are discussed at some length in chapters 5 and 6.

Notes

1 *Report of Committee to Review the Functioning of Financial Institutions*, Cmnd 7937, 1980.
2 One of the functions of prudential regulation is to ensure that they are not disappointed.
3 The index-linked national savings and securities issued by the British government, whose values are linked to the retail prices index, are an exception.
4 Including capital gain as well as income.
5 The role of rates of interest in resource allocation is discussed further in chapters 5 and 16.

2

Finance in Britain

In this chapter we shall look briefly at the structure of the British financial system at the present time. It reflects on the one hand the preferences now of asset-holders and liability-issuers for the various kinds of financial instrument, and on the other the legacy of the assets and liabilities which have been created, the institutions built up and markets developed in the past. We shall then go on to examine three aspects of the process by which saving is channelled to investors through the financial system: first, the extent of the saving and investment which takes place in the economy; then the question of who saves and who invests; lastly, the flows of funds through financial institutions and markets as money passes on its way from savers to investors. At this stage we do no more than sketch the outline of the picture in order to draw attention to the salient features; more detailed discussion and analysis will be found in subsequent chapters. But before embarking on this task it is necessary to be aware of the economic context in which financial activity has been taking place in recent years.

The economic context

For the UK the second half of the 1980s was a period displaying strong economic growth and rapid financial development, the latter being part of a worldwide phenomenon. Conditions in Britain were unlike those of the preceding decade, and they are unlikely to recur during the remainder of this century.

The 1970s had been a turbulent period in the world economy, with the UK being no exception. After the severe recession of 1974–5 economic growth picked up again to peak in 1979, but inflation, which had reached 27 per cent at one time in 1975, was never really brought under control. It fell to under 8 per cent in the middle of 1978 but was rising again in 1979. The new Conservative government in 1979 tightened monetary policy severely and there was a sharp recession in 1980 and 1981. However, this was followed by growth of between 2 and 4 per cent a year from 1982 to 1986, which accelerated to over 5 per cent in both 1987 and 1988. There was a slowdown in 1989, with the economy moving into a recession in 1990–1.

For a variety of reasons, including *inter alia* an increase in indirect taxes in the June 1979 Budget and further sharp increases in oil prices, inflation rose to over 20 per cent in 1980, but dropped again quite quickly under the influence of the tight monetary policy, reaching a low point of under 3 per cent in 1986. However, the rapid economic growth at the end of the decade was associated with rising inflation, which peaked at 10 per cent in the autumn of 1990.

The boom in the second half of the eighties was associated with a high rate of monetary and credit expansion. There were very substantial increases in house prices, particularly in the south of the country, fed by a readily available supply of mortgage loans. These conditions were the result of deregulation, bringing the banks, which had previously played only a relatively minor part, into the mortgage market and giving the building societies much greater access to funds. Where previously there had often been some degree of informal rationing of mortgage loans, by the second half of the eighties this had been replaced by keen competition amongst lenders. Demand in the housing market was stimulated by relatively low interest rates, the prospect of capital gains and (particularly in 1988) tax reductions which boosted confidence and increased the disposable incomes of potential borrowers.

It was not only housing on which consumers were spending money. Private consumption spending rose by nearly a quarter in volume terms between 1985 and 1989, a rate of growth considerably greater than that of the economy as a whole, and which could not possibly be sustained. This spending too was supported by high levels of consumer borrowing, part of it being mortgage borrowing secured on housing. The general expansion of economic activity led in turn to an investment boom by industrial and commercial companies, including huge investments in offices and new shopping developments, also financed mainly by bank credit. However, this demand-led economic expansion was also reflected in rising inflation, in a swing in the balance of payments from approximate balance in 1986 to a deficit approaching 4 per cent of gross domestic product (GDP) in 1989, and in rare surpluses in the government's financing position as buoyant tax revenue exceeded the growth of government spending. The expansion was eventually brought to a halt by a period of monetary restriction beginning in the second half of 1988.

The second half of the eighties was marked also by major changes in the financial system, both in the UK and abroad. On the one hand there was a trend towards deregulation – for example, institutions which had been precluded from engaging in certain types of business were permitted to do so. On the other there were changes in the system of regulation, affecting both institutions and participants in financial markets. A notable example in the UK was Big Bang, the name given to changes in the dealing and other arrangements introduced in the UK securities markets in October 1986.

The worldwide financial system was characterized by the development of new financial products and markets, and a stock market boom which developed in the mid-eighties was brought to an end by the crash of October 1987. The over-optimism and high profits of the boom years were followed by caution and excess capacity subsequently, with adverse consequences for the profitability of the institutions concerned. Moreover, banks and other deposit-taking institutions in a number of countries were caught up in a similar process, engaging in lending which proved in retrospect to be unsound. As a result, a more cautious attitude to financial activity was in evidence by the beginning of the 1990s.

Institutions and markets

Tables 2.1 and 2.2 show some of the assets and liabilities of the most important categories of financial institution in Britain. Banks and building societies (table 2.1) are the dominant deposit-takers in the economy, with domestic sterling deposits at the end of 1989

Table 2.1   Banks and building societies: domestic sterling deposits and lending, end-1989

	Deposits	*(£ billion)* *Commercial lending*
Banks	290	353
Building societies	155	156
Total	445	509

Source: Financial Statistics, February 1991, tables 6.1, 6.9

Table 2.2   Investing institutions: assets, end-1989

	(£ billion)
Life assurance companies	248
Pension funds	250
General insurance companies	40
Unit trusts	57
Investment trusts	24

Sources: Various – see tables in chapter 12

amounting to over 85 per cent of GDP in that year.[1] They compete for deposits in *retail* markets, where they seek to attract deposits from individuals and small businesses, and in *wholesale* markets, where the sources are mainly companies and other financial institutions. Bank deposits were almost twice as large as building societies' deposits, a proportion that had moved in the banks' favour during 1989 as a result of the conversion of the Abbey National Building Society into Abbey National Bank. Commercial lending by these institutions amounted to almost 100 per cent of GDP, with the banks accounting for 70 per cent of the total.[2] The deposit-taking institutions are discussed in chapter 11.

Life assurance companies and pension funds are the most important categories of investing institution (table 2.2), with assets in both cases amounting to some 50 per cent of GDP in 1989. A significant part of the life assurance companies' assets are held in respect of pension business, which has grown very rapidly in recent years. The assets of general insurance companies are much smaller, reflecting the shorter-term nature of their insurance contracts, but are significant in terms of the financial system, amounting to some 8 per cent of GDP in 1989. Unit and investment trusts are collective investment institutions which held assets amounting altogether to some 16 per cent of GDP at the end of 1989. Traditionally they have had a considerable emphasis on investment in foreign securities. In recent years unit and investment trusts have not been a quantitatively important medium for channelling new saving into investment in the UK, and a high proportion of their liabilities is in fact held by other investing institutions.[3] The investing institutions are discussed in chapter 12.

Table 2.3 illustrates the scale of the UK securities markets and sterling money markets – markets for certain short-term financial

Table 2.3   Sterling securities and money markets, end-1990

	(£ billion)
UK public sector stocks	116
Listed UK companies securities	
Bonds	44
Preference shares	16
Ordinary shares	445
Unlisted UK company securities	5
Sterling money markets	200

Sources: Various – see tables in chapter 14

instruments – which are considered more fully in chapter 14. UK institutions are also very active participants in the international securities markets, for which London, along with New York and Tokyo, are the three most important international centres. The total value of listed UK securities in the domestic markets at the end of 1990 was about 115 per cent of 1990's GDP. Public sector stocks accounted for under a fifth of the total valuation at the end of 1990, having fallen from over two-fifths ten years earlier, and of this about 20 per cent were index-linked gilt-edged stocks, whose capital value and interest payments are linked to the retail prices index. UK company bonds and preference shares accounted for less than 10 per cent, while ordinary shares comprised over 70 per cent of the total. Securities traded on the so-called Unlisted Securities Market – shares of mainly small companies which satisfied less exacting criteria than those with a full Stock Exchange listing – contributed less than 1 per cent of the total value, though having access to the securities market is by no means unimportant for the companies concerned.

The total value of the financial instruments traded in the sterling money markets was just over 35 per cent of GDP. Much of the business in these markets takes place between financial institutions, but banks could not function as they do in the absence of the money markets, which facilitate the movement of funds within the financial system and provide a stock of highly liquid financial instruments. For some ultimate borrowers they also act as a cheaper alternative to bank loans, and form a significant source of finance. The central institutions in these markets are the discount houses (or discount *market*) which act as market makers for most of the financial instruments traded.

Tables 2.1–2.3 do not cover all of the financial instruments or financial institutions in Britain. Notes and coin, national savings securities, other loans and equity investments are all extremely important, and there are a number of specialized institutions, such as venture capital companies and factoring companies, which have significant roles within the system.[4] There are also the important new markets in financial derivatives, which were developed during the 1980s. These are contracts based upon foreign exchange rates, interest rates, or security prices, which enable participants in the markets to take a view on the likely future course of interest rates or security prices. Alternatively, the markets can be used to offset some of the risks which are inherent in holding financial assets or issuing financial liabilities.

Saving and investment in Britain

We turn now to consider the part played by the financial system in the saving/investment process. Table 2.4 shows that for the ten years from 1978 to 1987 saving in Britain averaged about 17.5 per cent of GDP, with investment very slightly less.[5,6] Within this period saving varied comparatively little – by less than 2 per cent of GDP – but investment was more volatile, with a peak of nearly 20 per cent in 1979 and a trough of just over 15 per cent in 1981. At over 20 per cent of GDP in 1988 and 1989 the investment figures illustrate the strength of the boom at the end of the eighties, while the decline in saving in 1989 shows that the share of domestic consumption was rising at the same time.

The share of saving in the UK is low by international standards (table 2.5), with only the USA amongst the seven most important

Table 2.4 Saving and investment in the UK, 1978–89

| | (Per cent of GDP at market prices) | | | |
	1978–82 average	1983–87 average	1988	1989
Saving[1]	17.6	17.4	17.4	16.4
Investment[2]	17.3	17.2	20.2	20.2

Source: Blue Book, 1990, tables 3.5, 3.6
  [1] After deducting stock appreciation but before providing for depreciation
  [2] Gross domestic fixed capital formation *plus* value of physical increase in stocks and work in progress

Table 2.5   Saving in major industrial countries, 1980–89

	(Per cent of GNP)
Japan	31.6
Germany	22.5
Italy	21.9
Canada	20.7
France	20.4
UK	16.6
USA	16.3

Source: OECD

industrial countries having a lower propensity to save. Even the *peak* levels of saving in the UK in the eighties did not reach the *average* level in any of the other countries. Low saving and low investment tend to go together, and the share of saving in GDP in the UK has certainly not assisted Britain's economic performance.

For many purposes it is convenient to divide the economy into *sectors*, whose functions differ or whose activities are governed by different considerations. We shall employ a five sector classification: personal sector (households etc.); industrial and commercial companies; financial companies and institutions; public corporations; and general government (central government and local authorities). The needs and financial behaviour of these sectors will be discussed at much greater length later, but at this stage a brief description of the contribution of each sector to saving and investment in the economy, and of the financial flows between them, will help to set the scene.

Table 2.6 shows how saving and investment were divided between these sectors from 1978 to 1989. In the first five-year period the personal sector, which includes unincorporated businesses and non-profit making institutions as well as households, was the most important source of saving in the economy. That is the normal situation, and at an average of 8 per cent of GDP personal saving was much the same as in the mid-seventies. Since then it has fallen, to about 6 per cent on average in 1983–7 and to under 4 per cent on average in 1988 and 1989. This fall in the share of personal saving was the counterpart of the consumption boom in the second half of the eighties.

Investment by the personal sector includes the buildings, plant and equipment required by the business component of the sector as well as private house-building. At 4 per cent of GDP in 1978–82,

Table 2.6 Saving and investment by sector, 1978–89

(Per cent of GDP at market prices)

	Saving[1]				Investment[2]			
	1978–82 average	1983–87 average	1988	1989	1978–82 average	1983–87 average	1988	1989
Personal sector	8.1	6.2	3.2	4.3	4.0	4.7	5.8	5.2
Industrial and commercial companies	6.8	7.8	7.4	4.7	6.2	6.8	9.6	9.5
Financial companies and institutions	1.7	2.4	3.1	3.5	2.2	2.0	2.6	2.8
Public corporations	2.1	1.8	1.4	1.3	2.8	1.7	1.0	1.0
General government	-1.0	-0.8	2.3	2.6	2.2	1.9	1.2	1.7

Source: Blue Book, 1990, tables 3.5, 3.6
[1] After deducting stock appreciation but before providing for depreciation
[2] Gross domestic fixed capital formation *plus* value of physical increase in stocks and work in progress

investment was also in line with earlier experience – slightly higher, in fact, than in the previous five-year period. Thanks to the housing boom (and to council house sales which count as personal sector investment) it increased subsequently, with the result that at the end of the decade personal sector investment was significantly greater than personal sector saving.

Industrial and commercial companies are also usually responsible for a substantial part of the saving in the economy. Part of this is required simply to maintain the capital stock, and is reflected in the depreciation item in their accounts, while part reflects retentions out of profits. Saving by industrial and commercial companies therefore varies quite strongly over the economic cycle – it fell from 9 per cent of GDP in 1978 to 5.5 per cent in 1980 – but the average of a little over 7 per cent in the ten years from 1978 to 1987 was in line with previous experience. The sharp fall in 1989 reflected a combination of little profits growth and increases in dividends, net interest and tax payments. Investment, however, reached a peak in 1988 and 1989 (helped by a gradual movement of public corporations into the industrial and commercial company category after privatization). As a result, whereas saving had slightly exceeded investment on average from 1978 to 1987 – the normal situation in previous years – it fell far short of investment at the end of the eighties.

Financial companies and institutions are also investors in their own right, but in addition they invest in property for use by industry and commerce and in plant and equipment which is leased to other companies. In the decade before 1973 investment by financial institutions amounted to only about 1 per cent of GDP, but by the end of the eighties it was approaching 3 per cent. Their saving averaged about 2 per cent of GDP from 1978 to 1987, but rose to over 3 per cent in the last two years of the decade.[7]

Public corporations include the nationalized industries and certain publicly-owned enterprises. In the mid-seventies their investment averaged 3.5 per cent of GDP and it was still approaching 3 per cent in 1978–82. However, the privatization programme that converted most of the major public corporations into quoted companies shifted much of this investment into the industrial and commercial companies sector, so that by the end of the decade the remaining public corporations invested only 1 per cent of GDP. (After privatization most of the former public corporations increased their investment programmes, since they were no longer subject to constraints on public expenditure.) Saving followed a similar trend, though the decline was less rapid than the decline in investment.

General government consists of the central government and local authorities, and there is saving if current tax revenue exceeds *current* spending. In every year from 1978 to 1986 there was dis-saving by general government – local authorities consistently ran surpluses on their current accounts (i.e. they had positive saving) but the central government ran a current account deficit. In the ten years from 1978 to 1987 the dis-saving by general government averaged nearly 1 per cent of GDP. There was a remarkable turn-round at the end of the eighties, thanks to a combination of relatively strict control of public expenditure and buoyant tax revenue due to the rapid expansion of the economy. The result was that the central government had a current surplus averaging nearly 2 per cent of GDP in 1988 and 1989, with the local authorities adding another half per cent. Meanwhile tight control was kept on investment. In the mid-seventies this had averaged over 4.5 per cent of GDP, including a considerable local authority house-building programme. By 1978–82 it had been reduced to a little over 2 per cent, with a further decline subsequently.[8]

It is clear from table 2.6 that the sectoral distributions of saving and investment always differ, and may differ substantially. More-over, there is nothing immutable about the patterns observed. Nevertheless, it is normal for the enterprise sectors – industrial, commercial and financial companies and the public corporations together – to invest more than they save, and general government investment is normally greater than their saving. In contrast, the personal sector normally saves more than it invests, and one of the principal tasks for the financial system is to channel the surplus savings to the other sectors of the economy. The position at the end of the eighties, with the personal sector investing more than it saved and the general government sector in the opposite situation, was very unusual, and the overall excess of investment over saving was of course mirrored by a large (and unsustainable) deficit in the current account of the balance of payments.

Financial surplus or deficit

When an economic agent (for example a household, firm or government authority) has saving which exceeds its investment we say that it has a *financial surplus*; even if all its investment was financed from its own saving there would be a surplus left over to be used to acquire financial assets or repay debts. In the contrary case, when investment exceeds saving, we say that the agent has a *financial deficit*. Thus in table 2.6 the excess of personal sector saving over investment is a measure of the personal sector's financial surplus.

The surpluses and deficits (which have a negative sign) for all the sectors for 1978 to 1989 derived from table 2.6 are shown in table 2.7, which also includes the 'overseas sector' and the 'residual error'. The former shows the extent to which the UK increases its indebtedness to the rest of the world (i.e. the overseas sector has a financial surplus) or builds up its claims on other countries,[9,10] while the latter is simply an accounting item.[11] Table 2.7 shows clearly the importance of the personal sector as a source of finance for other sectors in the economy at the beginning of the eighties, as well as the dominant position of the public sector (public corporations and general government) as a net borrower. It also demonstrates how the position was reversed by the end of the eighties, with the personal and industrial and commercial companies sectors drawing on the savings generated by the public sector and, especially, overseas.

Table 2.7   Sectoral financial surpluses and deficits in the UK, 1978–89

| | *(Per cent of GDP at market prices)* *Financial surplus (+)/deficit (−)* | | | |
	1978–82 *average*	*1983–87* *average*	*1988*	*1989*
Personal sector	4.0	1.5	−2.6	−0.9
Industrial and commercial companies	0.6	1.0	−2.2	−4.8
Financial companies and institutions	−0.4	0.4	0.4	0.7
Public corporations	−0.7	0.1	0.4	0.3
General government	−3.2	−2.7	1.1	0.9
Overseas sector	−1.2	−0.3	3.2	3.7
Residual error	−0.9	—	0.4	—

Source: Blue Book, 1990, tables 3.5, 3.6

The sectors' financial surpluses and deficits provide some indication of the extent to which the financial system has the task of shifting funds between broad sectors of the economy. For that reason they are important. But they do not tell the whole story, because funds also have to be transferred between lenders and borrowers within each sector, and because a great deal of financial activity is caused when people rearrange their assets or liabilities. For example, a very high proportion of households' investment in owner-occupied housing depends upon mortgage borrowing, so that the savings of some are being channelled through the financial system to provide funds for others within the same sector. Again, although self-financing is much more prevalent amongst enterprises, a deficit of the industrial and commercial companies sector as a whole is made up of surpluses of some companies outweighed by deficits of others, so that in this sector, too, financing activity greatly exceeds the net deficit of the sector as a whole. Within the public sector, however, financing is much more highly centralized, with the saving of some public sector entities being made available for investment by others without passing through the financial system. The surplus or deficit of the public corporations and general government together is therefore a reasonably good indicator of the resources they supply to, or the demands they make upon, financial institutions and markets.

Transactions in financial assets – the flow-of-funds table

An economic agent's financial surplus or deficit provides a link between the agent's saving and investment in physical assets on the one hand and its transactions in financial assets on the other. An agent with surplus saving is in a position to acquire additional financial assets or to repay debt, while an agent with a deficit must either borrow more or reduce financial asset holdings. We can show this schematically as follows:

Saving − investment = financial surplus

= increase in financial assets
− increase in financial liabilities

= net acquisition of financial assets.

For the purpose of this equation a financial deficit is treated simply as a negative financial surplus, and decreases in financial assets or liabilities are treated as negative increases.

Table 2.8 shows an illustrative example. Suppose a company has saving of £100 000 and investment of £200 000 in a year, and suppose that its financial assets and liabilities consist of bank deposits and loans respectively. The upper part of the table shows that its financial surplus is −£100 000, i.e. it has a financial *deficit* of £100 000.

There are a number of ways in which it can arrange its finances, of which two are shown in the lower half of table 2.8. Example A

Table 2.8 Saving, investment and transactions in financial assets and liabilities

	A		B	
				(£ thousand)
Saving			100	
less Investment			−200	
Financial surplus			−100	

	A		B	
Change in bank deposits (asset)	50 (increase)		−50 (decrease)	
less Change in loans (liability)	−150 (increase)		−50 (increase)	
Net acquisition of financial assets	−100		−100	

shows the company as *increasing* its bank deposits by £50 000 (investment in a new activity may well entail an increase in liquid assets), so that loans have to rise by £150 000, to match the financial deficit and increase in assets. Alternatively (example B) the firm might have financed the deficit by running down bank deposits (−£50 000) and borrowing only £50 000. In either case the *net* acquisition of financial assets is −£100 000 (increase in assets *less* increase in liabilities), equal to the financial surplus for the firm. The financial surplus provides a constraint which the company's financial transactions are bound to satisfy.

A picture of the financial activities of each sector can be obtained by listing its transactions in all the available financial assets and liabilities; taken together these must, of course, be consistent with the sector's financial surplus or deficit. This procedure can be carried out for every sector in the economy – the financial instruments employed in the economy have to be classified into a limited number of categories, such as sterling deposits or loans for house purchase, and the transactions by all the sectors in each of the categories have to be shown. A table in which the rows show categories of financial instrument and columns show the sector's transactions in each instrument is called a flow-of-funds table. The flow-of-funds table then presents a complete and consistent statement of the financial transactions between the sectors of the economy.

Table 2.9 is an example of a flow-of-funds table, which shows the flows of funds in the UK during the years 1985–9, expressed as percentages of GDP. The sectors are familiar, although public

Table 2.9 Flows of funds, 1985–89

(Per cent of GDP at market prices)

	Personal sector	Industrial and commercial companies	Public sector	Financial companies and institutions	Overseas sector
Sterling deposits, notes and coin	6.5	1.8	0.1	−10.6	2.1
Life assurance and pension funds	5.5	—	−0.1	−5.3	—
Public sector debt	0.1	−0.1	0.8	−0.7	−0.1
UK company securities	−2.0	−0.9	−1.1	0.9	3.1
Overseas securities	0.3	1.9	—	3.2	−5.4
Unit trust units	0.2	—	—	−0.2	—
Sterling bank lending	−2.1	−3.4	—	6.6	−1.0
Loans for house purchase	−7.0	—	—	7.0	—
Foreign currency deposits (net)	—	−0.8	—	−0.5	1.3
Investment abroad (net)	−0.1	0.9	—	−0.1	−0.6
Miscellaneous loans etc.	0.4	−0.5	−0.2	−0.2	0.5
Total financial transactions	1.8	−1.0	−0.6	—	−0.2
Balancing item	−2.2	−0.4	0.2	0.6	1.9
Financial surplus	−0.4	−1.4	−0.4	0.6	1.7

Source: Blue Book, 1990, tables 11.2–4, 11.12, 11.15

corporations and general government have been grouped together as the public sector, because so much of their financing is centralized. With so many different financial instruments it is inevitable that there should be a high degree of grouping in the figures. Thus, for example, all sterling deposits – i.e. bank and building society deposits – have been aggregated together. The bottom line shows the financial surpluses and deficits derived from the national income accounts, and the discrepancies between the estimates of transactions in financial assets and these totals are included in the 'balancing item'.

Since the flow-of-funds table is a complete description of financial transactions, all identified transactions of each sector must be allocated to one or other of the rows in the table. Acquisitions of assets or reductions in liabilities are shown as positive, and reductions in assets or increases in liabilities are negative. Since each *column* shows the transactions for one sector, the sum of the transactions items – the net acquisition of financial assets – is of course equal to the financial surplus or deficit for that sector.

Each *row* of the table shows the transactions by all of the sectors in that particular category of financial instrument. The sum of all the entries in each row is therefore normally zero, because financial instruments are simultaneously liabilities of their issuers and assets of their holders. For example, if the personal sector increases its holdings of sterling deposits as an asset (a positive entry in the sterling deposits row), banks and building societies must at the same time be increasing their liabilities to the personal sector (an equal negative element in the deposits entry for the financial companies and institutions sector).[12]

The flow-of-funds table helps us to pick out some of the major characteristics of finance in the UK.

On average the personal sector added 6.5 per cent of GDP each year to its holdings of sterling deposits, notes and coin. This increase in its holdings of highly liquid assets was slightly more than the money channelled into life assurance and pension funds (5.5 per cent). But at the same time the sector was a net seller of company securities to the tune of 2 per cent of GDP a year, it borrowed much the same from the banks (excluding house purchase loans), and loans for house purchase amounted to a massive 7 per cent of GDP each year (compared with about 4 per cent of GDP spent on new dwellings and purchases of land and dwellings from other sectors).

The total identified financial transactions added up to 1.8 per cent of GDP a year, compared with a financial *deficit* for the sector of 0.4 per cent derived from the national income accounts. The discrepancy reflects errors and omissions in *both* the financial transactions and the national income accounts, and we cannot say with any confidence where they have arisen. One implication is that the personal sector may not, after all, have had a financial deficit in this period – it is quite conceivable that there was actually a small surplus.

Industrial and commercial companies do appear to have had a financial deficit and were net borrowers overall. But they devoted nearly 2 per cent of GDP a year to building up their sterling deposits and much the same to acquiring overseas securities. Investment abroad also made a net demand on funds, with UK companies' overseas investment exceeding that of foreign companies in the UK by almost 1 per cent of GDP. The main source of finance was sterling bank lending (over 3 per cent of GDP), with securities issues adding nearly a *net* 1 per cent – that is, securities issues exceeded securities acquired in takeovers by this amount. Foreign currency deposits (net) show the increase in these deposits *less* any increase in foreign currency borrowing. In this period borrowing exceeded the rise in deposits by 0.8 per cent of GDP a year, no doubt to help to finance acquisitions of overseas securities and investment abroad.

The only major items in the public sector column are net sales of company securities of a little over 1 per cent of GDP a year and net purchases of public sector debt of a little under 1 per cent. The former reflects the proceeds for the government of the privatization programme, the latter the fact that the bulk of these proceeds could be used to retire government debt.[13]

The increase in the sterling deposit liabilities of financial institutions in this period averaged over 10 per cent of GDP a year, double the flow of funds into life assurance and pension funds. The principal uses of these funds by the financial institutions were loans for house purchase (7 per cent), sterling bank lending (6.6 per cent), purchases of overseas securities (over 3 per cent) and purchases of UK company securities (less than 1 per cent); holdings of UK public sector debt fell by 0.7 per cent of GDP a year.

These figures illustrate two important features of the period. First, the rate of growth of both deposits and loans was very high, reflecting the economic boom. In more stable economic conditions, with only moderate inflation, they would be lower.

Secondly, the high proportion of long-term funds devoted to overseas investment reflected a trend towards greater international diversification of investment portfolios. In quantitative terms, this is of no great importance so long as overseas investors are acquiring

UK securities to much the same extent as UK investors are acquiring overseas – there was in fact some, though by no means a completely compensating, flow of this kind. But it does mean that UK capital markets are more vulnerable to changes of mood and swings of fashion in international markets than was the case when domestic funds flowed largely into domestic markets. Changes of sentiment, reflecting political or other factors, are liable to have substantial effects on conditions in capital markets.

Purchases of UK securities by the overseas sector averaged just over 3 per cent of GDP in this period, against sales of overseas securities to UK residents of 5.4 per cent. Sterling deposits with UK banks etc. exceeded sterling bank lending by about 1 per cent a year, while the inflow through foreign currency deposits and lending (1.3 per cent) was slightly larger. Overseas direct investment in the UK was less than UK investment abroad, by 0.6 per cent of GDP a year. However, these figures need to be treated with caution because the balancing item amounted to nearly 2 per cent of GDP – it is not easy to observe and record either international trading or financial transactions comprehensively and accurately. The sum of the recorded financial transactions (−0.2 per cent) implies a small current account *surplus* for the period, whereas the figures for the current account of the balance of payments show a *deficit* of 1.7 per cent of GDP.

The flow-of-funds table provides the organizing framework for the analysis of the financial system in this book. When we examine the behaviour of the major users of the system – all the non-financial sectors – we shall be examining the columns of the table in more detail. When we turn to institutions and markets we shall focus in each case on only a small number of rows. In every case there are balance sheet constraints to be satisfied – a sector's financial transactions are constrained by its (true) financial surplus or deficit, an institution's transactions by the equality between changes in assets and liabilities, a market by the fact that for every buyer of a financial instrument there must be a seller. And it is in the process of ensuring that all these constraints are satisfied that interest rates and asset prices are determined.

Notes

1 These deposits represent only about 30 per cent of the banks' deposits, the bulk being in foreign currencies – see chapter 11.
2 There is a small amount of overlap in both deposits and commercial

lending, as a result of transactions between banks and building societies.

3 It would therefore be misleading simply to add the figures for all the categories together to obtain a total for all the investing institutions in table 2.2.

4 These are discussed in chapter 13.

5 So far as possible throughout this book, saving and investment are measured after deducting stock appreciation, which is largely a consequence of inflation and is automatically absorbed by an increase in the value of stocks. They are also measured *gross* – that is no deduction is made for capital consumption (or depreciation).

6 The figures refer to domestic saving and domestic investment, the difference (in principle) being the surplus on the current account of the balance of payments.

7 Estimating the profitability of financial institutions according to national accounts conventions is a peculiarly difficult exercise, so the figures for saving by financial institutions should be treated with an appropriate degree of scepticism!

8 The decline shown by the figures is a little misleading because council house and other asset sales are treated as negative investment. But the fact remains that there was a genuine squeeze on investment.

9 The financial surplus of the overseas sector is therefore equal to the current balance of payments (with sign reversed) adjusted for capital transfers.

10 The sum of the sector surpluses and deficits in each year should in principle be zero, since total saving (including the net acquisition of foreign assets) must equal total investment. In practice there is a discrepancy, equal to the residual error in the national income accounts.

11 It is the difference between the income and the expenditure estimates of GDP.

12 Since the sum of the financial surpluses of all the sectors is (minus) the residual error in the national income accounts, the bottom row does not add to zero and the balancing items add to the same total.

13 Or more usually, to avoid the need to refinance maturing government debt.

Part II

Theory of the financial system

In Part II our task will be to examine the ways in which the financial system interacts with saving and investment in the economy, and the real and monetary factors which determine interest rates. Borrowers and lenders, sellers and buyers of securities, have access to markets for funds in the broad sense; i.e. they can issue liabilities or acquire assets on 'market' terms, including interest rates. The relevant markets may be informal, such as the retail deposit market, or organized, such as the securities market, and access on 'market' terms does not mean that all vestiges of monopoly power are ruled out or that the market is free of government intervention; the rate of interest charged to a borrower is likely to reflect the strength of competition amongst lenders for his business, regulations which affect cost, and any government subsidies. But access to markets does imply that the rates of interest charged to individual borrowers or paid to lenders are not *arbitrary*, that economic agents in similar situations are accorded the same treatment, and that borrowers and lenders have some choice regarding their sources and uses of finance.

We begin in chapter 3 by considering the ways in which financial institutions and markets help to mobilize saving in the economy and channel savings to those who are likely to make best use of them, and follow this in chapter 4 with asset transformation – the task of transforming risky and illiquid liabilities into safe and liquid assets – and cost reduction. In these two chapters 'the' rate of interest is the price which balances the supply of funds (saving) with the demand for funds (investment) – it is an abstraction from the range of rates actually attached to different financial instruments.

We then move on to examine interest rates. Chapter 5 sets out in broad outline the factors which determine the interest rate on long-term assets, before turning to the structure of interest rates on financial instruments with different maturities, exposure to risk, and vulnerability to inflation. The analysis of chapter 5 is developed further in chapter 6, with particular attention being paid to the factors influencing short-term interest rates and the links between worldwide and domestic factors in the determination of interest rates.

3

Mobilizing saving

Chapter 1 drew attention to some of the ways in which financial institutions and markets promoted saving and investment. It was partly a matter of improving the opportunities available to savers, who, as a result of the financial system, were able to obtain higher yields on their savings and to hold them in safer and more liquid forms; partly of altering savers' preferences, so that saving ranked higher in their list of priorities; and partly of giving potential investors access to funds on the scale they required, at a cost which they could afford, and on terms which were acceptable to them. In this chapter we consider the mobilization of saving – the functions of providing facilities for saving, of gathering savings together, and of making saving available to investors.

In what follows we shall assume that saving and investment are brought into balance in the market for funds, as illustrated in figure 3.1. The level of saving, S, is assumed to increase and of investment, I, to fall as the rate of interest, r, rises; the justification for these assumptions will emerge later. In figure 3.1 the equilibrium level of saving and investment is OA, and the equilibrium rate of interest is r_0. Anything which shifted the saving schedule to the right would raise the equilibrium level of saving and investment and lower the rate of interest (e.g. an increase in desired saving represented by a shift in the savings schedule from S to S' would increase actual saving and expand investment to OA' and lower the rate of interest to r_1), and anything which shifted investment to the right would also increase saving and investment but raise the rate of interest (e.g. a shift from I to I' would increase saving and investment to OA'' and raise the rate of interest to r_2); and vice versa for leftward shifts in the saving and investment schedules.

We shall begin by investigating saving and investment in a rudimentary economy in which individuals are unable to borrow or

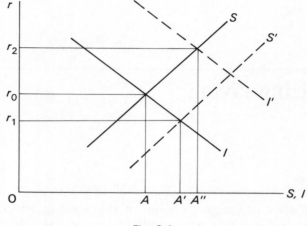

Fig. 3.1

lend and are therefore constrained by their own incomes and the investment opportunities open to them. We shall then consider the effect on savers of breaking this budget constraint by allowing them to purchase financial assets or to borrow at some given rate of interest, and we shall examine how this aspect of financial institutions' activities influences the propensity to save. After that we shall turn to investors, the main borrowers of funds, and investigate the effects of giving them access to whatever funds they can usefully employ at the going rate of interest. Finally we shall draw the threads together to see how saving, investment and the rate of interest are affected by the existence of a financial system.

Saving and investment in the absence of a financial system

Consider first an economy without financial institutions or markets. No actual economy is as poorly endowed with financial opportunities as this,[1] but it is nevertheless useful to examine the factors which would influence saving and investment in a very simple, hypothetical economy. We shall work with a two-period model, and we shall assume that every economic agent is both a producer and a consumer. As a producer the agent has to choose in the first period between using resources to produce goods for consumption in that period or for investment in order to augment the output of consumption goods in the second. As a consumer, the agent has preferences concerning the time-pattern of his consumption; if he chooses to consume less today it is because he expects to be compensated by a higher level of consumption tomorrow. We assume further that if he neither invests nor disinvests our economic agent will have a given output of consumption goods (or endowment of income) in each period. The decisions taken by the economic agent will depend upon: the *income* from existing resources in the two periods; the *opportunities* to vary the pattern of consumption between the two periods by investment or disinvestment; and the agent's *preferences* relating to consumption levels in the two periods.

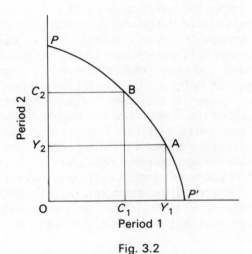

Fig. 3.2

The income from existing resources and opportunities of changing the pattern of income through investment or disinvestment are illustrated in figure 3.2. The point A, with incomes OY_1 and OY_2, shows the income in periods 1 and 2 respectively. PP' is a production possibility curve which shows the terms on which, through investment, consumption can be transferred between the two periods; by giving up some of the consumption available in period 1 the economic agent is able to increase his consumption in period 2.[2] If he chooses to move to point B this means that his consumption in the first period is OC_1, and in the second is OC_2. That part of his endowment of income which is not consumed in period 1 is his saving (C_1Y_1 in figure 3.2) and this is also a measure of his investment. As a result of saving C_1Y_1 he is able to add C_2Y_2 to his consumption in period 2.

Notice that the ratio of C_2Y_2 to C_1Y_1 decreases as C_1Y_1 increases; as the level of investment rises the marginal return to investment normally falls. The return to investment can be expressed as a rate of interest, r. The additional consumption gained as a result of investing C_1Y_1 in period 1 is $(Y_2C_2 - C_1Y_1)$, so that:

$$r = (Y_2C_2 - C_1Y_1)/C_1Y_1$$
$$= (Y_2C_2/C_1Y_1) - 1$$

or

$$Y_2C_2/C_1Y_1 = 1 + r.$$

Y_2C_2/C_1Y_1 is simply the average slope of PP' between A and B, showing that the slope of the production possibility curve is equal to $(1+r)$. In this instance r can be either positive or negative.[3]

Economic agents have preferences regarding the time-pattern of their consumption and these preferences can be represented by an *indifference map*, as in figure 3.3. Each curve represents combinations of consumption in the two periods, between which the individual is indifferent. Thus since the points X and X' lie on the same indifference curve (I_1) this implies that the individual is equally happy with consumption OC_1 in period 1 and OC_2 in period 2 as he would be with consumption OC_1' and OC_2' in the two periods respectively. Any point on a higher curve (such as I_2) is preferred to any point on a lower. If the economic agent's needs in the two periods are perceived to be the same, the curves will be symmetric about the 45° line; and they will also be convex to the origin because

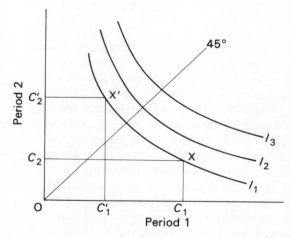

Fig. 3.3

the consumer will be willing to depart from an equal consumption pattern only if the increased consumption of one period is sufficient to compensate him for the reduction in the other.[4]

The economic agent's preferences and opportunities can be put together to show what combination of consumption in the two periods he will choose, and this is done in figure 3.4. Given his income at A, the production possibility curve PP' shows the maximum achievable combinations of consumption in the two periods, and the preference map indicates that the highest attainable indifference curve is I_2, where the agent is at point B on PP'. At this point consumption will be OC_1 and OC_2 in periods 1 and 2 respectively. Since income in the first period is OY_1 the saving (consumption forgone) amounts to C_1Y_1, and this is invested to produce output of Y_2C_2 in the second period. The implied rate of interest on saving is therefore $[(Y_2C_2/C_1Y_1) - 1)]$.

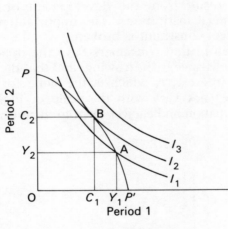

Fig. 3.4

There is no reason to believe that the production opportunities or preferences of all the economic agents in a rudimentary economy of this kind would be identical, and, with lending and borrowing ruled out, each agent would have to make the best of his own position. This means that the implied rates of return on investment would vary, agent to agent, according to each agent's own production possibilities and preferences. There would be no possibility of transferring resources from those agents who could only achieve a low rate of return on investment to those who were able to invest more productively. Moreover, in practice many individuals have very limited opportunities for carrying out real investment projects, almost to the point where no such opportunities may exist at all. In a rudimentary economy such an individual would be constrained to have a time-pattern of consumption which was the same as that of his income; i.e. he would be constrained to remain at point A on indifference curve I_1 in figure 3.4.

The rate of interest and saving

Now consider the effects of creating a financial system which allows lending and borrowing to take place. For this purpose we shall divide economic agents into two groups – consumers, who have no productive opportunities, and producers, whose sole concern is with production.[5] It is the consumers who are responsible for saving in the economy. The precise mechanism for saving is immaterial at this stage; it could result from the development of either financial markets or financial institutions. The important point is that the individual's budget constraint is broken.

Suppose therefore that consumers have the opportunity to save by lending or to dis-save by borrowing, and that they are faced with a fixed rate of interest, r, which is the same for borrowers and lenders and does not vary with the scale of their borrowing or lending. Their situation and choices open to them can be represented by figure 3.5.

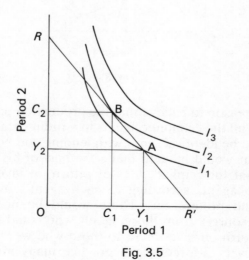

Fig. 3.5

The point A represents the consumer's income, OY_1 and OY_2 in the two periods respectively, and the line RR', which passes through A, represents his consumption opportunities, replacing the production possibility curve for the consumer. The slope of RR' is $(1+r)$, the rate at which consumption in one period can be exchanged for consumption in the other.[6] If $r = 0$, RR' is a 45° line; if the slope is greater (less) than 45°, r is positive (negative). The individual is able to shift from A to the point B on indifference curve I_2, where he consumes OC_1 in period 1 and lends the balance of his income for that period C_1Y_1. This enables him to consume OC_2 in period 2, using the second period income, OY_2, and the repayment with interest of the loan, Y_2C_2. Thus the ability to borrow or lend relaxes the consumer's budget constraint and allows him to improve his position.

It is clear from figure 3.5 that the amount of saving in period 1 (and correspondingly dis-saving in period 2) will depend upon the slope of the line RR'; i.e. upon the rate of interest, r. At some rates of interest the consumer would choose to be a lender, while at others he might choose to borrow. Figure 3.6 enables us to investigate how lending and borrowing are likely to vary with the rate of interest; i.e. to examine the relationship between saving and the rate of interest.

Suppose that as before the consumer's income is represented by the point A. If the interest rate is represented by the line R_0R_0', which is tangential to I_1 at A, he will neither save nor dis-save in period 1. With a higher rate of interest, shown by R_1R_1', the

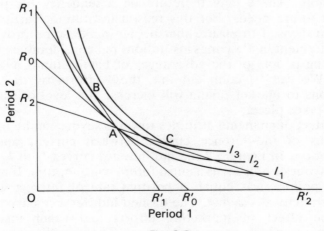

Fig. 3.6

consumer would choose to save by moving to B on I_2; and with a lower rate, shown by R_2R_2', he would dis-save by moving to C on I_3.

In the vicinity of point A, the consumer's income in the two periods, there is no doubt that a rise in the rate of interest raises the level of saving or reduces dis-saving – there is a positive relationship between saving and the rate of interest. But this positive relationship does not necessarily continue indefinitely as the rate of interest increases. It is possible that a very high rate of interest would lead to a lower level of saving than prevailed at a somewhat lower rate, though a rate of interest higher than that shown by R_0R_0' could never lead to actual dis-saving.[7] Though this qualification must be borne in mind, the fact that a positive relationship between saving and the rate of interest must prevail over at least part of the range is the justification for drawing an upward-sloping saving schedule in figure 3.1.

So far the theory does not allow us to conclude that opening financial markets where none existed previously would necessarily increase saving. At the same time as opportunities for saving become available so do opportunities for borrowing, and if the rate of interest turned out to be low it is theoretically possible that more consumers would avail themselves of the chance to borrow than would choose to save. Whether this is likely to happen in practice is a question which we reserve for later discussion.

A financial system comprises institutions as well as financial markets, and financial institutions have an additional effect on saving; they affect peoples' attitudes towards it. To many people present needs seem urgent, and those of the future are uncertain and remote. There may therefore be a tendency for people to discount future needs. For this reason institutional arrangements are often devised to ensure that people make some provision for their retirement, and savings institutions put considerable effort into persuading people of the advantages of having funds available in future. We can be confident that these efforts by the financial institutions to market saving will increase the level of saving that actually takes place.[8]

The effect of changing attitudes towards saving can be illustrated by means of indifference curves between current and future consumption. In figure 3.7 the indifference curves I_1 to I_3 reflect a bias in favour of present as against future consumption. If income in the two periods was equal, a positive rate of interest would be needed to deter dis-saving. The dashed indifference curves I_1' to I_3' show the effect of marketing efforts and other institutional arrangements which encourage saving. These indifference curves

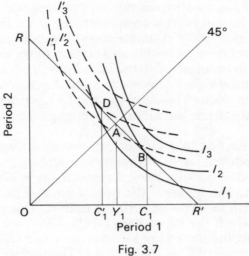

Fig. 3.7

are flatter, because by heightening perceptions of future needs the additional period 2 consumption which is required in order to persuade people to cut their consumption in period 1 has been reduced. As before, RR' shows the savings opportunities which are available, and it can be seen easily that the level of saving for any given interest rate is increased. For example, with the income shown at A and the interest rate represented by RR', in the absence of marketing the consumer would choose to move to B, with dis-saving of Y_1C_1. But when the slope of the indifference curves has been changed by the marketing effort he chooses instead to move to D, giving saving of $C_1'Y_1$. The effect of the marketing effort is therefore to raise the level of saving at any rate of interest.

The rate of interest and investment

We turn now to the effects of making the facilities of the financial system available to producers. We imagine that the producer has a certain amount of resources available, and that these can be used to produce either consumption or investment goods. Investment goods produced in period 1 are used by the producer to make consumption goods in period 2.

The producer will now concentrate on maximizing the value of his (or her) production, regardless of the time-pattern of his own consumption needs. His consumption in the first period is not determined by his own production of consumption goods at that time, because he can borrow to supplement any deficiency or lend any surplus. Again, the consumption goods produced in the second period can either be used for his own consumption in that period or sold to pay off debts incurred in the first. Thus, while consumption is limited by the total value of his production, decisions concerning the allocation of productive resources in the two periods can be taken quite separately from decisions concerning the time-pattern of consumption.

The value attached to a unit of consumption goods depends on when it is produced, and the relative valuation of consumption goods produced in periods 1 and 2 respectively is measured by the rate of interest. The higher is the rate of interest the less output in period 2 is worth in terms of period 1 output. This is illustrated in figure 3.8, in which the set of lines labelled RR' are lines of equal value, all having the slope $(1+r)$ so that the value OR on the period 2 axis is $(1+r)$ times OR' on the period 1. The further is the line RR' from the origin the greater is the value represented, so R_0R_0', R_1R_1' etc. are in ascending order of value.

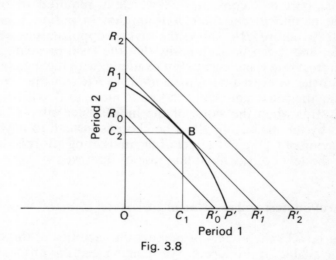

Fig. 3.8

In order to maximize the value of his output the producer will choose to produce OC_1 and OC_2 of consumption goods in periods 1 and 2 respectively, thus placing himself at B on PP' where it is tangential to R_1R_1', the highest attainable value line. Measuring investment in terms of consumption goods output forgone, investment is C_1P'. The yield on additional investment at B is just equal to the rate of interest.[9]

It is easy to see from figure 3.8 how the level of investment will vary with the rate of interest. A fall in r, which implies that the set of RR' lines will be flatter, shifts the point B towards the period 2 axis and increases the level of investment. Conversely, a rise in the rate of interest will reduce investment, which is therefore an inverse function of the rate of interest (as indicated by the falling investment schedule in figure 3.1).

We cannot yet say whether investment in the new situation will be higher or lower than it was in the rudimentary economy. Clearly, if producers had to provide for their own consumption needs there would be some who were unable to take full advantage of investment opportunities; these producers will invest more because the prevailing rate of interest will be lower than the rate of return at the margin of their investment previously. On the other hand, some producers will now invest less because projects which were previously marginal offer too low a return, and it pays them to produce consumption goods in period 1 instead. The net effect depends on how high the interest rate turns out to be. However, we can say that the average quality of the investment that takes place will rise. For it is the producers with opportunities to earn a rate of return higher than the rate of interest who will invest more, whereas those investing less will be those whose investments were comparatively low-yielding.

The possibility of borrowing resources also extends the production opportunities open to the producer, who can augment his own resources for investment in the first period, with the loan to be repaid out of part of his period 2 production. This is of the utmost importance, because it means that the scale of investment is not limited to what the investor can find from his own resources, and large-scale investment offers a potentially much higher rate of return than many small-scale projects.

This is illustrated in figure 3.9, in which the production possibility curve PP' extends beyond the vertical axis (reflecting the possibility of borrowing) and exhibits economies of scale in the range XZ; i.e. in this range the marginal return to investment increases. If the producer was restricted to investing his own resources he would choose to move to B_0, where the value of his output would be OR'_0. But by borrowing OC_1 for investment he can invest a total of C_1P' in period 1, to yield OC_2 of consumption goods in period 2; i.e. he can move to B_1 on PP' and take advantage of the economies of scale. This allows him to produce a higher value of output, OR'_1. Since many of the more attractive investment possibilities entail investment on a scale which greatly exceeds the investing company's

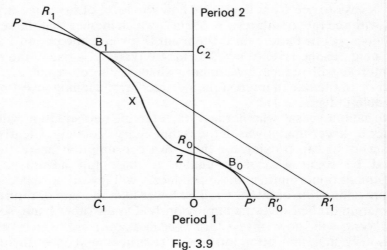

Fig. 3.9

own resources in any year, the financial system, which facilitates such investment, contributes greatly to its productivity.

Intermediation and investment

These effects, which result from the breaking of the budget constraints facing savers and investors, are known as *intermediation effects*. They justify the slopes of the saving and investment schedules in figure 3.1. These are now repeated in figure 3.10, which illustrates the effects of intermediation on saving, investment and the rate of interest. The vertical line AB represents the levels of saving and investment in the absence of financial markets; these are of course equal. Saving and investment are shown as independent of the rate of interest, because in the absence of financial markets no uniform rate of interest exists – each economic agent has his own implied rate of interest at the margin of his own saving and investment (as illustrated in figure 3.4), but there is no reason to suppose that different agents will have the same implied rate. In contrast, when financial activity is possible, we can expect to have the customary upward-sloping saving schedule and downward-sloping investment schedule as shown. In figure 3.10, S and I intersect at the equilibrium rate of interest, r_0, with saving and investment at OD. In this figure, D falls to the right of B, indicating higher levels of saving and investment when intermediation is possible than in a rudimentary system.

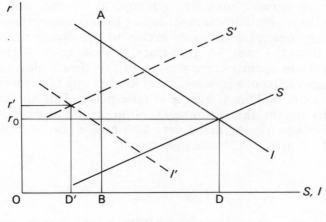

Fig. 3.10

This is much the most probable outcome. The provision of opportunities for saving and active marketing of savings facilities are likely to raise the level of saving and so push *S* out to the right. And the mobilization of saving to finance large-scale investment raises the investment schedule. It is therefore unlikely that the introduction of a financial system would reduce saving and investment. But it is a theoretical possibility that cannot be ruled out altogether. In figure 3.10, *S'* and *I'* have been drawn to intersect at a level of saving and investment *OD'*, which is less than *OB* in the rudimentary case. Nevertheless, even in this case, the effect on future output would not necessarily be adverse, because the financial system would still help to raise the average productivity of the investment which did take place.

The problem is that the opening of financial markets and institutions gives *consumers* as well as producers access to credit, so that the net supply of saving may actually be reduced. This is unlikely to be a permanent phenomenon, but it can occur temporarily for some years after a change is made. For example, financial deregulation in the UK greatly increased consumers' access to credit in the 1980s. Rationing in the mortgage market was virtually eliminated, with the result that a surge of borrowing for house purchase permitted substantial equity withdrawal (i.e. dis-saving) from the housing market. Allied to easier access to consumer credit generally, this contributed to a marked reduction in the personal savings ratio in the second half of the decade.

Some countries, however, attempt to ensure that financial markets do promote investment rather than consumption. Governments may restrict consumers' access to the financial markets or ensure that the cost of consumer borrowing is high. Similar discrimination against certain types of investment deemed by the government to be of a comparatively low priority (e.g. investment in land or some buildings) may also take place. This allows governments to obtain the advantages of improved opportunities for saving, whilst ensuring that a very high proportion of that saving is directed towards productive investment.

Notes

1 We are assuming even the absence of money as a medium of exchange.
2 The reverse process, shifting consumption from period 2 to period 1, is more difficult, but can occur to some extent through the consumption of capital.
3 Which would imply that the additional consumption gained in period 2 was less than the amount given up in period 1.
4 This is the assumption of a diminishing marginal rate of substitution in consumption.
5 Consumer/producers may be regarded as taking consumption and production decisions separately.
6 Strictly speaking the slope of RR' is *minus* $(1+r)$.
7 An increase in the rate of interest has both income and substitution effects. It is possible that the income effect may lead the consumer to demand more consumption in period 1 and less in period 2, thereby discouraging saving. The substitution effect of an increase in the rate of interest will always tend to increase saving.
8 We should note, however, that institutionalized saving may change the shape of the indifference curves and the relationship between saving and the rate of interest. Thus the objective of a pension fund is to provide a *target* level of income for its members. The higher the rate of interest the lower the level of annual contributions required to achieve this target; i.e. an increase in the rate of interest reduces the required level of saving. This was illustrated in the UK in the late 1980s, when pension funds reduced their contribution levels in response to the high rates of return on investment earned in the preceding years.
9 That is, at B on PP', the additional period 2 output obtained by forgoing one unit of period 1 output is $(1+r)$.

4

Asset transformation

When we took a preliminary look at the financial system in chapter 1 we noted that financial institutions and markets had the dual functions of transferring resources from savers to investors and of helping both these groups to obtain financial instruments with the characteristics they wanted.

Savers' needs are in fact very varied. While some are prepared to put money away for a long time and to accept a certain degree of risk, the majority are most concerned with the safety of their savings and put a premium on liquidity – the ability of turn them into cash at short notice. Investors' requirements also cover a very wide range; for some it is long-term capital which is required, preferably without any obligation to repay if a project proves unsuccessful, while for others funds may be required for only a short period and can be repaid with a high degree of certainty. The needs of some savers and some investors do not therefore necessarily conflict, though even when no conflict exists the financial system has the task of bringing those with matching requirements together. However, taking saving as a whole there is a strong bias towards a preference for safety and liquidity, whereas on the investment side the principal need is for long-term finance which must frequently be exposed to a significant degree of risk.

In the absence of financial institutions and markets some compromise would have to be found. This would inevitably be unsatisfactory to both parties, and would be liable to reduce the levels of saving and investment in the economy. Moreover, the processes of bringing savers and investors together and agreeing terms would be costly, and this too would be likely to depress investment activity. Thus, in addition to the function of releasing savers and investors from budget constraints which we discussed in the last chapter, the financial system also has to transform the risk-bearing liabilities of ultimate borrowers into safe assets for lenders, to transform long-maturity liabilities into liquid assets, and to reduce the costs incurred in the saving/investment process.

In this chapter we examine how these functions are carried out. We deal first with risk, and show how unnecessary risks can be avoided and those that remain can be borne by those savers most willing to take risk. Then we go on to maturity transformation and liquidity. Finally we consider the means employed to cut transactions costs and show how a reduction in these costs benefits savers and investors and raises the level of financial activity in the economy.

Risk transformation

Investment is an inherently risky activity, though the degree of risk depends upon the form the investment takes. The results of business activity are always unpredictable, and while businessmen may attempt to reduce risk – for example by diversifying their activities, integrating with suppliers or customers, or entering into long-term contracts – they cannot eliminate risk altogether. The costs and benefits of investment by public authorities are equally uncertain. Constructing and equipping a new hospital may cost much more than anyone expected at the time the decision to build was taken; the running costs may turn out to be higher than anticipated; or the need and therefore usage may turn out to be less. Even investment in housing carries an element of risk: too much may have been paid for the land, or the area may decline, perhaps as a result of a recession in local industry, with a consequential fall in the value of property.

In every case somebody has to bear the risk. With public authority investment it is the taxpayer, because the government taps the savings market by issuing loans and guarantees the saver against loss. With houses the risk is shared between the owner and the mortgagor, though the latter bears little risk unless the sum lent lies close to the market value of the property. In the case of business investment the risk is borne by the owners of the financial assets which form the firm's capital, but the capital is usually divided into debt and equity, and the risk is not borne equally by both parts. The debt component is relatively safe, often secured on some of the firm's assets or by 'covenants' inserted into loan agreements; these covenants usually give the lender the right to immediate repayment if the firm fails to carry out its obligations. The business risk – the variability of income or capital value associated with business activity – is therefore concentrated on the firm's equity, to which the benefits of a good performance accrue or which absorbs the first slice of any loss.

This division of companies' liabilities into distinct categories with very different degrees of risk exposure is vitally important to the working of the financial system, because it permits savers and institutions who are averse to risk to specialize in low-risk financial instruments, whilst leaving other savers or institutions whose needs do not inhibit the holding of risky assets to specialize in the function of risk-bearing. It is parallelled by a distinction between *default* risk and *equity* risk.

Default risk is attached to debt: it is the risk that the borrower will default on his or her obligations, that he or she will fail to pay interest or to repay the loan itself when it is due. The probability of default is a measure of default risk and a safe asset is one for which this probability is zero; i.e. there is complete confidence that interest will be paid and capital repaid as agreed at the outset. The holders of debt instruments such as deposits or loans normally wish to ensure that the default risk is low (loans) or even negligible (deposits), and the charge for a loan will include a premium – fixed at the time the loan is granted – to compensate the lender for the risk of loss. Thus, while the rate of interest which a borrower must pay for a loan reflects the risk of loss contemplated at the time the loan is granted, it does not normally depend on how successful he turns out to be in using the funds profitably.

Equity risk derives from the uncertainty surrounding the income which will be earned by business assets. Because the income is uncertain the future value of the assets themselves cannot be predicted exactly, and neither can the remuneration which the holder of equity assets will receive. The return to the equity-holder is therefore related to the profitability of the enterprise in question. If the enterprise is successful equity assets will maintain or increase their value, whereas if it is a failure the value of the equity will be reduced or even lost altogether.

While the conceptual distinction between default risk for debt and variability of return for equity is useful, it is not in fact absolutely clear-cut in practice. Default does not necessarily imply total loss to the lender; it is really a question of varying amounts of loss with different probabilities. And very occasionally, when the risk entailed in a project seems too high for a straightforward loan, lenders may nevertheless agree to grant the loan, but on condition that they receive some additional income if the project is successful.[1]

Default risk

Risk transformation is one important function of deposit-taking institutions like banks and building societies. The depositors who hold the institutions' liabilities must be able to regard them as absolutely safe. The institutions' loans, however, inevitably bear some default risk. Their ability to transform these risky assets into riskless liabilities depends on three things: the risk of loss on each loan; controlling their risks; and providing sufficient capital of their own to absorb any unexpected losses.

Lenders go about the task of trying to ensure that the probability of any individual loan going into default is low in a number of ways. First, they consider the purpose of the loan, and whether they think it is legitimate. Legitimate purposes would include house purchase, investment by a firm in new plant and equipment or stocks, purchase of consumer durables, or the temporary finance of a peak in a consumer's spending. But to make a loan which was intended to enable a borrower to live beyond his means, or to allow a business to maintain its working capital during a period of continuing and persistent losses, would usually be regarded as unjustified. Secondly, the lender considers the borrower's income. In the case of a house mortgage or a consumer instalment loan, the lender wishes to be satisfied that the borrower has sufficient income to pay the interest and make capital payments on the agreed terms, without undue strain. In the case of a loan to a business, the lender will wish to be satisfied that the borrower has sufficient income to meet the terms of the loan, either from his other activities or from the income generated by assets purchased with the loan itself. In reaching a decision the lender will often rely heavily on his judgement of the borrower, rather than on the precise project for which the loan is required. Thirdly, the lender may look for security over assets. If the borrower should be unable to carry out his commitments under the loan agreement, the lender with a charge over marketable assets such as buildings or marketable securities may be able to recover his loan, albeit with some cost and delay. Alternatively, the security may in effect be provided by a firm's existing activities; if the firm is itself in a position to absorb losses, the loan may not be at risk. Finally, the lender may reduce the risk of loss by writing 'covenants' into the loan agreement, so that he is able to demand immediate repayment of the loan if there is a serious risk that the firm will be unable to carry out its obligations. In any event, unless the lender is reasonably confident that he will get his money back he is unlikely to accede to a loan request.

The second method through which deposit-taking institutions limit the risk of loss is by pooling risks. Deposit-taking institutions try to make a large number of small loans rather than a small number of large ones, because, although this does not reduce the expected loss in their portfolio of loans overall, it does give considerably improved predictability and limits the *maximum* loss for which the institution has to allow. By making a large number of loans institutions can expect their actual loss experience to be very close to the average loss rate for that type of business, whereas if only a small number of loans were made the institution might have the misfortune to find that an unusually high proportion had gone sour.

Table 4.1 Loan losses where $p = 0.01$

Number of loans	Expected number (%) of losses	Maximum tolerable[1] number (%) of losses
10	0 (0)	1 (10)
100	1 (1)	4 (4)
1 000	10 (1)	19 (1.9)
10 000	100 (1)	126 (1.26)

[1] Probability of greater number <0.005

The effect of spreading risks on the maximum loss which an institution need contemplate, for various sizes of loan portfolio, is illustrated in table 4.1. It is assumed that the chance of default on any single loan is 1 in 100 (i.e. the probability of default, p, is 0.01) and the risks are *independent*, in the sense that the fact that one borrower defaults on a loan makes it neither more nor less likely that other borrowers will default too. The first two columns of the table show how the number and percentage of losses respectively which the institution might expect on average rise as the number of loans made by the institution increases from 10 to 10 000. But the institution may be unlucky and find that more borrowers default, so it has to guard against the possibility that more than 1 per cent of its loans will fail: with 1000 loans it might reasonably expect that on average ten would be lost, but if it was lucky it might lose only five and if it was unlucky it could lose fifteen or more – if it was exceptionally unlucky it might even experience, say, forty losses.

The institution can never entirely rule out the possibility that losses will be greater than it has allowed for. What it can do is decide on the risk it is prepared to take that losses will exceed the amount for which it has provided, and make allowance for losses accordingly. In table 4.1 it has been assumed that the institution is prepared to accept a 1 in 200 chance that it will suffer losses greater than the maximum number for which it has allowed. The third column of the table shows how this maximum tolerable number of losses increases with the number of loans, and the final column expresses those losses as a percentage of loans granted.[2] It can be seen very clearly that with a small number of loans the maximum percentage loss with which the institution has to contend is substantially above the average level of 1 per cent – for example, 4 per cent if 100 loans are made – but as the number of loans increases the maximum tolerable loss moves steadily closer towards the average. By the time an institution had 10 000 loans in its portfolio it could rely on its loss experience being little worse than the average for that type of loan.

This conclusion, however, does depend critically on the default risks being independent and on the institution's ability to control the level of risk on each loan successfully (to 1 per cent in this example). Achieving an adequate spread of risk is not merely a matter of making a large number of loans. Banks try to ensure that their loans are not concentrated too heavily in any single branch of economic activity or any single area of the country, and they also seek to restrict the maximum size of any single loan, because clearly the risk of one large loan is much greater than that of the equivalent number of small loans.

Examples of the problems which may arise from interdependent risks are not difficult to find – concentration of lending has been a potent cause of bank failures. Texan banks had loan portfolios which depended heavily on the local economy in general and the oil industry in particular. When the oil industry struggled the entire Texan economy was in trouble and many banks failed. Banks in New England were similarly exposed to the local property market, and failed when property prices collapsed. Such concentration of lending is not confined to the United States – building societies in the UK lend predominantly to the housing market and would be vulnerable to any general and sustained fall in UK house prices.

Controlling the average level of risk is, however, just as important as ensuring that risks are well spread. There is evidence to suggest that bankers are no less prone than other businessmen to swings of confidence that affect their perceptions of risk, and that their judgements are not always well-founded. A prime example of risks being misjudged was lending to developing countries in the late 1970s. This was followed by over-optimism about business prospects and over-reliance on insecure asset values in the latter part of the 1980s. In both cases the banks were faced with much higher average loss levels than they had bargained for.

The expected default risk will normally be incorporated in the charge made for a loan. If a bank expects that on average 1 per cent of its loans to a particular category of borrower will be lost each year, then a charge of 1 per cent will be included in the rate of interest paid by such borrowers on loans. This loading for default risk will of course vary between categories of loans, corresponding to the different levels of loss anticipated. But while institutions can include a premium for the *expected* level of losses in the charges they make to borrowers, in the nature of things they cannot charge for unexpected losses.[3] The importance of judging the *average* level of risk correctly cannot be over-stressed.

The protection for depositors against unpredicted losses lies in the capital and reserves (the equity) of the financial institution. Losses in excess of those predicted are borne by the institution's own capital, and the liabilities to depositors are threatened only if losses are so high that all of the institution's capital is used up. In order to provide adequate protection to depositors the size and concentration of loans in an institution's portfolio is often related to the scale of its own capital and reserves, with limits enshrined in regulations governing the institution's operations. For example, it is not regarded as safe for banks in the UK to make loans amounting to more than 10 per cent of their own capital to any single borrower, and excessive concentration of loans for one single activity (e.g. property development) is also frowned upon. Regulators also stipulate the minimum capital backing which the institution must hold against its asset portfolio as a whole, account being taken of the composition of the portfolio.[4]

No matter how well an institution may spread its risk there remains a significant danger that it will experience unexpectedly heavy losses. Its average loss experience may rise because it fails to control its risks properly or, as is more likely, because of a change in the general level of losses associated with the kinds of business in which it is engaged – there is little that any single bank can do to protect itself entirely from the effects of economic fluctuations. There are relatively few losses from business failures in a boom, but chickens come home to roost in the ensuing recession when companies fail to earn the profits they had expected, asset values are undermined, and individuals are unable to service their debts.

Institutions with large and diversified portfolios are in fact much more vulnerable to fluctuations in loss experience for this kind of reason than they are to excessive losses due to the inherent uncertainty attached to individual loans. The premium for default risk has to take account of the loss experience over the cycle as a whole.

The ability of financial institutions to transform risky loans into safe deposits depends, then, upon the three factors we have discussed. They need to *control* risk and incorporate an allowance for probable losses in the charge they make for loans; they must *spread* risk to guard against the possibility that loans to some customers or categories of customer will lead to unusually heavy losses; and they must ensure that their own *capital* is adequate to absorb any losses they may incur through a failure to control risk properly, adverse economic conditions, or concentration of lending in their portfolios.

Equity risk

Financial institutions and markets also transform equity risk in the economy. The principal institutions which perform this function in the UK are the investment and unit trusts, which provide specialized fund management services, and the life assurance and pension funds, which manage very large asset portfolios corresponding to their liabilities to policyholders or members respectively. The key to transforming equity risk lies in diversification – the spreading of assets over a number of different holdings. Spreading ensures that there will be some degree of offsetting between losers and winners, so that the saver avoids the extremes and can reasonably expect his return to reflect the average performance of the kinds of investment made.

Suppose that a person invests £1000 in the ordinary shares of a firm. The value of the investment in a year's time – that is the price of the shares plus any dividends received – is uncertain. Let us call this v. The value, v, may have risen above £1000 or fallen below it. However, the investor will believe that some ranges of value are more likely than others, and we can draw a frequency distribution showing the probability or likelihood he attaches to v lying in certain ranges in a year's time. These probabilities reflect nothing more than the saver's guesses as to the future values; for example a probability of 0.4 that v will lie in a certain range implies that the saver thinks that there is a 40 per cent chance of this outcome.

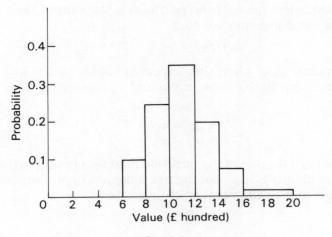

Fig. 4.1

Figure 4.1 illustrates one possible frequency distribution. For example, the probability that v will lie in the range £800–£1000 is shown as 0.25. With this frequency distribution the average value[5] of v would be £1098.

Where the outcome of an investment is unpredictable, as it is in this example, the investment is clearly risky. To conform with everyday usage we shall say that the risk increases with the spread of the frequency distribution; a risky investment is one in which the possibility of an outcome either much greater or much less than the average is substantial. The most common measure of risk is in fact the *standard deviation* of the frequency distribution, a measure which increases as the spread widens.[6]

The frequency distribution of v is usually shown as a continuous curve, as illustrated in figure 4.2, with the arithmetic mean, or *expected value*, written as μ and the standard deviation as σ.

Suppose now that instead of making one single investment of £1000 with expected value μ and risk σ, the saver makes n investments of £1000 each with expected values $\mu_1 \ldots \mu_n$, and risks $\sigma_1 \ldots \sigma_n$. Suppose further that the investments are *independent*, in the sense that the value of each one of them at the end of the year is entirely unaffected by the values of all the others. If we write the value of the whole portfolio as V, with expected value μ_p and standard deviation (risk) σ_p, it can be shown that

$$\mu_p = \mu_1 + \mu_2 + \ldots + \mu_n,$$

i.e. the expected value of the portfolio is the sum of the expected values of the n investments, and

$$\sigma_p = \sqrt{(\sigma_1^2 + \sigma_2^2 + \ldots + \sigma_n^2)}.$$

In the special case where the expected values and risks of the n investments are all the same, say μ and σ respectively, this reduces to

$$\mu_p = n\mu$$
$$\sigma_p = \sigma\sqrt{n};$$

i.e. the expected value of the portfolio increases in proportion to the number of elements in it, but the risk increases in proportion only to the square root of the number of investments.

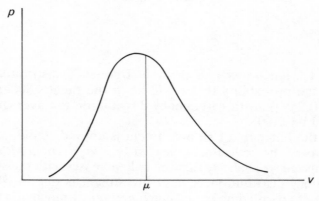

Fig. 4.2

Now let us use this example to examine how diversification reduces risk. Compare the risk *per £1000 invested* of investing a capital sum on the one hand in a single asset and on the other in equal amounts of n assets, each with the same risk σ. In the case of the single investment the risk will be σ as before, but if n investments are made the risk per £1000 falls to $\sigma/\sqrt{n}$; that is, the spread of the frequency distribution is reduced by a factor of $\sqrt{n}$.[7]

Figure 4.3 illustrates the effect of diversification on the frequency distribution of the return to investment. The frequency distribution of v illustrates the distribution for each single investment of £1000, while that of V/n shows the corresponding distribution per £1000 of the entire portfolio. It can be seen that if all the individual investments have the same expected value μ, the distribution of V/n also has the expected value μ but that it is more concentrated than

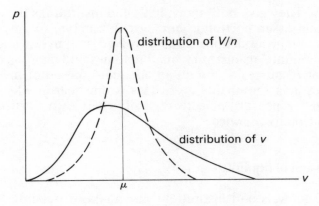

Fig. 4.3

the distribution of v, and will also generally become more symmetric about μ than the individual distributions.[8] Thus diversification – the spreading of assets over a number of separate holdings – reduces the risk to which the holder is exposed.

The relationship between the risk of a portfolio and the number of securities amongst which it is divided depends crucially on the assumption that the values of the individual securities are independent. In general this is unlikely to be the case; for example, during a boom share prices tend to rise together so that a high value of one investment is associated with high values of others. Interdependence of this kind, known as *positive covariance*, increases the risk of the portfolio as a whole.

On the other hand, the example which assumed that the risks of the individual securities were independent, understates the extent to which it may be possible to reduce risk through diversification. Risk can be reduced even further if the portfolio is divided between assets whose values tend to deviate in *opposite* directions from their expected values. For example, if two companies in some industry are in keen competition and each accounts for a substantial share of the market, an improvement in the profitability of one due to a gain in market share will be matched by reduced profitability for the other company. By holding shares in both companies the saver would be able to eliminate that part of the risk attached to variations in market share. When a gain in the value of one share is associated with a loss in the value of another, we say that there is *negative covariance*. Negative covariance within a portfolio reduces risk.[9]

Financial markets, which allow the equity of a company to be broken down into smaller lots, make diversification a practical possibility. They give both individuals and institutions the ability to divide their asset portfolios amongst a number of investments. However, the transactions costs involved in buying and selling securities militate against very small holdings and many savers have insufficient resources to obtain an adequate spread of investments themselves at a reasonable cost. This is one reason why financial institutions, which are able to diversify their own portfolios, can offer an attractive service.

The provision of liquidity

Financial markets and institutions also make it possible to satisfy simultaneously both investors' needs for permanent or long-term capital and the desires of many savers for a high degree of liquidity in their assets. Since the financial institutions which transform maturities and provide savers with liquidity rely to some extent on the existence of good asset markets, we shall consider first the ways in which the markets contribute to liquidity.

When there is an active market for a financial asset a holder is able to obtain cash before the asset's maturity date, which may be some way off in the case of bonds, and indeed does not exist at all for irredeemable securities including ordinary shares. An active market, with many competing buyers and sellers, also means that the holder can rely on receiving a fair price at the time he sells. This will not in general be the same as the value of the asset at maturity (where applicable), but it is fair in the sense that the seller does not have to bargain from a position of weakness at the time he wishes to make the sale. The provision of liquidity – the ability to turn securities into cash at short notice – is one of the principal functions of organized financial markets.

Markets operate successfully when transactors have differing needs, a variety of motives for dealing, or differing views about the value of securities. It is such differences which generate trading activity and which make it likely that a seller of a security will be able to find a buyer without difficulty. For example, in the ordinary share market, at any time there are likely to be sales made by executors for estates, who have to raise cash in order to pay inheritance tax, and purchases by pension funds, which are receiving an inflow of contributions to invest. In the interbank market one bank which has access to deposits but no immediate need for additional cash will lend to another with excess loan demand. In the gilt-edged market a pension fund, which prefers to hold long-dated securities, will sell stocks for which the remaining term is short, perhaps to a bank, which is anxious to increase the more liquid part of its portfolio. Or, returning to the share market, two institutional investors may hold differing opinions about the future profitability of a particular company, and the pessimist will sell the shares to the optimist.

Transactions in securities can and do take place outside organized markets, but the existence of an organized market which brings together a large number of potential transactors in securities is one means of providing liquidity and of making it easier for buyers and sellers to deal. For example, in the sterling money markets the brokers are in touch with a large number of institutions or other clients, some of whom may have spare funds whilst others are likely to be short of funds. By dealing through the broker each institution can make contact easily with a suitable counterpart, and it is the broker's range of contacts which makes it possible for the single client to place funds or obtain funds readily.

In some markets, such as the stock market, there are professional market makers – economic agents who find the price at which buying and selling orders match or who are themselves prepared to buy or sell on request. In the German stock exchanges, for example, these market makers simply record buying and selling orders and calculate the price at which they will be equal. In Britain, by contrast, the market makers in ordinary shares, bills and bonds quote prices at which they are prepared to buy or sell securities, and hold a stock of the asset in question. By being prepared to act as principals and to vary the size of these holdings they provide immediate liquidity in the market, allowing sellers to make a sale without delay. Changes in the prices they quote maintain the balance between supply and demand in the slightly longer term.

The main providers of liquidity amongst the financial institutions are the deposit-taking institutions like banks and building societies. They contribute to the liquidity of the financial system by issuing liabilities (deposits) with a maturity shorter than their assets. In order to do this they rely on the law of averages, as it affects their depositors and borrowers, structured asset and liability portfolios, including assets with varying degrees of liquidity, and access to financial markets, in which some of these assets can be sold before maturity and in which new funds can be gathered.

The application of the law of averages to default risk has already been discussed, and it was shown that by making a large number of loans an institution could avoid the risk that its experience would depart far from the general average. The same principle can be applied to the deposit-taking activities of clearing banks or building societies. They know that in any period some of their depositors will wish to encash their deposits, but they can be reasonably confident that at the same time others will wish to make new deposits with them. In the case of banks, while they must assume that some borrowers will wish to make greater use of their overdraft facilities, the demands of others are likely to fall. Institutions therefore need liquidity only to cover the *net* position. The *maximum* demand for cash against which the institution needs to guard is determined by the same considerations as before. A large number of depositors reduces the maximum percentage deposit loss which is likely, and independence between depositors also reduces deposit variability. Indeed, negative covariance may help to reduce the institution's liquidity requirements. For example, a clearing bank, which has both individuals and shops amongst its customers, knows that a reduction in the deposits in one group is likely to be partly offset by an increase in the deposits of the other.

Cash inflows and outflows will not match exactly; some variability in the cash demands by an institution's depositors remains. By holding structured asset and liability portfolios the institution ensures that it can honour its liabilities. The institution must keep a proportion of its assets in a liquid form, some highly liquid to deal with short-term variability in its cash needs, and some less so but which can be realized if there is a persistent need for cash – due, for example, to a steady deposit loss or a sustained rise in the demand for loans. The liquidity of the institution's portfolio ought, there-fore, to reflect the volatility and maturity structure of its liabilities, as well as the nature of its assets. Where deposits are volatile and other assets, such as overdrafts, are variable, the institution must maintain a high level of liquidity.

Institutions, such as banks, which have access to the wholesale deposit markets do not need to rely exclusively on liquid asset holdings to ensure that they have sufficient liquidity. The banks are generally able to draw on the wholesale market to a greater or lesser degree at their own discretion, an element of flexibility which diminishes their need for liquid assets. The wholesale market also enables them to structure the maturities of some of their liabilities – by lengthening the average maturity they reduce their vulnerability to unexpected cash outflows.

Maturity transformation by financial institutions depends ultimately on their continued access to markets, particularly markets for deposits. Institutions must be able to remain competitive in the (informal) market for deposits, for if they do not they are liable to suffer a persistent loss of deposits. For this reason many deposit-taking institutions lend at variable rates of interest with the rate set by means of a link to some standard rate, which in turn moves with deposit interest rates. Thus if the deposit rate becomes uncompetitive, the institution is able to raise both deposit and lending rates together, without the risk that its own profitability will be endangered by a narrowing of its margins. Such a link may be formal, as in the case of bank overdrafts quoted as base rate plus a fixed margin, or it may be a matter of practice, as with the building societies which generally make significant changes to their deposit and loan rates at much the same time.

Continued access to the deposit market depends also on the maintenance of an institution's reputation. This is particularly important for banks which rely to a significant extent on deposits from the wholesale markets, where the standing of the borrower is crucial. If even a shadow of doubt is cast over the soundness of a financial institution it is liable to find itself faced with a withdrawal of deposits and an inability to obtain new deposits in the market. This is what happened in Britain during the secondary banking crisis in 1974–5, when many institutions which otherwise appeared to be sound experienced considerable difficulty in renewing deposits and had to seek help from the Bank of England and the clearing banks. Similar problems have caused the US authorities to support major banks which have got into difficulties.

Financial institutions also have a role to play in *interest rate transformation*. Some borrowers (lenders) have a preference for borrowing (lending) at variable rates of interest – rates which will vary in line with the prevailing rates of interest in future. Others prefer to fix the interest rate for extended periods. Financial institutions (and markets) provide facilities which enable the ultimate users of the financial system to satisfy their preferences. The financial system does this partly by providing both savers and investors with financial instruments which meet their needs, and partly by accepting some imbalance between the interest rate characteristics of their own liabilities and assets.

When, however, financial institutions lend for long periods at fixed rates of interest and finance their lending by borrowing at variable rates of interest they take a risk. If interest rates rose sharply during the currency of their loans they might face disaster because, as already noted, to remain competitive in the deposit market they would have to raise their interest rates on deposits and so operate at a loss. That is what happened to a considerable number of Savings and Loan Associations in the United States at the beginning of the 1980s. Most institutions try to limit this risk by ensuring that interest rate changes will impinge more or less equally on both sides of their balance sheets: short-term deposits are matched by variable rate loans, fixed rate deposits may be sought to match fixed rate lending. Alternatively, the new financial markets in interest rate instruments (see chapter 14) can be employed to assist this process. Banks and other financial institutions can use these markets to hedge interest rate risk[10] as far as they think necessary.

This means in practice that institutions can meet the preferences of individual clients, but it does not deal with any imbalances in the financial system as a whole. However, borrowers' and lenders' preferences regarding the interest rate characteristics of financial instruments are seldom absolute – they can be changed if the price is right – and any significant overall imbalances will be reflected in the relative interest rates on fixed and variable rate instruments.

Reducing transactions costs

Financial markets and institutions also assist the users of the system by reducing the transactions costs they face – the time and trouble as well as the actual expense of conducting business. They do this in a number of ways. First, they provide convenient places of business, to which savers with funds to lend and borrowers in search of money can go, thereby avoiding the need to seek out a suitable counterpart on each occasion. The cost of providing these services should not be underestimated – branch networks and the information systems required to support financial activity require very substantial commitments of people, premises, and of communications and computing technology. Secondly, the financial institutions provide standardized products, thereby cutting the information costs associated with scrutinizing individual financial instruments. Thirdly, they specialize and operate on a substantial scale, which enables them to acquire expertise and cut costs through the use of tested procedures and routines. Finally, there are regulatory bodies watching over the markets with the object of maintaining the quality of the financial instruments traded and of ensuring that market participants conform with accepted codes of behaviour. This gives confidence to the users of the market and frees them from the need to collect the information and carry out the detailed analysis which would be required in order to make their own assessments.

The financial system in Britain relies on competition between financial institutions and within financial markets to keep down operating costs. It is competition that determines the margins between deposit and lending rates which banks can earn on their business, and low-cost competitors undercut their rivals in order to expand their share of the market. Institutions which have persistently higher costs than their competitors are likely to go out of business. In some instances, however, competition in the past – though much less so nowadays – was muted as a result of agreements amongst the participants; the effects of such agreements on operating costs within the financial system is a subject to which we shall return later.

In chapter 3 we made the simplifying assumption that the rate of interest facing borrowers and lenders was the same. In reality, however, the cost to a borrower is higher than the return received by the lender because it is the gross cost (interest + expenses) which is relevant to the former and the net return (interest − expenses) which is relevant to the lender. Figure 4.4 illustrates the effect of transactions costs on financial activity.

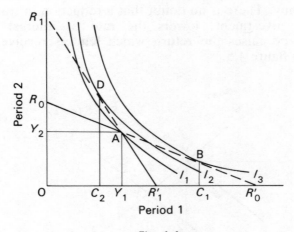

Fig. 4.4

As before let us suppose that an individual has income given by point A in the diagram; i.e. OY_1 in period 1 and OY_2 in period 2. However, now instead of being faced by a single rate of interest he receives the rate r_0, represented by R_0R_0', if he acts as a lender, but has to pay the rate r_1, represented by R_1R_1', if he is a borrower. The individual's opportunity line is therefore R_0AR_1' in figure 4.4, and with the indifference curve shown in the figure he would choose to remain at point A, neither borrowing nor lending. If the borrowing rate had been r_0 he would have chosen to move to point B and to borrow Y_1C_1, whereas if the lending rate had been r_1 he would have moved to D and lent C_2Y_1. Transactions costs, which open up a gap between borrowing and lending rates, therefore discourage financial activity.[11] Clearly the closer r_0 and r_1 are together – i.e. the lower are transactions costs – the more likely it is that either borrowing or lending will take place.

By reducing the transactions costs faced by borrowers and lenders, the financial system cuts the gross cost of funds to borrowers and raises the net return to savers. On the normal assumptions about savers' and investors' behaviour the lower cost to borrowers will raise the level of investment and the rise in the return to savers will raise the level of saving.

Asset transformation and the levels of saving and investment

We shall conclude this chapter by analysing the effects of asset transformation on savings and investment and on the rate of interest in the economy. There is no doubt that a reduction in transactions costs raises investment, lowers the rate of interest paid by borrowers, and raises the return which lenders receive. This is illustrated in figure 4.5.

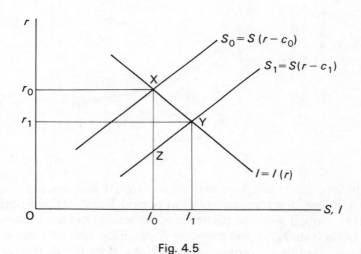

Fig. 4.5

It is necessary at this stage to distinguish between the rate of interest paid by the borrower, which we shall continue to denote by r, and that received by the lender, which we shall denote by $r - c$, where c covers the operating and any other transactions costs incurred by borrowers and lenders. In figure 4.5 the investment schedule is shown as a declining function of r, as before, and the saving schedule is a rising function of $(r - c)$. In the initial position, in the absence of financial institutions and markets, we suppose that transactions costs amount to c_0, and the equilibrium is at point X, with investment (equal to saving) OI_0 and the rate of interest at r_0. Now suppose that the financial system reduces transactions costs to c_1, the difference between c_0 and c_1 being represented by XZ. The saving schedule therefore moves to S_1, and investment rises to OI_1 with the rate of interest paid by borrowers falling to r_1. As figure 4.5 shows, the reduction in the rate of interest from r_0 to r_1 is less than the reduction in transactions costs XZ, so the net return to savers also increases.

The effects of risk and maturity transformation are less clear-cut. There is no doubt that they will increase borrowers' demands for funds. Firms which are able to match the maturity of their assets and liabilities and which have good access to equity capital can limit risks arising from the structure of their financing, and this makes it possible for them to contemplate embarking on more risky investment projects. This is illustrated in figure 4.6. The position before asset transformation is available is shown by the schedules labelled I and S, giving a level of investment OI_0 and a rate of interest r_0. The effect of asset transformation on investment is to shift the I schedule to I' and this alone would raise investment to OI_1 and the rate of interest to r_1.

Unfortunately, however, we cannot deduce from *a priori* argument that asset transformation will increase the level of saving. The problem lies in the precautionary objective for saving, because

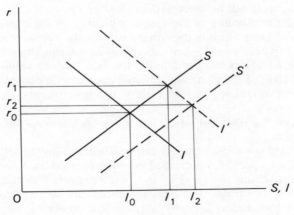

Fig. 4.6

improved liquidity and lower risk mean that the amount of wealth required to satisfy precautionary needs is reduced. It is therefore theoretically possible that asset transformation might reduce the level of saving. However, there are two reasons why this is unlikely in practice. First, the improvement in the characteristics of the financial instruments available to savers must make saving more attractive, especially saving through the financial system as opposed to accumulating physical assets. Secondly, in the absence of suitable financial instruments people may choose not to save but instead employ other social arrangements to provide for their support. For example, it may be customary for people who are in need to fall back on family and friends, rather than to attempt to accumulate sufficient wealth to stand on their own feet. If these effects are dominant, the saving schedule will shift from S to some position such as S' in the diagram, investment will rise further to OI_2 and the rate of interest will fall to r_2 (which may even lie below r_0).[12] Thus in normal circumstances we can expect asset transformation to encourage both saving and investment and to raise the level of investment in the economy.

Notes

1 In other words, they demand an element of equity return for taking on equity risk.
2 The number of losses has been calculated using the Poisson or normal distribution, as appropriate.
3 To the extent that losses affect the strength of competition subsequently banks may, however, be able to recoup them out of higher margins.
4 The regulations will be discussed in chapter 11.
5 That is, the mid-points of the ranges weighted by their probabilities.
6 The standard deviation is the square root of the *variance* measured as $\Sigma f(v - \mu)^2$ where v and μ are the values and mean value of the share respectively and f is the probability attached to each value, v.
7 Of each £1000 of the portfolio, £1000/n goes in every asset. So the risk of each investment is σ/n, and with n such investments $\sigma/_p$ is equal to $(\sigma\sqrt{n})/n = \sigma/\sqrt{n}$.
8 If n is large the distribution of V/n takes on the shape of the *normal* distribution.
9 The effects of covariance on risk can be illustrated in the following way. Suppose that a portfolio is divided between two shares X_1 and X_2 in the proportions a_1 and a_2 ($= 1 - a_1$), with expected values μ_1 and μ_2 respectively. Suppose that the variances are σ_1^2 and σ_2^2 and the covariance (defined as $\Sigma f(v_1 - \mu_1)(v_2 - \mu_2)$, where f is the probability of v_1 and v_2 occurring together) is σ_{12}. It is convenient to write σ_{12} in

terms of the correlation R_{12} between X_1 and X_2, since R_{12} lies between -1 and $+1$:

$$\sigma_{12} = R_{12}\sigma_1\sigma_2.$$

If the total return on the portfolio is V, with mean μ_p, and variance μ_p^2,

$$\mu_p = a_1\mu_1 + a_2\mu_2$$

and

$$\sigma_p^2 = a_1^2\,\sigma_1^2 + 2a_1a_2R_{12}\sigma_1\sigma_2 + a_2^2\sigma_2^2.$$

If the values of the shares are independent, $R_{12} = 0$, and this reduces to

$$\sigma_p^2 = a_1^2\sigma_1^2 + a_2^2\sigma_2^2.$$

Its maximum occurs when the values of the shares are perfectly correlated (as, for example, with two shares in the same company), in which case $R_{12} = 1$ and

$$\sigma_{max}^2 = (a_1\sigma_1 + a_2\sigma_2)^2.$$

If there is a perfect negative correlation ($R_{12} = -1$) the variance of V is at a minimum, and

$$\sigma_{min}^2 = (a_1\sigma_1 - a_2\sigma_2)^2.$$

The general result is that the greater the negative covariance of v_1 and v_2 the lower is the variance of V.

Notice that the risk also depends on the values of a_1 and a_2, the proportions of the portfolio held in each share. For the special case of $R_{12} = -1$, the risk attached to V can be eliminated altogether if a_1 and a_2 are chosen so that $a_1/a_2 = \sigma_2/\sigma_1$.

In practice it is impossible to eliminate risk completely through diversification. Some part of the uncertainty connected with the value of equity depends on the performance of the country's economy as a whole (or of the whole world economy for an international portfolio). General prosperity will affect the general level of equity values, as will changes in financial or political conditions. Uncertainty connected with the market as a whole is known as market risk, and cannot be diversified away. What diversification can eliminate is the risk attached to particular companies, namely the risk that they will perform well or badly relative to the market as a whole.

10 In practice the ability to hedge interest rate risks through futures and other financial instruments is limited by the capacity of the markets.
11 It should be noted that taxes, which cause a divergence between lending and borrowing rates of interest, have a similar effect.
12 If the greater ease of satisfying the precautionary objective had the dominant effect, S would shift to the left, with the rate of interest rising and investment turning out to be at a level lower than OI_1 – conceivably even lower than OI_0.

5

Interest rates

In this chapter we shall begin by looking at the factors which determine the general level of interest rates and then go on to explain some of the reasons why the interest rates on financial instruments differ – for example differences in risk, term to maturity, vulnerability to price level changes, and transactions costs. At the end of the chapter we shall discuss the relationship between interest rates on financial instruments and economic efficiency.

The level of abstraction in this chapter is high. For example, we discuss interest rates in *the* economy, without even a sideways glance at international influences and constraints. However, the aim is practical – to provide a general framework for analysing the consequences for interest rates of phenomena such as a sudden increase in the demand for capital, a rapid expansion of money and credit, and changes in inflationary expectations. In the next chapter we shall attempt to bring the discussion much closer to the actual institutional and international market structures.

The function of the rate of interest, r, in equating saving and investment, has already been noted. Figure 5.1 repeats part of figure 3.1, which illustrates how r is determined by the intersection of an upward-sloping savings schedule and a downward-sloping investment schedule. A rise in the profitability of investment or a fall in the desire to save will shift the relevant schedule and raise the equilibrium rate of interest. For example, in the market for securities an increase in the profitability of investment encourages firms to raise capital by issuing more securities, thus depressing their price and raising the rate of interest.[1]

In discussing the mechanism through which saving and investment are brought into balance we normally stress the part played by rates of interest on financial instruments – the *cost* of funds. Though other

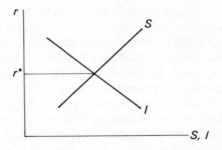

Fig. 5.1

terms of credit (e.g. some forms of qualitative rationing) are sometimes also important, their role has diminished as competition within the financial system has become keener. In any event, changes in these other terms are usually temporary – a response to a transient disequilibrium between the demand for funds and what financial institutions are willing to make available – rather than permanent; lasting changes in the flows of saving or investment generally have their impact on the cost of funds.

The interest rate and the market for loanable funds

It is now time to broaden our analysis of interest rate determination to allow for *monetary* influences. We therefore distinguish between long-term assets such as the securities traded in capital markets, equity in businesses and physical assets such as houses, and short-term assets such as 'money', exemplified by bank and building society deposits. The rate of interest, r, is the yield on long-term assets.

An important feature of 'money' is that either the amount available or the general level of interest rates paid on monetary assets is set by the monetary authorities – in the UK it is the level of interest rates, which the authorities influence through their operations in the money markets. We are not concerned in this book with the techniques of monetary policy; suffice to say that the authorities' freedom of choice regarding the interest rates they set is heavily constrained by other policy objectives. The rates of interest on monetary assets are also the main determinants of the rates charged for credit – the loans which form the counterpart of deposits in the banks' and building societies' balance sheets.

Money plays a distinctive role in the determination of long-term interest rates because, unlike long-term financial assets, changes in money holdings are often unplanned; they are not the consequence of conscious decisions as to how much money should be held. If, for example, an employee is asked to work additional overtime his income, and hence his money balances, will be more than he expected. If a firm's sales fall below its expectations its revenue will be reduced and its money balances will run down accordingly. Or again, if the vendor of a house receives a higher price than he expected his money balances are augmented. Changes in economic agents' money balances will of course affect their *future* behaviour, but some time is likely to pass before they alter their expenditure or buy or sell other financial assets in order to return their money holdings to a planned level. In the short-run, therefore, the individual economic agent's money holdings may diverge substantially from equilibrium. The same goes for money holdings in aggregate, and it is quite possible for the supply of money and the demand for money – interpreted as the aggregate amount that people would choose to hold in equilibrium – to be out of balance.[2]

Consider then the market for *loanable funds*; i.e. funds which are available for investment in long-term assets. The sources of supply and demand are as follows: for supply, saving, planned reductions in money holdings, increases in the supply of loans from monetary institutions; for demand, investment, borrowing for consumption, planned increases in money holdings, reductions in the supply of loans from monetary institutions.

Saving, which is the main continuing source of supply of loanable funds, arises in all sectors of the economy and may take many forms. Personal saving may consist, *inter alia*, of contributions to pension funds, the repayment of mortgage loans, the purchase of securities, or additions to deposits with building societies and banks. Business saving comprises retained profits and, most important, depreciation charges; what is not reinvested in the business is usually held temporarily in monetary form. The government too may contribute to saving in the economy by raising more in taxes than it needs for its own current expenditure, with the proceeds going to finance part or all of the public sector's investment and any surplus being available to buy in government securities.

The supply of loanable funds is augmented by any reduction in economic agents' desired money holdings. Money balances, which have previously been built up temporarily, may be employed in purchasing securities or other long-term assets. Any increases in bank or building society lending (which will of course be matched by an increase in their deposit liabilities, money) also adds to the supply of loanable funds.

Investment is the principal source of demand for loanable funds and it is also to be found in all sectors of the economy. People borrow to buy houses, industrial companies to pay for factories and equipment, and governments need money for many forms of capital spending, including hospitals, schools and roads to name only a few. Some investment is financed directly out of current saving but much is financed by borrowing or a reduction in money holdings. Consumers buying durable household goods, or even just borrowing to pay for a holiday, also contribute to the demand for loanable funds, as do public sector bodies with current account deficits to finance.

The same goes for firms which issue securities in order to build up their money balances, whilst the use of money balances – whether raised through securities issues or generated from current income – to repay bank or building society loans diminishes their supply.

We can simplify the factors affecting the market for loanable funds by treating borrowing for consumption as an offset against gross saving and regarding the changes in the demand for money and supply of loans as net figures. Defining

S = saving
I = investment[3]
ΔL = increase in the supply of loans
ΔM_d = increase in the planned demand for money

the equation for balance in the market for loanable funds (LF) is

$$S + \Delta L = I + \Delta M_d.$$

Each of these terms is a function of interest rates, both the yield on long-term assets, r, and the rate on monetary assets, i, set by the monetary authorities. Given the latter the equation determines r.

Although the change in the monetary institutions' total liabilities (money) must equal the change in their total asset (loans),[4] in the short-run there is no reason why ΔL and ΔM_d should be equal. The difference is unplanned changes in money holdings. It follows that S and I may also be unequal in the short-run.[5] In the long-run, however, since unplanned changes are gradually eliminated, ΔM_d and ΔL must move together, leaving the balance equation as

$$S = I.$$

Now consider the effect of increasing bank lending. This adds to the funds available in the capital market, so that instead of S in

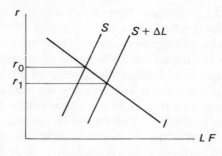

Fig. 5.2

figure 5.1 we have $S + \Delta L$. The effect of incorporating the increase in loans is therefore to reduce the rate of interest in figure 5.2 from r_0 to r_1.

To see how this comes about, suppose that instead of raising new funds from the stock market companies borrow from their banks. The additional bank lending relieves the pressure of demand for funds in the securities market, the price of securities will rise and the rate of interest fall accordingly.

A rise in the demand for money will have the opposite effect. It adds to the funds required from the capital market (or diverts funds which would otherwise have been channelled into the market). Figure 5.3 shows that the effect is to raise the rate of interest from r_0 to r_1. This is what occurs if long-term investment institutions, such as life assurance companies and pension funds, decide to build up their liquidity in a period of uncertainty about the future, rather than investing in the capital market.

All the elements of demand and supply for loanable funds have been brought together in figure 5.4. It is clear that the effect on the rate of interest of any shift in S, ΔL, I or ΔM_d will depend on the elasticities of *both* lines. The less elastic (steeper) is $S + \Delta L$ and

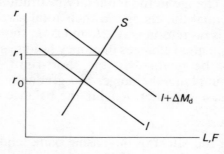

Fig. 5.3

the more elastic (flatter) is $I + \Delta M_d$ the greater will be the effect on the rate of interest of any shift in investment demand or the demand for money.

To make this concrete, suppose that the supply of bank loans is highly elastic in the short-run, as will be the case if the authorities set the rate of interest and do not respond quickly to an increase in bank lending. Then an increase in investment demand will be financed largely by bank lending and will have little impact on securities market yields. If, however, the authorities impose a stricter control on monetary growth, and raise short-term interest rates quickly when bank lending expands, $S + \Delta L$ will be inelastic and the increase in investment demand will lead to a substantial rise in long-term yields.

The initial effect of the reunification of East and West Germany on interest rates provides a good illustration. Reunification was expected to result in both an increase in investment, to re-equip East Germany with modern capital, and a reduction in saving as the standard of living in East Germany was raised well in advance of any corresponding increase in output. In terms of figure 5.4, the $I + \Delta M_d$ was shifted up and the $S + \Delta L$ line was shifted to the left. Moreover, the latter was inelastic because it was known that the German central bank would not permit excessive monetary expansion. Short- and long-term interest rates in Germany rose accordingly.

The opposite situation occurred in the UK in the great credit expansion of 1987 and 1988. It is now generally accepted that, faced with very strong demand for funds (high I, low S), the UK authorities kept short-term interest rates too low, with the result that bank and building society lending (ΔL) grew extremely rapidly. This contributed to the stock market boom prior to the crash in October 1987, to its subsequent recovery, and to the domestic and commercial property market booms in that period.

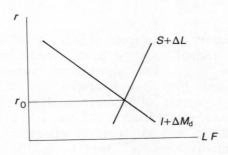

Fig. 5.4

The situation illustrated in figure 5.4 is only a short-run equilibrium. For unless planned saving equals investment and the planned increase in money holdings equals the increase in loans from monetary institutions, the economy as a whole will not be in equilibrium and the situation will be one of constant change. For example, if S is less than I and ΔL is greater than ΔM_d people will be receiving more income and building up larger money balances than they intended; this will lead them to change their planned levels of saving and investment, as well as the planned composition of their financial asset portfolios in the future. (An excess of investment over planned saving, associated with bank lending and an unplanned build-up of money balances, is in fact a classic recipe for an inflationary boom!)

The structure of interest rates

Until now we have assumed that interest rates on all financial instruments could be proxied by a single rate for long-term assets, r, and a single rate for monetary assets, i. In reality, however, interest rates vary widely amongst financial instruments and between borrowers. Why do some borrowers pay more than others? Why do equity shares yield more than property? Why do both yield less than gilt-edged securities? Why are the yields on long-dated securities different from those on short-dated? These are some of the questions which must now be answered. As our benchmark we shall take the risk-free rate of interest on government securities of the appropriate term; there is no default risk and the flow of income (in money terms) is certain. We begin, therefore, by considering the factors which influence the term structure of interest rates.

Term

The interest rate on any category of security varies with its *term* or maturity. The normal situation is that long-term securities bear higher rates of interest than short-term, because of the bias of borrowers towards long-term liabilities and of lenders towards short. The higher rates of interest on long-term securities are needed to persuade either lenders or borrowers to depart from their preferred maturities and to provide a margin out of which those financial intermediaries which help to bridge the gap through maturity transformation are able to cover their costs. The differences in interest rates which are needed for this purpose are known as *liquidity premia*, and these may be expected to rise with the term of the security.

But the term structure is also affected by other important considerations, which result from time to time in short rates exceeding long – a situation which is at first sight perverse. When deciding whether to lend for long or short periods savers must take account not only of the interest they will earn initially but also of the interest rates which they expect to prevail in future. They can choose between making a single investment for a long period at a rate of interest fixed at the outset, or of making repeated short-term investments at whatever short rates prevail during that period. Ignoring liquidity premia, the rate of interest demanded by a long-term investor will therefore depend on what he would hope to earn from a series of short-term investments – his expected return by the end of the period from the two alternatives must be the same. It follows that the rate of interest on long-term securities must be some kind of average of the short rates which are expected to prevail in future. The links between long rates and expected future short rates are known as *expectations* effects.

It is expectations effects which explain why short rates are sometimes higher than long. If high short rates are thought to be temporary, so that people generally expect them to be lower in future, the average short rate during the period of a long-term loan will be less than the current short rate, and the difference may more than offset the effect of liquidity premia on the term structure of interest rates.[6]

Default risk

The risk that a borrower may default on his obligations affects the rate of interest he must pay for a loan, which includes a 'loading' for risk. In many instances lenders distinguish a relatively small number of risk categories, and put potential borrowers into the category which they think appropriate, the loading in the interest rate the borrower is charged reflecting the risk of loss for that category.[7] Banks draw a distinction between 'blue chip' companies and those to which they attribute a higher risk. *Project* loans, where any security has to be found in the project itself, carry a higher risk loading than loans for which more reliable security is available. Instalment loans from banks generally incorporate a lower risk-loading than similar loans from finance houses, because the risk of default is generally lower for the customers of the former. Commercial bills which have been accepted (i.e. guaranteed) by a bank yield less than trade bills which have no similar guarantee. When loans are negotiated individually the risk-loading may be a factor in the negotiation; for example a company seeking a loan for an investment project may attempt to persuade its bank that it deserves to be placed in a more favourable risk class.

Note that default risk is by no means the only or most important factor influencing the margin by which the cost of loans exceeds the risk-free rate of interest. The loading must also take account of the administrative costs incurred by the lender, which, particularly for relatively small loans or loans involving extensive documentation, may substantially exceed the loading for risk; and there must also be a profit margin to enable the lending institution to service its own capital.

Equity risk

Before considering the way in which equity risk is incorporated in asset yields we must first consider how the yield on equity – a somewhat elusive concept – is measured.

The cost to a company of issuing equity shares is determined by the dividends it is expected to pay in future. If the dividend was expected to be constant, we could express the cost as the dividend divided by the net proceeds per share issued. But dividends are not usually expected to be constant, so some allowance must be made for anticipated changes in dividend payments.

Dividends may in fact be expected to change for several reasons. First, the company may be thought to have entered a period of unusual prosperity or unusual difficulty, which will affect its profitability and dividend payments. Secondly, most companies aim to retain part of their profits in order to develop their business, and to the extent that they are successful this can be expected to lead to gradually rising dividend payments. Thirdly, in a period of inflation the money values of the company's income, expenses and profits may be expected to rise broadly in line with the price level – an expectation that may of course be disappointed for extended periods – so inflationary expectations are also reflected in anticipated dividend payments.

There is no very good reason to expect dividends to change in a regular fashion from year to year, even though many companies do attempt to maintain some stability in their dividend payments; but fortunately it is possible to convert erratic changes in dividends into a mathematically equivalent constant annual rate of growth. If this rate is g and the dividend yield is d, the cost of equity capital to the company can be expressed as $(d + g)$.[8]

The cost to the company is the same as the return which the holders of equity shares expect to receive. To see this, consider the total return to a shareholder over a period of a year from a company whose dividend yield is d and for which the dividend is expected to grow by g from one year to the next. If the general level of interest rates is constant the rise in dividend will lead to a proportional increase in the price of the shares, so that in the course of the year the shareholder receives a dividend yield of d plus capital appreciation of g, and this rate of return continues so long as dividends grow and are expected to continue to grow at the rate g.

In general the equity yield $(d + g)$ will be higher than the risk-free long-term rate of interest r, because the flow of income from equity shares is uncertain and asset-holders demand some compensation for their exposure to risk.[9] The yield margin over the risk-free rate will reflect the intensity of risk-aversion amongst asset-holders in general – the greater their reluctance to accept risk the higher the margin must be.

The yield which asset-holders expect to earn on the shares of equally risky companies should in principle be the same; otherwise they would have an incentive to sell the shares of the lower-yielding companies and buy those of the higher, and this would alter the relative share prices until the yields were equal. This does not imply that *dividend* yields will be equal, because the expected growth of dividends varies from one company to another, and this is reflected in the dividend yields on their shares – a low dividend yield implies that the rate of growth of dividends is expected to be high, a very high dividend yield implies an expectation that the dividend is likely to be cut.

High-risk companies – those for which expected profits in future are very uncertain – may need to pay more for equity capital than low-risk companies. However, the margin need not necessarily be large because the asset-holder with a large portfolio can eliminate the extra risk through diversification. Indeed, there is a possibility that very risky investments may appeal to the gambling instincts of some investors, and so attract funds more readily than safer investments for which the maximum likely return is lower; if this occurs the average yield on highly risky investments would be less than on safer holdings.[10]

It is important to note that only part of the risk associated with equity shares can be eliminated by diversification. A diversified portfolio will enable the investor to be confident that his assets will yield the same as the average of the market,[11] but they do not give him any protection against a decline in profitability as a whole, or against a fall in equity prices as a result of an increase in the general level of interest rates. Strictly speaking, therefore, it is the extent to which the yield on the shares of a particular company is expected to vary with general market movements which determines the risk attached to that share, and which is reflected in the risk-loading in the yield demanded by asset-holders.

Inflation

We must now distinguish between *nominal* and *real* rates of interest. The nominal rate is the rate of interest expressed in money terms, whereas the real rate makes an adjustment for the effect of changes in the general price level. Suppose that a one-year loan bears a rate of interest of 15 per cent, and that during the course of the year the general price level in the economy rises by 12 per cent so that the loan itself and the interest received is worth 12 per cent less at the end of the year than at the beginning. Then at the end of the year the lender has £115 per £100 lent, but in terms of the prices prevailing at the beginning of the year this is only £(115/1.12); i.e. £102.67. The real rate of interest is consequently only 2.7 per cent.

If the rate of inflation is low the relationship between the nominal yield, r, the real yield, r^*, and the expected rate of inflation, $\dot{p}$, is:[12]

$$r = r^* + \dot{p}$$

As we have already seen, expected inflation accounts for part of the difference between the dividend yield on equities and the yield on gilt-edged securities. Bonds are claims to nominal income flows, whereas ordinary shares and property are claims to flows of real income, because dividends and rent are expected to rise broadly in line with the price level in future. As a result, the expected yields on claims to real income flows include a growth element for inflation.[13]

It is often most helpful to think of the long-term rate of interest as the *real* rate, r^*, earned on physical assets. This is determined by the real and monetary factors discussed earlier. The *nominal* rate on long-term bonds will then incorporate an allowance for expected inflation. Thus the oil price increases in the summer of 1990, which led to heightened inflationary fears in the USA, were reflected in higher bond yields. Similarly, as the UK's adherence to the

Exchange Rate Mechanism leads to the belief that the average rate of inflation in the UK will be lower in future, so UK bond yields can be expected to fall.

Cost and profits

The rates of interest charged to borrowers and the cost to the company of raising equity capital must also include an allowance for transactions costs. Transactions costs are usually subject to economies of scale – they rise less than in proportion to the size of transactions – so that the loading for transactions costs is larger for small loans, or small issues of equity capital, than it is for large. The transactions costs of raising new capital are sometimes charged as a separate fee, rather than being recovered in the form of a higher interest rate. But the loading for servicing costs (e.g. the cost of monitoring a loan and of collecting payments at the due dates specified in the loan agreement) are usually built into the interest rate charged. Differences in transactions costs are one important reason why loans to the banks' retail customers bear higher rates of interest than do wholesale loans.

The rate of interest charged for a loan by a financial intermediary will also include an element for profit to enable the intermediary to service its own capital. Banks, for example, put their own capital at risk when they make loans. In principle the amount of a bank's own capital required will reflect the risk of the loan, but in practice the approach adopted by regulatory authorities is to specify the minimum capital backing for broad categories of loan.[14] The amount which the intermediary can hope to earn on any particular loan is influenced by the strength of competition which it faces. For example, in the market for wholesale bank loans there is a very large number of potential lenders, and competition is extremely keen. Borrowers are prepared to shop around and take funds from those lenders who offer them the most favourable terms. In the retail bank loan market price competition is more restrained, because borrowers place more weight on the maintenance of the goodwill which goes with long-established relationships with their banks and are generally reluctant to shift from one bank to another as a result of a failure to negotiate a small reduction in interest rates. Indeed, the ability to obtain a loan at all, and the terms regarding repayment and security attached to it, are usually of much greater importance in the eyes of the borrower.

Costs and profit margins may be influenced by agreements

between lenders, though these are now rare in the UK, and government regulations may also affect transactions costs. Most restrictive agreements and regulations have the effect of raising these costs.

The allocation of funds

Putting all these elements together, the rate charged for a loan of any term will be made up of the following components: risk-free rate for that term, plus loading for default risk, plus loading for servicing costs, plus loading for profit. Similarly, the dividend yield required for an issue of equity shares will include: real yield required on a risk-free perpetuity,[15] plus loading for equity risk, minus allowance for real growth of dividends. The rates charged for loans of differing terms reflect liquidity premia and expected future rates of interest, and nominal and real yields are linked by expectations of inflation.

Suppose now that competition within the financial system was sufficient to ensure that lenders were unable to earn excess profits, and suppose further that lenders were in a position to assess risks accurately. Then the price which borrowers had to pay for funds would reflect the going risk-free rate of interest for the appropriate term, the costs incurred in connection with their loans, and an appropriate loading for risk. The allocation of funds would be 'efficient' in the sense that each borrower had to pay a price which reflected the going rate for funds in general and the specific costs and risks associated with his own business. The same would apply to equity capital.

If firms chose to raise money for all projects which were able to earn at least enough to meet the financing costs, and did not go ahead with lower-yielding projects, this efficiency in the supply of funds would feed through into an efficient allocation of investment. By finding the rate of interest which equated saving and investment in the economy, and charging in addition for specific risks and costs, the financial system would price funds according to their opportunity costs. It would then be left to the potential borrowers to determine the allocation of resources amongst competing investment projects, in the light of their own estimates of the likely returns.

Funds, in other words, would go to the highest bidders. If there was an increase in demand for mortgages by potential house-owners they would be prepared to pay more for mortgages, so building societies would raise their deposit and mortgage rates, putting upward pressure on interest rates generally. Funds would be attracted from, say, the banks, some of whose borrowers would be unwilling to pay the higher rates of interest. Or again, improved industrial investment prospects might encourage firms to raise additional equity capital, and this too would result in funds being drawn away from alternative uses.

How closely the British financial system approximates to this ideal has been a matter of considerable debate, and we shall consider the matter more fully in chapter 16. At this stage, however, there are a number of points to note. That differences in the strength of competition, and consequently of costs and profitability, of different segments of the market can detract from efficiency is obvious. But while such differences do occur in practice to some extent in Britain, they are unlikely to be factors of major importance. More significant, perhaps, are questions to do with the assessment of risk. It has often been asserted that financial institutions in Britain lack the competence to assess risk properly, and are consequently unduly conservative in their lending practices. Moreover, it is said, the long-term institutions place too much emphasis on current dividends and on the outlook for companies in the short-term. If these allegations are true they would imply that the system did not allocate resources efficiently, but would be biased against projects which were risky or which yielded their return only gradually and over a long period.

Questions have also been raised over the extent to which rates of interest do in fact balance saving and investment in the economy. It is suggested that the general level of interest rates might be inappropriate to prevailing economic conditions. This could be caused by a faulty monetary policy, a malfunctioning of the capital market, or other structural deficiencies in the economy. Whatever the cause, interest rates which were too low would be associated with more investment than was desirable, and excessively high interest rates would curb investment unnecessarily. However efficient the allocation of the investment that did take place, the allocation of resources as a whole would be out of balance.

Finally, this concept of efficiency itself may require qualification. Is profitability, or the return to the private economic agent, the right criterion for deciding whether or not investment should take place? It is sometimes argued that other criteria are also relevant. For example, a proposal to set up a business in an area with heavy unemployment might be justified, even if the profitability measured in conventional terms on the capital invested was lower than could be obtained on alternative projects elsewhere. This is one instance where social returns and private returns may diverge, and it can be argued that efficient allocation would reflect the former rather than the latter. How best to take account of such divergence is another matter to which we shall return in chapter 16.

Notes

1 Recall the inverse relationship between asset prices and interest rates.
2 The same applies to the demand for and supply of bank loans; e.g. there may be unplanned utilization of overdraft facilities. For simplicity, however, we assume that all unplanned changes are reflected in money holdings.
3 S and I must be defined consistently. Thus if I is gross investment S must include depreciation.
4 Abstracting from any changes in the institutions' non-monetary liabilities, e.g. their capital.
5 Note that S is *planned* saving in this context – a behavioural concept. It is not identical to the national accounts concept of saving, which would also include *unplanned* changes in money holdings.
6 At the time of writing, three-month sterling interbank deposits yielded 11 per cent and long-dated gilt-edged securities yielded just over 10 per cent, reflecting the view that short-term interest rates were likely to average less than 10 per cent in the following twenty years.
7 Sometimes this classification is carried out on a formal basis by bond rating services which classify companies into risk categories.
8 The dividend yield is (dividend)/(share price). The transactions costs of issuing the shares have been ignored.
9 The position may be reversed in periods of inflation when the uncertainty attached to inflation may make 'risk-free' assets expressed in nominal terms seem riskier than equity shares.
10 There is some evidence of this phenomenon in the USA.
11 Or better if he is successful in selecting companies whose performance is better than the market as a whole expects.
12 Strictly $(1 + r) = (1 + r^*)(1 + \dot{p})$.
13 At the time of writing the dividend yield on ordinary shares was a little under 5 per cent on average, while long-dated securities yielded around 10 per cent. If we suppose that the dividend yield includes a loading of 2 per cent for equity risk and that the real growth of dividends is expected to average 1 per cent per annum in future, then the risk-free real yield would be given by $(5 + 1 - 2) = 4$ per cent. The implied allowance for inflation would thus be $(10 - 4) = 6$ per cent.
14 Banks also require capital support for the lower-yielding liquid assets they need to hold in order to be able to raise the funds for lending; and they have in addition to recover the costs of any compulsory non-interest bearing reserves – see chapter 11.
15 A perpetuity is an undated security – one which promises a guaranteed annual payment *in perpetuity*.

6

Interest rates: further development

In this chapter we begin by examining in more detail some of the concepts employed in our analysis of interest rates, in particular the concepts of *money* and of the *yield* on long-term assets. We then turn to the factors which motivate and constrain a country's monetary authorities in determining short-term interest rates, before considering the effects of international linkages, including the key influence of exchange rate uncertainty in determining the interest rates on deposits and bonds. We conclude with a discussion of interest rate determination within the Exchange Rate Mechanism (ERM) of the European Monetary System and in a possible future European monetary union.

Money and long-term assets

So far the discussion has been conducted in terms of, on the one hand, *long-term assets* and, on the other, *money*, without attempting any precise definitions. It is not in fact possible to define any hard and fast list of financial instruments which fall into each category, because in reality financial instruments (and long-term physical assets) form a spectrum without any natural divisions. The financial instruments regarded as *money* in this context have therefore to be distinguished by reference to the behaviour of their holders and the proximate determinants of the interest rates on them. Specifically, financial instruments which are used as temporary stores of value and whose interest rates are largely determined by the monetary authorities qualify as *money*. At the other end of the spectrum are the *long-term assets* which people treat as investments – permanent stores of value or sources of income – whose yields are determined primarily by market forces, including of course the secondary repercussions of monetary forces, as discussed in the previous chapter. In between are assets bearing some of the characteristics of both money and long-term assets, gilt-edged securities with a maturity of five years being an example.

To qualify as money, assets must be capable of being used as a temporary store of wealth, pending a decision on its permanent disposition. This does not, of course, exclude the use of the same assets to hold wealth permanently – it simply means that the assets also perform a buffer role in asset-holders' portfolios. The most important categories in the UK are bank and building society deposits, including deposits which can be withdrawn only after a short period of notice or subject to a small penalty. But notes and coin also play a (small) part, as do financial instruments such as Treasury bills, commercial bills and some types of national savings.

To perform satisfactorily as a temporary store of value a financial instrument must exhibit a negligible default risk, a high degree of capital-certainty, and ease of conversion into means of payment. Company treasurers who invest their company's liquidity in risky assets must expect to lose their jobs if borrowers default or assets fall in value, and interest rates should be fixed only for short periods, so that value is not lost if interest rates rise. So while deposits with reputable financial institutions are 'in', unit trust units, ordinary shares, long-dated gilts and commercial property are clearly 'out'.

The second key characteristic of money in this context is that its rate of interest is largely determined by the monetary authorities. In the UK the Bank of England exerts its most direct influence on the rates of interest on Treasury and commercial bills, via its dealing rates in the market, and on loans to the Discount Market.[1] In turn, the rates of these key financial instruments largely determine the rates paid on the broad range of short-term financial instruments which are close substitutes for them. Thus a significant change in the Bank of England's dealing rates in the bill market feeds through almost immediately into wholesale deposit and lending rates, with retail rates usually following a little later. This does not of course mean that the rates offered by all the institutions are identical – some movement is taking place all the time as individual institutions alter their competitive stances in the market or revise their views about the likely course of interest rates in the future. But these factors account for relatively small variations around the general level of rates, and it is this general level which changes in response to the authorities' actions.

The precise technical mechanism through which the monetary

authorities in any country exert their influence is not important in this context – in the USA short-rates are influenced mainly through operations in the federal funds market, in some other countries through changes in key official rates. The important point is the fact that significant changes in the rates of interest on monetary instruments emanate from the monetary authorities.

The planned demand for money has been the subject of much theoretical and empirical investigation. We do not need to go into the details, it being sufficient to state that the demand for money, broadly defined as it is here, can be expected to grow with both national income and wealth, to be sensitive to the rates of interest on monetary assets relative to those on long-term assets, and to be affected by 'confidence'. Great uncertainty about the future, in particular fears that adverse economic conditions will be experienced, increases the demand for monetary assets.

The growth of national income and wealth accounts for rather stable trends in planned money holdings, whereas the effects of changes in confidence or movements in relative interest rates brought about by actions of the monetary authorities may be more abrupt. In the short-run these may therefore have significant impacts on long-term interest rates. Moreover, changes in the planned demand for money in any period also reflect discrepancies between actual and planned holdings at the outset. Economic agents do not generally try to eliminate the whole of such discrepancies quickly; but spare money burns a hole in the pocket, and abnormally high levels of money holdings create a demand for long-term assets (e.g. takeovers of other companies). Similarly, shortages of money lead individuals and firms to cut their expenditure on goods and services, to sell or issue long-term securities, and to dispose of physical assets.

The yield on long-term assets

The concept of the yield on long-term financial assets has already been discussed in general terms. On fixed-interest securities it is simply the ratio of the interest payments to the price of the security,[2] while on ordinary shares the principle is the same, though in this case the dividend payments have to be adjusted for future growth. For any given stream of interest or dividend payments, a fall in the long-term rate of interest implies a rise in the price of the security.

Most long-term assets are physical assets without, in many cases, corresponding financial assets. Private owner-occupied houses are a key example – there is no financial instrument corresponding to the owner's equity in the house. Similar considerations apply to privately-owned businesses, for although there may well be share capital it is not traded on a market and the information from which to calculate a yield is not readily available. In such cases it makes more sense to focus on asset prices – house prices and the prices paid for entire businesses – than to attempt to identify yields directly.

In the case of housing the income has to be imputed. It can be thought of as the rental (net of costs) which the house would command if rented on the open market. As with ordinary shares this may contain an element for real growth (the district may become more popular or land generally may be in short supply) and an allowance for rents rising with inflation. The imputed yield would then be the rental value, adjusted for growth and inflation, divided by the price of the house.

In most parts of the UK the house letting market is very thin, and the only element we can observe with any confidence is house prices. To see what is happening to long-term yields in the housing market we therefore have to rely on the inverse relationship between prices and yields. In the absence of any change in the imputed rental stream, a rise in house prices is equivalent to a fall in yields.

The theory developed in chapter 5 for long-term interest rates can be applied to the housing market. If, other things equal, there is an increase in bank and building society loans (ΔL) the rate of interest on long-term assets will fall (i.e. in this context the price of those assets – houses – will rise); and if nervousness about the business outlook leads to an increase in the demand for money (ΔM_d) and causes people to hold off buying houses, the price of houses will fall (i.e. the yield rises).

The same approach can be applied to the market for business assets. A business which promises to generate some given income flow will fetch a higher price when interest rates are low than when they are high. Monetary factors, which affect long-term interest rates generally, are reflected in the prices of business assets.

Short-term interest rates and monetary policy

In chapter 5 we saw how, in the short-run, the rate of interest on long-term assets was determined by a combination of saving, investment, and monetary factors. In the long-run, however, balance had to be achieved both between saving and investment on the one hand and between the (planned) demand for and supply of money on the other. In the short-run, the rates of interest on short-term assets set by the monetary authorities clearly had an important influence on long-term rates, but the factors affecting these rates were left unspecified. It is now time to fill this gap and investigate the factors which determine short-term rates of interest.

The monetary authorities attempt to set the level of short-term interest rates so as to achieve certain goals, which are related principally to price stability (or the control of inflation), the level of economic activity, and exchange rates. To see how they behave, consider what happens if monetary factors are not in equilibrium, specifically if $\Delta L > \Delta M_d$. The growth of lending means that money balances will be increasing faster than the planned demand for money, and this credit expansion will affect the demand for goods and services directly, as well as holding down long-term asset yields with further indirect consequences for demand for goods and services. Moreover, if the situation persists for some time, money holders will seek to run down their excess money balances, adding yet again to demand in goods and asset markets.[3]

The consequences of all this demand will be a rise in both nominal income – the money value of currently produced goods and services – and asset prices. Depending on the amount of spare resources in the economy, the former may well be associated with a rise in general inflation – the nearer is the economy to full employment the greater the extent to which a rise in nominal income will take the form of price increases rather than increases in real output.

A similar process takes place if $\Delta L < \Delta M_d$; i.e. the increase in lending is less than the increase in the (planned) demand for money. This will have a deflationary impact on nominal income and asset prices, whose consequences for the economy will depend on the degree of downward price flexibility in goods and (especially) labour markets. The greater the price flexibility the greater the impact on price trends and the less the impact on economic activity.

We can turn now to the actions of the monetary authorities, who set the short-term interest rates. They select the level of short-term rates (or, in practical terms, decide to *change* the level) by reference to their success in achieving their goals. Ideally they would like to combine high economic activity with price stability, but the shocks which occur in the real world usually make this impossible to achieve completely. So priorities come into play, and these vary from one country to another and from one period to the next.

In Germany, for example, the Bundesbank has the reputation of giving a high priority to the avoidance of inflation, reflecting what is thought to be the preference of German society at large. This means that they are prepared to raise short-term interest rates if they judge that inflation is too high or threatens to increase, and they will do this even at the cost of a decline in economic activity. In the USA the priority between the goals for inflation and economic activity is more evenly balanced. In the UK the evidence suggests that, provided inflation is not threatening to rise out of control, the authorities have in the past given higher priority to economic activity than to inflation – though in recent years it has not always been easy to distinguish between the effects of policy objectives and the consequences of misjudgements about the actual situation.

In setting short-term interest rates the monetary authorities react to their perception of economic developments. The growth of 'money' (however defined) may be used as a guide, or even as a rule. Money holdings which are growing faster than some predetermined rate may be taken as a signal that interest rates should be raised. However, it is unusual for monetary authorities to rely on monetary growth alone in determining their policies; more commonly they react to their perception of the economic situation overall, based upon a wide range of economic indicators. Their actions reflect their judgements about the dangers which they face: thus, in 1988 when the Federal Reserve Board in the USA judged that they were threatened by rising inflation, interest rates were raised, and in the second half of 1990 when recession was judged the greater danger interest rates were cut.

While the monetary authorities have considerable scope for judgement in the short-run, in the long-run their freedom of action is heavily constrained. For if they choose to set short-term interest rates at 'too' low a level, nominal income will expand and sooner or later inflation will pick up. This is a highly unstable situation, because rising inflation feeds expectations of further rises in future, so that a constant nominal rate of interest implies declining real rates – adding to the pressure of demand in the economy. In order to control the inflationary pressure the authorities are compelled to raise interest rates eventually, indeed by more than would have been needed if interest rates had not been set too low initially. Only when the inflationary expectations have been eliminated can the correct equilibrium level of short-term rates be restored. This is exactly what occurred in the UK when interest rates were held too low in 1987 and 1988 – the eventual rise, to 15 per cent in 1989, was much greater than it need otherwise have been.

The general conclusion stands that in the long-run interest rates are determined by the need to balance saving and investment, and this condition applies equally to long- and short-term rates of interest. However, in the short-run, other factors have an important bearing on short-term rates, and through them influence the yields on long-term assets. While the monetary authorities are by no means unconstrained in their choice of level for short-term rates, monetary influences do play a substantial part in determining interest rates in financial markets.

International linkages

So far we have discussed saving, investment and monetary factors within *an* economy, without addressing the question of the relevant boundaries for this purpose. This is an important omission. To what extent, for example, are interest rates in Britain determined by specifically British factors, and to what extent by the surrounding international environment? The answer depends on the exchange rate arrangements and other factors which govern the degree of international financial market integration.

Consider first the conditions which prevail in a country which has a single fiscal system, single currency and unified financial markets. Within such a country funds can flow freely from one region to another, and will do so in response to the ebb and flow of demand. When, for example, the development of North Sea oil created a high demand for funds in Aberdeen, interest rates in Aberdeen did not rise relative to the rest of the country; instead, the necessary funds were made available in Aberdeen at the going rate of interest through the normal financial institutions and markets. The commercial risks had of course to be evaluated in the usual ways, but there was no question of political risks or special tax barriers impeding the flow of funds. The general level of interest rates varies little within a country.[4]

This situation can be contrasted with that which applies in international financial markets, where the free flow of funds may be impeded by three factors: exchange risks, fiscal and other regulatory barriers, and political considerations.

Foreign exchange risk is the first factor leading to fragmentation in international financial markets. It is particularly important in the deposit and bond markets. Consider the position of a British investor choosing between holding short-term deposits in sterling and US dollars for some period. If he holds a sterling deposit, at the end of the period he will have his deposit plus the interest earned on it; if a dollar deposit, the same plus any capital gain or loss due to a change in the sterling/dollar exchange rate. Since future exchange rate movements, particularly over short periods, are subject to a very high degree of uncertainty, and capital gains or losses due to exchange rate changes are likely to be much greater than interest receipts, the uncertainty creates a barrier which impedes international capital flows.

This permits the monetary authorities in different countries to set short-term interest rates at different levels. Their freedom of action is, however, limited both by the direct effects of higher or lower interest rates on the spot rates of exchange and by the foreign exchange market's perception of likely exchange rate trends.

The stance of monetary policy has a direct effect on the strength or weakness of the exchange rate. High interest rates discourage domestic credit expansion and tend to draw in funds from abroad, thereby strengthening the exchange rate. In contrast, an easy monetary policy, associated with low interest rates and rapid growth of credit, weakens the exchange rate by stimulating the demand for imports and discouraging inflows of funds. Since strength or weakness of the exchange rate feeds through quite quickly into domestic price inflation the monetary authorities cannot ignore these effects.

The second limitation arises from the fact that the spot and forward prices for a currency in the foreign exchange market must compensate for the interest differential between financial instruments of the same term.[5] But these rates in the foreign exchange market may be limited by international agreements or longstanding practices – membership of the European Exchange Rate Mechanism (ERM), the link between the Hong Kong dollar and the US dollar, and the relationship between the Austrian schilling and the deutschmark are all examples – and they may also reflect the market's assessment of how economic forces will drive exchange movements in the future. The monetary authorities of a country whose currency is expected to depreciate will have to set interest rates above those which are available on stronger currencies. Thus a persistently high rate of inflation, or a persistent balance of payments deficit, may give rise to currency weakness which has to be compensated by high domestic interest rates.

Fears and expectations of exchange rate changes also cause the interest rates on longer-term bonds to differ from one country to another. These expectations may be very persistent and are usually related to past experience of inflation. Thus fears that the French franc might one day be devalued against the deutschmark have led to the rate of interest on government bonds in France being higher than those in Germany. In recent years, as these fears have receded the interest margin has narrowed. In other cases it is the expectation rather than merely a fear of devaluation which is the key factor. Countries with high rates of inflation are expected to devalue periodically against countries with low rates, and their bond yields reflect this fact.

Exchange rate movements are less significant as a barrier to international long-term equity investment, if only because in the long-run it is expected that major exchange rate changes will broadly reflect differences in inflation.[6] The value of equity investments in domestic currency terms is expected to rise in line with the general price level, thus compensating for any decline in the exchange rate.

The upshot is that foreign exchange risk does not constitute an effective barrier to the international capital flows which tend to equalize the *real* yields on equity instruments. But differences in inflation and other factors which affect exchange rates both permit differences between countries in the *nominal* yields on debt instruments and help to explain why they exist.

Fiscal and regulatory barriers also help to delimit the boundaries within which interest rates are determined. Exchange controls which impede capital flows are the leading example, though in the industrial world these are now of comparatively little significance. For the most part they have been abolished, and even when they existed multinational companies' ability to circumvent them and to borrow in the cheapest market minimized their effects. Regulations governing the assets held by some major categories of financial institutions, such as insurance companies in some countries, do still have a limiting effect.

The same can be said of taxes paid by asset-holders. These affect the prevailing levels of interest rates because international investors are concerned with the yield they receive *after* tax, and their activities tend to equalize the post-tax yields on the securities they hold. Thus in 1989 the threatened imposition of a with-holding tax on the interest on securities in West Germany led to an immediate increase in German bond yields.

Political risks may also be an important impediment to capital flows. Investors depend ultimately on the law to enforce their property rights – the right to receive their capital back, to the interest they have been promised, or to their share of the profits earned on an equity investment, as the case may be. Property rights may not be well-established or easy to define, as is still the case in some East European countries today, and foreign investors always face the risk that *force majeure* may deprive them of their rights. By and large, investors from countries with a history of political stability can have greater confidence that they will enjoy the fruits of investments in their home countries.

Again, within the major industrial countries, political risks pose few barriers to international investment – the risks are not thought to be high and can in any case be limited through diversification. But in the developing world and in countries which do not enjoy a high reputation for political stability, political risks may act as a powerful deterrent to inward capital flows.

All this suggests that there is no simple answer to the question of defining the boundaries of the region within which interest rates are determined. Nevertheless the fiscal and structural barriers which help to divide markets tend to be structural in character and to account for differences in yield *levels*:[7] they do not isolate individual countries from the effects of worldwide trends. Political risks have similar consequences, though the perception of such risks can change quite quickly in response to political developments, and provide a reason for yield trends to differ between countries.

The integration of markets means that there is quite a strong tendency for real yields to move in concert on a worldwide basis. The effects of changes in saving and investment flows in one country or region spill over into others. Thus the effect of the reunification of Germany, which virtually eliminated Germany's substantial savings surplus, was not confined to interest rates in Germany, but spilled over into all the world's major capital markets (thus greatly moderating the effects which would otherwise have been observed on yields in Germany itself). The same goes for monetary influences: the very tight monetary policy pursued by the US authorities in 1980 drove up real rates of interest across the world, just as the more expansionary monetary policies pursued generally in the second half of the 1980s contributed to the worldwide stock-exchange boom and asset price inflation in that period.[8]

In these respects real equity yields and real long-term bond yields are subject to the same real and monetary forces. But inflationary expectations, to the extent that they are reflected in likely exchange rate trends, also have an important bearing on the *nominal* yield on bonds, and these expectations are specific to the countries or currencies concerned. Thus the nominal yields on bonds, in addition to being subject to common movements due to changes in worldwide real yields, are also influenced by purely domestic factors

– fears that inflation will rise, that monetary policy will be tightened, and so on. In practice these domestic factors may often prove to be the more important influence.

Where the possibility of exchange rate movements is high in the short-run, countries enjoy an even greater degree of independence from world trends in setting short-term interest rates. Again, countries cannot opt out altogether from worldwide shortages or surpluses of savings. Nor, as we have seen, can they avoid the consequences of persistently high expected rates of inflation causing currency weakness. But, so long as the exchange rate consequences are acceptable, exchange rate variability does permit a country to pursue a monetary policy and set short-term interest rates at a level which differs from those elsewhere.

The ERM and monetary union

The extent to which a country's exchange rate is free to vary and the way in which the authorities manage it clearly have important consequences for short-term interest rates. Britain's membership of the ERM is no exception. It affects UK interest rates in three ways: membership places obligations on the monetary authorities to keep sterling within its ERM bands, these bands limit the scope for exchange rate movements and hence the interest differentials relative to other currencies, and the implied commitment to bring UK inflation more closely into line with inflation in other ERM member countries influences expectations in the financial markets.

Countries within the ERM agree a set of central parities for their currencies against all the other currencies in the system. Fluctuation bands, normally 2.25 per cent on either side of the parity, are determined and each country agrees to take whatever action is needed to prevent the exchange rates for its currency falling outside the fluctuation bands. Appropriate action includes exchange market intervention, interest rate policy, or other aspects of economic policy. In principle both of the countries involved must take action when there is a danger of a limit being breached, but in practice the country whose currency is most out of line with the others in the system as a whole is expected to take action well before this point is reached. Some countries, currently (1991) the UK and Spain, operate with a wider 6 per cent band as an interim measure whilst others, for example Belgium and the Netherlands, maintain a much narrower fluctuation margin relative to the deutschmark.

Realignments of the central parities within the system can take place by general agreement, but are discouraged.

Membership of the ERM means that the monetary authorities always have to take account of the exchange rate in setting short-term interest rates; and if there is any significant chance of the central parities within the ERM being altered the exchange rate becomes the overriding factor. Short-term interest rates have to be set high (or low) enough to counter market fears of any realignment. Thus fears that sterling's central values within the ERM may be reduced weaken sterling and compel the UK authorities to hold interest rates at a level which offsets this weakness – the interest margin on sterling over other stronger ERM currencies has to be wide enough to compensate for the risk of depreciation. Conversely, if sterling was expected to rise beyond the upper ERM limit, sterling interest rates would have to be held down to discourage inflows into sterling.

We can see just how important the obligation to maintain parities can be by considering what may happen in a period when there is considerable uncertainty about future exchange rates. Suppose that in the run-up to a general election the market expected that sterling would be devalued after the election by, say, 5 per cent. Assuming that the devaluation would take place immediately after the election and that the date was known, six months before the election an annual interest differential of 10 per cent would be required to compensate holders of sterling for the risk of loss. The closer the election, the larger the margin needed. Of course it would not be *certain* that sterling would be devalued and a change in the parity would not necessarily mean an equivalent, or even any, change in the actual rate. Moreover, if sterling was towards the lower limit in its band there would be a chance of appreciation to balance part of the risk of loss. Precise calculations of the interest differentials required to support the currency are therefore impossible. But it is clear that high interest rates must be at least a part of a policy to support sterling in these conditions. Moreover, the narrower the band within which the exchange rate can vary, the greater the reliance that has to be put on interest rates to provide the necessary support. With the option of permitting sterling to fall constrained by ERM membership, interest rate policy in the short-run is governed by exchange rate considerations to an even greater degree within the ERM than it would be outside.

For countries operating with the standard 2.25 per cent bands the pre-eminence of the exchange rate in determining short-term interest rates diminishes in more stable conditions. Suppose that there is no serious question over the maintenance of the parities. Then the scope for a currency to vary within the bands enables the monetary authorities to give priority to domestic considerations in fixing short-term interest rates, provided that they do not want to move too far out of line with the rates available on other currencies. What this means in practice is that the authorities in countries whose currencies are strong within the ERM have the freedom to cut interest rates on domestic grounds, whereas in countries whose currencies are weak interest rates can be raised. But by and large there is little scope for cutting interest rates on weak currencies or raising them on strong.

The scope for independent interest rate policies is, of course, influenced by the width of the band. Those countries operating a policy of targeting the deutschmark within a very narrow margin have little option but to follow changes in deutschmark interest rates slavishly; those using the standard 2.25 per cent band have more freedom of action; and a 6 per cent band allows still more. The degree of independence depends too on the importance of the country, and currency, concerned. The Bundesbank in Germany can raise deutschmark interest rates even when the mark is strong, because other countries are likely to have to follow suit.

Membership of the ERM affects the foreign exchange market's expectations of future exchange rate levels. There is a clear obligation on members to pursue policies which are likely to make future realignments unnecessary and in particular to bring about a convergence of rates of inflation.[9] As it becomes apparent that a relatively high inflation country intends to honour this commitment the interest margin on its securities over those from stronger currency countries narrows.

When, however, the financial markets are nervous about the possibility of a currency realignment in future, interest rate policy is constrained by its effect on market expectations. Participants in financial markets are looking continually for evidence of a government's resolve to control inflation, and a cut in interest rates may be interpreted as evidence that commitment is lacking. In that case the effect of an interest rate reduction on inflationary expectations, and hence on the exchange rate, would be much greater than if confidence was unaffected.

The broad thrust of the ERM is therefore towards the unification of financial markets. It is not only the real yields on long-term assets which will be equalized (and be dependent largely on worldwide conditions, as we have seen) but also the nominal yields on bonds and short-term deposits. The monetary conditions relevant to their determination are those of the core members of the ERM as a whole (led by Germany), and while variations in short-term interest rates amongst the members will persist so long as exchange rates can vary, short-term rates will follow a common trend. The scope for interest rates in the individual member countries to vary reflects the width of the fluctuation bands and, crucially, confidence that the existing parities will be maintained. In setting short-term interest rates the core members will of course continue to be constrained by their desire to achieve high levels of economic activity and to avoid inflation.

The trend towards unification will be taken one step further by monetary union amongst the members of the ERM. Monetary union implies that there will be either a single currency or *permanently* fixed exchange rates, so that foreign exchange risk within the area is eliminated, and that there will be a single monetary authority for the area as a whole. In the absence of foreign exchange risk the same level of short-term interest rates will be found throughout the area, with any residual differences reflecting variations in costs, risks, or market imperfections.

The factors which determine interest rates will therefore be common to the entire area. The real yields on long-term assets will be determined principally by worldwide savings and investment and by the general ease or tightness of monetary policy. These yields will influence the nominal yields on deposits and bonds, which will also be determined by monetary conditions within the area.[10] The conditions for interest rate determination within a European monetary union will thus be comparable to those which exist in a single country today.

Notes

1 Apart from setting the interest rates on notes, coin and bankers' deposits with itself at zero.
2 With an appropriate adjustment for any premium or discount to the price of the security at maturity.
3 There will also of course be implications for the exchange rate, to be discussed in the following section.
4 There are two principal caveats to enter. First, fiscal policies which discriminate between the regions of a country will affect the cost of funds for some borrowers. Secondly, comparing one region with another, differences in costs or in the strength of competition amongst the financial institutions may affect margins.
5 Otherwise there would be opportunities for risk-free covered interest

arbitrage. The attempts to profit from these opportunities would alter prices in the foreign exchange markets until the cost of forward cover (the difference between the spot and forward prices for the currency) equalled the interest differential.

6 In line with the purchasing power parity theory of exchange rates.

7 These differences will change when the barriers themselves change.

8 The integrated nature of world capital markets accounts for the high degree of correlation between different equity markets which is observed in the short-run, as well as for common medium-term trends in the yield basis. The markets in individual countries do, however, also reflect the prospects for the companies whose shares are quoted, and these frequently differ considerably from one country to another. For example, the prospects for economic growth at the time of writing (1991) differ sharply between Germany and Japan on the one hand and the USA and UK on the other. These domestic factors also have an important bearing on share price trends.

9 Persistent differences in rates of inflation are the most important causes of substantial changes in exchange rates.

10 On the twin assumptions that capital is able to flow freely between the area of the single currency and third countries, and that the exchange rates are also allowed to vary freely.

Part III

The users of the system

In this part the behaviour of the users of the financial system is examined in greater depth. The financial facilities required by the various categories of user reflect the nature of their economic activities, which differ between persons, industrial and commercial companies, and the public sector. In the following chapters the behaviour of each of these sectors is considered in turn, while their linkages with the overseas sector are brought together in the last chapter of this part.

In normal conditions the personal sector is the most important source of saving in the economy, and households also have substantial demands for funds, especially in connection with home ownership. Saving and investment by the personal sector are discussed in the next chapter – the reasons why people save, how much they save, the forms in which they choose to hold their savings, consumer borrowing for house purchase and other purposes, and the forces underlying the consumer boom of the second half of the eighties are all considered.

For industrial and commercial companies, which are the subject matter of chapter 8, it is the ability to raise finance which matters most. The factors which influence the structure of companies' balance sheets and their needs for equity and debt finance are dealt with first, before we turn to examine the trends in their sources and uses of funds over a 30-year period and highlight the heavy dependence on external finance, especially from the banks, at the end of the eighties. The special financing problems of small companies are discussed briefly at the end of the chapter.

Each of the three components of the public sector – the central government, local authorities and public corporations – has its own financing needs, though the impact on the financial system is consolidated to a high degree in central government financing arrangements. In chapter 9 the trends in the saving, investment and financing of the individual sectors are discussed, before we examine the impact of public sector borrowing (or debt repayment) as a whole on the financial system and the economy.

Chapter 10 on the 'overseas' sector brings together all the changes in assets and liabilities involving transactions between the UK and foreign residents. As the international economy has become more integrated these have assumed increasing importance for industrial and commercial companies, portfolio investors and the banks.

7

Personal saving and investment

The personal sector has traditionally been the chief source of saving in the UK capital market. Personal sector saving has usually exceeded its investment by a considerable margin, with the financial surplus being made available to other sectors of the economy. While business saving has generally been larger in absolute terms it has less impact on the capital market because so much is employed in investment within the firms concerned.

In the second half of the 1980s, however, the personal sector broke with tradition. The consumer boom was associated with a fall in personal saving to under 5 per cent of GDP on average in 1985–9, and this was in fact slightly less than personal sector investment (also 5 per cent) in the period – the traditional financial surplus disappeared. The sector did continue to build up financial assets by 11 per cent of GDP a year on average, much the same as ten years previously, but only by borrowing nearly 9½ per cent of GDP a year, or twice as much as it had before. While some people were building up assets, others (or sometimes the same people) were borrowing heavily, often in order to buy a house or using a house as security.

The personal sector divides its financial assets between those which are safe and have a high degree of liquidity, catering for short-run needs and providing some security against the uncertainties of the future, and longer-term assets held for their income-producing qualities or to provide for known future needs such as retirement. In chapter 1 we took a preliminary look at the reasons for saving and the ways in which people's motives influence their choice of financial assets. Our task in this chapter is to examine these matters in greater depth, in order to account both for the personal sector's asset holdings and for the flows of funds which they supply to and draw from the financial system.

Personal sector wealth

The 'personal' sector in the United Kingdom includes not only households and individuals, as might be expected, but also the business activities of sole traders and partnerships, such as farms, retail shops and independent professional men and women, and private non-profit-making bodies such as charities, trade unions and clubs. However, individuals and households account for about 90 per cent of personal sector wealth, and while the factors which influence the behaviour of the other components are often different from those affecting private persons, with few exceptions the figures give a reasonably accurate picture of household behaviour.

Table 7.1 shows the personal sector's assets and liabilities at the end of 1989. Net wealth – i.e. the difference between the sector's assets and liabilities – amounted to more than £2100 billion, about six times personal disposable income (PDI) in 1989.[1] Physical, or *tangible*, assets comprised 58 per cent of net wealth; this does not include the value of consumer durable goods – cars, furniture etc. – which are excluded from the official wealth figures. Non-marketable tenancy rights (see below) make up 8 per cent, financial assets 53 per cent, and borrowing 18 per cent.

Dwellings accounted for nearly 90 per cent of the personal sector's tangible assets at the end of 1989, though it is worth noting that this figure would fall to under 80 per cent if consumer durables were included. The other tangible assets are mainly used for business purposes, namely agricultural, commercial and industrial land, and stocks, vehicles and equipment.

Non-marketable tenancy rights reflect the difference between the values of certain properties with sitting tenants and their values with vacant possession. These rights are not marketable, but tenants who purchase their properties as sitting tenants can sell them subsequently with vacant possession, thus realizing their value. In the local authority sector the rights are reflected in the discount to open market values at which tenants can purchase their homes.

At the end of 1989 the personal sector's holdings of financial assets were worth over three times its disposable income. The most liquid categories – notes and coin, deposits with banks and building societies, and national savings[2] – accounted for just under a third of the total. Direct holdings of securities and loans, whether to the government, UK companies or overseas bodies, amounted to only a sixth, much less than indirect holdings of these assets through unit trusts, life assurance and pension funds, which amounted to nearly

Table 7.1   Balance sheet of the personal sector, end-1989

	(£ billion)
Tangible assets	
Dwellings	1097
Other land and buildings	103
Stocks, vehicles, equipment	35
Total	1235
Non-marketable tenancy rights	167
Financial assets	
Notes and coin	13
Bank and building society deposits	284
National savings	35
Other government securities and loans	35
UK company securities	153
Overseas securities	11
Unit trust units	23
Equity in life assurance and pension funds	509
Domestic trade debtors	35
Other	33
Total	1130
Liabilities	
Loans for house purchase	256
Other lending by financial institutions	87
Domestic trade creditors	30
Other	23
Total	395
Net financial wealth	734
Net wealth	2137
Memorandum item	
Consumer durables	160

Source: Financial Statistics, February 1991, table S2

half of total financial assets. Much of the balance consisted of trade and other debtors – assets held in connection with business activities. Just over 10 per cent of the bank and building society deposits are held by the non-household components.

Most of the sector's liabilities are incurred in order to finance the purchase of physical assets, and at the end of 1989 liabilities amounted to just under a third of the value of tangible assets. Much the most important form of liability was loans for house purchase, equal to nearly a quarter of the value of dwellings. Other lending by financial institutions, which comprised just over 20 per cent of all liabilities, is used mainly for the purchase of consumer durables, stock and vehicles. Nearly half of this other lending (which is mainly from banks) relates to business activities, as does part of the creditors item.

There were substantial changes in the composition of the personal sector's balance sheet in the 1980s (table 7.2). First, thanks principally to booms in both house and share prices, and in spite of the decline in the savings ratio already noted, the ratio of net wealth to personal disposable income rose from 4.4 to 6.1. People felt better off, and spent more. Secondly, there was an increase in owner-occupation, as local authorities sold homes to their tenants and the incidence of private rented accommodation continued to decline: the combined shares of ownership of dwellings and tenancy rights in net wealth remained the same, but the division between them moved strongly in favour of ownership. Thirdly, there was a noteworthy increase in the share of financial assets, partly offset by an increase in borrowing, particularly house purchase loans. The most likely explanations are the end of rationing in the house mortgage market – access to funds became much easier – and a narrowing of margins in financial intermediation. Lastly, within

Table 7.2   Personal sector balance sheet trends, 1979–89

	1979	*1989*
Net wealth to PDI ratio	4.4	6.1
Shares in net wealth (%)		
Dwellings	45	51
Tenancy rights	15	8
Financial assets	41	53
Financial liabilities	13	18
Shares in financial assets (%)		
Liquid assets	40	29
Securities	19	20
Life assurance and pension funds	33	45
House purchase loans to dwellings ratio (%)	17	23

Sources: table 7.1; *Financial Statistics*, February 1981, table C financial assets there was a decline in the share of liquid assets and a corresponding rise in the share of life assurance and pension funds – a consequence of capital appreciation within life assurance and pension fund portfolios and the increasing attraction of equity instruments to savers in a period when returns on existing investments were high.

Motives for saving

A person's wealth represents the accumulation of his own saving over the years, capital appreciation on his assets, and any gifts or bequests he may have received. People save for a variety of motives. First, a certain amount of short-term saving takes place to meet seasonal or other peaks in spending, for example summer holidays, Christmas presents, consumer durables, or simply anything which demands a substantial cash outlay at one time. This kind of saving is really nothing more than short-run cash flow management – a building up or running down of money-holdings in order to iron out fluctuations in income and spending. The financial assets held in this connection are generally cash or deposits.

Secondly, people save out of a sense of precaution; they aim to build up a nest egg for emergencies. They might, for example, wish to guard against the misfortune of losing their jobs or having to accept short-time working for an extended period, during which their income would be much less than they had been accustomed to. Or they might want to hold a reserve in case, quite unexpectedly, their house or car had to undergo expensive repairs. Savings held for precautionary reasons often also take the form of deposits, but other liquid assets such as national savings or even short-dated securities all fill the bill.

Thirdly, people save for their old age or to ensure that, if they die young, their dependants are looked after. These motives for saving are extremely important, and are the fundamental reason for the strength of life assurance and pension funds in Britain. But there are other ways of achieving the same objectives. Ordinary shares and fixed interest securities, designed to preserve the value of capital and provide a satisfactory income after retirement, are often held for this purpose; a substantial proportion of the building societies' deposits are held by people saving for retirement; whilst others choose to save by purchasing their own home or investing in their own business.

Concern to provide for old age or dependants shades into a

straightforward desire to accumulate capital. People enjoy the ownership of wealth, for the security it gives and for the opportunities it provides, without necessarily wishing either to spend the income derived from their wealth themselves or, indeed, to sell the assets at some stage to finance their own consumption. Capital accumulation normally takes the form of business assets, marketable securities of all kinds, houses, and, to a more limited extent, deposits. In the past, the desire to build up a thriving private business has been a particularly powerful motive for saving.

Lastly, people will save in order to provide for their own comfort and pleasure. They accumulate wealth in the form of houses, motor cars, or consumer durables, not because they hope to derive any money income from them, or even to avoid expenditure of other kinds, but because they enjoy living in a well-furnished spacious house or having the freedom and convenience which a car provides.

Theories of saving

Enumerating the motives for saving helps us to understand why people save and gives some guidance on the form that saving will take. But it tells us very little about *how much* people will choose to save or how their saving will be affected by factors such as interest rates, income or wealth. These matters are the central concern of theories of saving.

Table 7.3 shows personal saving as a percentage of PDI from 1970 to 1989. While the precise figures must be taken with a pinch of salt – the error margin in estimates of saving derived from national accounts statistics is large – they indicate that personal saving was on an increasing trend during the 1970s, reaching a peak in 1980 and 1981. In the first half of the 1980s the savings ratio averaged about 12 per cent, but it fell sharply to average only 6 per cent at the end of the decade. A rise in the personal savings ratio was a common phenomenon in many countries in the mid-seventies – one which took economists by surprise – and led to attempts to refine existing theories of saving in order to account satisfactorily for what occurred.

The rise in personal saving at that time seemed to run counter to Keynesian theory, which stressed the link between personal saving and current income. If income rose, saving would rise too, but more than in proportion to income, whereas if income fell saving would suffer a disproportionate cut. In times of prosperity people would be slow to adjust their spending habits to their higher levels of income,

Table 7.3 Personal saving as a percentage of personal disposable income, 1970–89

	(Per cent)
1970–74 average	9.2
1975–79 average	10.7
1980	13.1
1981	12.5
1982	11.4
1983	9.8
1984	10.5
1985	9.7
1986	8.2
1987	6.6
1988	5.4
1989	6.7

Source: Economic Trends, Annual Supplement, 1991

whereas when times were bad they would draw on the precautionary balances they had accumulated earlier. This Keynesian approach provided insights into the ways in which changes in personal saving were likely to be induced by fluctuations in economic activity; but it has proved less satisfactory in suggesting how personal saving would react to other shocks to the economic system.

Subsequent theories of saving put greater stress on long-run income concepts, and linked saving to personal wealth rather than to current income. An individual's standard of living is determined not only by his current income, but also by his wealth and the income which he expects to earn in the future. For a typical person, the time-pattern of income during his life-span will not coincide with the time-pattern of his consumption; saving in some periods balanced by dis-saving in others permits him to match his consumption with his needs.[3] This approach encompasses several of the motives for saving discussed earlier (e.g. saving to meet seasonal peaks in consumption, saving by young couples to buy or furnish houses, and saving for retirement). Moreover, since the amounts required for all these purposes reflect a person's standard of living and are linked to long-run income, this approach suggests that an individual's desired holdings of financial assets should move broadly in line with the trend of income. The notion of a desired wealth/income ratio can also be extended to liquid saving held for precautionary reasons.

The effect of the rate of interest on the level of saving has already been discussed in chapter 3. Two potentially contrary effects were noted. On the one hand a rise in interest rates made saving more attractive, because it increased the saver's command over resources in the future; there was a positive substitution effect. On the other hand, because interest rates were higher it was possible to provide for known or estimated future needs with a lower level of saving; there was a negative income effect. The substitution effect is likely to be rather weak because, as the discussion of motives has shown, much of saving does not depend on the carrot of a real return. However, as already noted in chapter 3, the possibility of a negative income effect is much more than a theoretical curiosity, and may in fact be quite important in practice – when a pension scheme provides pensions which are related to the members' final salaries, the size of the fund which has to be accumulated and the level of contributions are reduced by increases in the rate of interest.

To these two effects we must now add the effect of interest rates on the values of existing assets. When real interest rates fall existing assets – bonds, equities, houses – appreciate in value and their owners feel better off. Less new saving is required to achieve target wealth/income ratios and, perhaps more important, incentives for dis-saving by those who can now afford it are created. Since personal saving is the difference between gross saving and gross dis-saving, this can have a powerful effect. In particular, in the UK in 1987 and 1988, house price inflation, caused partly by lower interest rates, was undoubtedly a major cause of the decline in the personal savings ratio. Falling interest rates, ready access to credit and an active housing market made it easy for owner-occupiers to convert part of the equity in their homes into consumption in these years – just as the high interest rates, which helped to depress housing values, and low turnover in the housing market inhibited equity withdrawal and raised the personal savings ratio in 1989 and 1990.

It is not, of course, only interest rates that affect the value of assets. Changes in profitability or in rents (imputed in the case of owner-occupied housing) are just as important as determinants of wealth/income ratios and feed through to household spending. They also have important consequences for the level of contributions to pension funds.

In the latter part of the 1970s, thanks to rapid inflation and the relatively poor stock market performance in this period, many pension schemes found that they had deficiencies, in the sense that the value of their funds was not sufficient to cover the liabilities to their members. As a result contribution levels had to be increased to eliminate the deficits over a period of years. This helped to increase the personal savings ratio at the end of the seventies. During the 1980s, however, strong stock market performances with rapidly rising dividends (especially in the UK) put this process into reverse. Schemes found that they had built up surpluses – their wealth was higher than was warranted by their future income needs – and reduced their contributions or omitted them altogether, thus contributing to the decline in the savings ratio in the second half of the decade.

Inflation is another factor which has a powerful effect on personal saving. First, it generally affects relative rates of return, with nominal rates of interest rising, at least initially, by less than the rate of inflation. This makes assets such as money and bonds relatively unattractive – frequently the real return becomes negative – in comparison with physical assets such as buildings or ordinary shares which can be expected to maintain their real values. The proportion of saving flowing towards physical assets tends to increase.

But inflation also affects saving through its influence on wealth/ income ratios – in this case the ratio of liquid assets to income. First of all, inflation means that in order to maintain a target ratio of liquid assets to income, people have to add to their liquid assets each year to keep up with the increase in their nominal incomes, and the higher the level of inflation the more they have to add. This counts as saving. For example, if people hold liquid assets amounting to 80 per cent of annual PDI and if inflation runs at 10 per cent, they would have to save nearly 8 per cent of their income simply to prevent a reduction in this ratio. As we have seen in chapter 5, nominal interest rates in an equilibrium situation would also include a premium of 10 per cent for inflation – all of this extra income on their liquid assets should in principle be saved.

Secondly, inflation which is not fully anticipated and which is not matched by correspondingly higher interest rates erodes the real value of liquid assets. In the course of the 1970s the ratio of liquid assets to income fell from about 90 per cent to 73 per cent, with two-thirds of the fall occurring in 1974 and 1975 – RPI inflation in these years was 16 and 24 per cent respectively, much higher than had been expected. This erosion had to be made good subsequently, not of course immediately when the impact on consumption in a short period would have been too severe, but over a period of years. A period of falling inflation, such as occurred in the first half of the 1980s, with real rates of interest comparatively high, provided the conditions for the erosion to be made good (see table 7.4).

The ratio of liquid assets to PDI continued to rise in the second

Table 7.4 Personal sector liquid assets as a percentage of personal disposable income, 1979–89

	(Per cent)
1979	73
1980	72
1981	78
1982	78
1983	80
1984	84
1985	86
1986	88
1987	90
1988	93
1989	94

Source: Blue Book, 1990, tables 4.1, 12.2

half of the 1980s, until by the end it was at its highest level for 25 years. This may have reflected an increase in the target ratio – inflation was lower than in the seventies, the interest rates on most liquid assets had become more attractive, and after the stock market crash in 1987 the comparative security of their value became more widely appreciated. However, it may also have reflected a temporary build-up of liquidity associated with the credit boom in the period; if so, it will be reversed gradually during the 1990s.

The last factor affecting personal saving is consumer confidence. The effect on borrowing of swings in confidence over the cycle can easily outweigh the Keynesian effects on gross saving. In the UK the rapid growth of disposable incomes in 1987 and 1988 led to a surge of confidence and extremely high levels of consumer borrowing, much of which was used to purchase consumer goods (including consumer durables) and services. This contributed to the low savings ratio. In other circumstances, slower growth of incomes, as in 1980 and 1981, caused consumers to draw in their horns, borrow less, and thus increase the level of net saving. It is not usually easy to distinguish these confidence effects from those of interest rates – high interest rates and weak confidence often go together – but it is arguable that shifts in the demand curve for credit due to confidence movements are at least as important in explaining changes in borrowing as movements along the curve due to changes in interest rates.

Choice of assets

Some of the major differences between financial assets are by now familiar – for example, differences with respect to liquidity, yield, and capital-certainty in nominal or real terms. Other characteristics of particular assets are also very important to their holders (e.g. the means of payment aspect of many deposits with banks and building societies). Contractual savings arrangements, through life assurance or unit trust savings schemes, are attractive to many people because they value the discipline to save which this imposes upon them. In deciding how their wealth will be divided amongst the physical and financial assets available to them, savers have to evaluate the characteristics of the assets in relation to their own needs.

It is convenient to divide the factors which influence the personal saver's evaluation of the alternative financial assets into three categories: structural factors, legislative factors, market factors. The structural factors relate to the motives for saving which have been discussed already. Everyone has some need of precautionary balances, but the amount required depends very much on the risks to which people are exposed. The National Health Service and other social security benefits are important structural factors which greatly reduce the need for precautionary balances. So is the State Retirement Pensions scheme, which make it unnecessary for individuals to provide so fully for themselves. Taking a broader perspective, a country's record of economic and political stability influences the ways in which people choose to save. In countries which have experienced very rapid inflation, in which those who held long-term assets have experienced a damaging erosion of their wealth, or which have suffered from serious political instability, people generally seek the freedom of manoeuvre which liquidity endows and have a very strong preference for short-term assets such as bank deposits. Structural factors, then, reflect a country's history and its general social arrangements.

Some of these arrangements are embodied in legislation, others are more deeply rooted in custom or convention. But in addition, there are legislative factors, which are not necessarily such permanent features of the economy but which also influence saving behaviour. The system of occupational pension schemes in Britain, with their associated tax arrangements is one example; these provide a very strong incentive for saving in this form, since contributions are a charge on gross income, the earnings of the funds are accumulated tax-free, a proportion of the accumulated fund can be paid as a capital sum at retirement, and the pension payments themselves are taxed as earned income. Until 'personal pensions', with similar tax treatment, were introduced in 1988 an employee who attempted to build up his own personal saving for retirement had none of these advantages. At one time life assurance too was encouraged through tax incentives, with the government granting tax relief or paying the insurance company a sum equal to a proportion of the gross premiums. These arrangements were discontinued in 1984, but until then individuals had a strong incentive to save through the medium of life assurance rather than, for example, investing directly in unit trusts. Even in the early 1990s life assurance still offers some tax advantages to wealthy investors, because the investment income and capital gains of life assurance funds are taxed at a lower rate (25 per cent) than the 40 per cent such individuals would have to pay themselves.

Tax arrangements also favour mortgage borrowing for house purchase. The taxpayer is permitted to charge interest on the first £30 000 of a mortgage against his gross income before tax; at the current standard rate of tax this reduces the effective cost of the mortgage by 25 per cent of the interest payment on this amount. This tax concession has encouraged endowment mortgages – i.e. mortgages in which the loan is repaid at the end of the period from the proceeds of a life assurance policy – because by avoiding earlier capital repayments the value of the tax concession is maximized. Together with the exemption of gains on owner-occupied housing from capital gains tax, these tax arrangements provide a powerful incentive for individuals in the UK to build up wealth in the form of owner-occupied housing rather than financial assets. However, Personal Equity Plans (PEPs), in which individuals can invest limited amounts annually and which are free of income and capital gains tax, and Tax Exempt Special Savings Accounts (TESSAs), which are also limited in amount but in which income is free of tax provided that capital is not withdrawn within a five-year period, have now widened the range of financial assets enjoying privileged tax treatment.[4] Legislative factors like these can in principle be changed fairly easily – but there is no doubt that while they remain in force they have a considerable influence on the pattern of personal saving.

The last group of factors affecting personal saving behaviour are market factors, notably the relative yields offered by different savings media. In choosing between two deposit-taking institutions, the saver will frequently choose that which offers the higher yield – quite small differences in interest rates (e.g. less than half a per cent) can have appreciable effects on the allocation of depositors' funds. Or in deciding with which life assurance company he or she should take out a policy a saver's attention will be drawn to the historical record. Other important market factors are the availability of branches, advertising and other forms of access to customers. Thus estate agents who are selling houses are in a good position to introduce clients to mortgage lending institutions, and the mortgage lenders can do the same for the providers of endowment assurance policies. Market factors have their main impact on the saver's choice amongst *similar* financial instruments.

Market factors have an important bearing on the allocation of saving in the short-run. If the demand for owner-occupied housing is high, whilst industrial demand for external finance is low, the rate of interest on building society deposits will rise relative to that paid by banks, and an above-average proportion of personal saving will flow to the former. Again, by offering high rates of interest on national savings and gilt-edged securities, the government is able to attract funds away from deposit-taking institutions. For example, a new issue of savings certificates may offer a tax-free yield which is attractive to higher-rate tax payers. However, in the long term the structural and legislative factors are the more fundamental. Whether interest rates are high or low, money continues to flow into life assurance and pension funds, and while the amount varies with economic conditions, the average level is determined by structural and legislative considerations. The experience of inflation and the tax advantages for owner-occupied housing combine to ensure that building societies, the financial institutions which specialize in the provision of housing finance, will face a continued high demand for funds. The structural and legislative factors are themselves determinants of the relative interest rates and other aspects of competition between institutions which prevail in the market for savings.

Personal borrowing

Personal borrowing is usually connected with the purchase of physical assets, though there is some borrowing for consumption, mainly by means of bank overdrafts or through the use of credit cards, and some for the purchase of financial assets or land. Dwellings are the predominant physical asset for which individuals borrow, but cars and many consumer durables are also often financed through instalment loans. Business assets financed by borrowing include not only tangible assets, such as the farmer's barn or the dentist's equipment, but also intangible assets, such as the lawyer's share in a partnership.

Home ownership is usually financed with the help of a mortgage loan from a building society, bank, or other mortgage lender. The maximum amount a purchaser can borrow is governed by the value of the property on which the loan is secured, by the purchaser's income, which determines how much he can afford for interest and capital repayments, and by the term of the mortgage. Loans on modern houses may be for periods of up to 30 years, but shorter periods are normal for older houses, and most lenders expect a loan to be repaid before the borrower retires. The arrangements for repaying loans vary. Traditionally borrowers arranged to make level monthly or quarterly payments of capital and interest combined, which would, however, be varied if interest rates changed, so in the early years of a mortgage relatively little capital was repaid. Nowadays endowment loans, with interest only paid during the currency of the loan and capital repaid in full at the end of the period, are more common. Variations include fixed-rate mortgages, in which the interest rate is fixed for periods normally up to three years, low-start mortgages, in which part of the interest normally payable in the early years is added to the loan outstanding, and pension mortgages, in which the repayment of the loan is linked to the maturing of a personal pension policy. When a house is sold the balance of the mortgage loan is repaid in full; the house-owner who is moving from one house to another negotiates a new loan for the house he or she is buying.

With mortgage loans so prevalent it is surprising at first sight to find that loans for house purchase amount to only about 25 per cent of the value of dwellings (see table 7.1). There are two main reasons: rising house prices have meant that owners have built up their equity in their house much faster than the capital repayments (if any) on their loans would suggest; and many older people who originally financed their home with the help of a loan have repaid in full.

The provision of mortgage finance to the personal sector on reasonable terms is one of the most important functions of the financial system in Britain today. Without it, personal sector investment in housing would collapse. It is, however, now a highly competitive market, without any trace of restriction, in contrast with the much more regulated system which existed ten years previously.

Developments in the housing market have important consequences for economic activity and inflation. Intense competition amongst lenders in 1987 and 1988 led to a considerable easing of the terms on which funds were made available – income multiples increased and loans of up to 100 per cent of value were not uncommon – thus contributing to the boom in house prices and the extremely high level of turnover in the housing market. This in turn fed the consumer boom and added to inflationary pressures. In contrast, the high interest rates prevailing in 1989 and 1990 resulted in a sharp drop in turnover and falling house prices, with repercussions on house-building, consumer demand and economic activity generally.

Credit facilities for the purchase of consumer durable goods are provided by banks, finance companies or the retailers themselves. The two principal forms are instalment loans and credit card credit. By making use of credit people are able to obtain the use of these goods earlier than if they had to save the whole purchase price in advance. In many cases this is clearly beneficial and, by and large, uncontroversial. For example, by using instalment credit people can improve the furnishings of their home and budget for the cost of doing so. Many people prefer to make regular commitments of this kind, which provide a discipline against impulse purchases with free cash which they might regret afterwards. It is in the lender's interest to avoid giving loans to people who cannot afford to service their debts.

It is often argued, however, that credit is too readily available – particularly when it is provided at the point of sale – and acts as a temptation to people to buy goods which they cannot really afford. The need to service their debts subsequently puts them under unduly severe financial pressure. It is suggested that lenders do not take sufficient care to ensure that borrowers can afford to take on the additional debt commitment.

There is no doubt that this does happen and that, in boom conditions when default rates are relatively low, the cost to lenders is not excessively high – though in a recession default rates climb sharply, and lenders who take insufficient care about the affordability of loan commitments tend to suffer heavy losses. However, whether there should be regulations to discourage the granting of credit to people who cannot afford it remains a much debated question. Regulations which made it more difficult for people to borrow more than they could afford would inevitably result in some other responsible borrowers being denied credit.

Credit card credit, which amounts to some 15 per cent of total non-mortgage borrowing by consumers, requires more self-control of the consumer, who has complete discretion over any borrowing up to the credit limit set by the lender. So long as the total credit taken is below the limit the minimum monthly repayment does not impose any external discipline. The flexibility and convenience of immediate access to credit is, of course, extremely valuable to the consumer. Again, it is in the lender's interest to avoid a high level of defaults, to avoid issuing cards to people who will not repay and to ensure that credit limits reflect the financial standing of the card holder – the penalty for errors being severe losses in recessions. But there is no doubt that access to credit *is* tempting, and that some people do use their cards irresponsibly. Whether that is sufficient reason to make cards less widely available is a moot point.

The personal sector also makes use of borrowing facilities for many other purposes, including bridging loans when people buy a new house before selling their old one, and loans to finance the fixed and working capital needed by traders and professional people, the payment of large tax bills before other assets can be realized, and everyday needs to tide people over until the next pay cheque is due. Much of this borrowing takes the form of a bank overdraft, technically repayable on demand and in practice reviewed at regular intervals, with interest charged at a rate which varies with the general market level.

The liabilities of the personal sector are all debts; the interest and repayment terms are settled at the outset – though the rate of interest may be either fixed or variable. The maturity of the debts is usually related to the assets acquired – long-term mortgages for house purchase, short- or medium-term loans for house improvements or the purchase of consumer durables or cars, and generally short-term credit for other purposes.

Personal sector financing

The financial transactions of the personal sector from 1985 to 1989 are shown in table 7.5. Personal sector saving accounted for about one-third of the total sources of funds, with loans for house purchase making up nearly half and the balance being other borrowing. Ten years earlier, in the period 1976–80, the proportions were very different. Then saving accounted for two-thirds, loans for house purchase a quarter, and other borrowing only 10 per cent. The figures for the second half of the 1980s demonstrate clearly the low level to which saving had fallen and the dependence of the boom on borrowing by the personal sector.

Interpretation of the uses of funds is complicated by the 'unidentified', or balancing, row in the table, which averages over

Table 7.5 Sources and uses of funds of the personal sector, 1985–89

	1985	1986	1987	1988	(£ billion) 1989
Sources of funds					
Saving	23.4	21.5	18.8	17.2	23.6
Loans for house purchase	19.0	27.0	29.3	40.3	33.7
Other borrowing	8.1	6.0	10.9	14.2	16.3
Total sources	50.5	54.5	59.0	71.7	73.6
Uses of funds					
Physical investment etc.					
Dwellings	12.2	14.5	17.9	22.3	20.8
Other fixed assets	3.2	3.3	3.7	4.4	5.2
Stocks	0.4	0.5	0.8	1.2	1.3
Capital taxes less grants	−0.4	0.0	0.3	1.2	0.7
Total physical investment etc.	15.4	18.3	22.7	29.1	28.0
Financial assets					
Liquid assets	21.5	23.6	24.9	39.4	39.0
Other public sector debt	0.8	1.2	1.1	−4.1	−3.5
Company securities etc.	−3.5	−2.1	−1.9	−9.3	−13.2
Life assurance and pension funds	20.5	21.5	22.4	23.3	30.0
Total financial assets	39.3	44.2	46.5	49.3	52.3
Unidentified etc.	−4.2	−8.0	−10.2	−6.7	−6.7
Total uses	50.5	54.5	59.0	71.7	73.6

Source: Blue Book, 1990, tables 4.2, 4.3

(minus) 10 per cent of the total. Of the rest, investment in physical assets comprised one-third and acquisition of financial assets two-thirds, in contrast with the balance sheet proportions (see table 7.1) in which physical and financial assets were much closer to equality. Inflation is the main explanation for this discrepancy; the value in money terms of physical assets increases in a period of inflation, whereas the financial assets include a substantial proportion with fixed nominal values.

Investment in dwellings made up over three-quarters of the sector's physical investment, and, as mentioned above, is highly dependent upon the availability of mortgage loans. It is noticeable that investment in new dwellings averaged only 60 per cent of loans for house purchase. When existing houses are sold their owners are able to realize part or all of their equity, and equity in existing houses is being used increasingly as security for borrowing for other purposes.

Turning to financial assets, it can be seen that, on average, liquid assets – cash, deposits and national savings – accounted for nearly 65 per cent of financial asset acquisitions, with life assurance and pension funds amounting to about half; sales of company and public sector securities acted as a partial offset. Again, these figures contrast with the balance sheet proportions in table 7.1, which show the value of life assurance and pension funds as 50 per cent greater than that of liquid assets, and, in spite of continual net sales, the value of securities amounting to two-thirds of liquid assets. The explanation lies in capital appreciation on security holdings, whether held directly by individuals or indirectly through life assurance and pension funds.

For many years now the personal sector has made net sales of company securities. This is probably largely a consequence of the incidence of inheritance tax, the changing arrangements in society for maintenance during retirement, and the tax concessions available for saving through institutional channels. Inheritance tax is levied on estates above a threshold, currently set at £140 000 (1991). Since substantial capital sums are frequently involved, payment of this tax usually entails the sale of securities. Once tax has been paid the recipients of bequests may also choose to hold their wealth in other forms, stimulated perhaps by the tax concessions available. The same goes for people who realize substantial capital sums from the sale of property or of private business interests. Moreover, whereas at one time many people of moderate means chose to purchase securities as a means of saving for retirement, most are now covered by occupational pension schemes or personal pension arrangements. In spite of efforts to widen share ownership through privatization issues, new purchasers of securities are not coming forward from within the personal sector in sufficient numbers to offset the sales of securities for the reasons indicated.

The value of the net sales of company securities is affected by security prices generally, because the timing of some realizations (e.g. of estates passing at death) is not dictated by prevailing prices. For these sellers, high securities prices mean high tax bills to be paid. But the sharp increase in net sales of company securities etc. in 1988 and 1989 probably reflects the loss of confidence in the stock market after the crash of 1987, together with the high rates of interest to be earned on liquid assets. For example, the demand for unit trust units, which had boomed in the years before the crash, fell to virtually nothing subsequently.

The flows of saving through life assurance and pension funds averaged about 5.5 per cent of GDP in this period. Their contribution to long-term saving in the economy is therefore of the highest importance. This sustained inflow of funds, coupled with the diminished importance of direct personal sector holdings of company securities, has created a situation in which the life assurance and pension funds now dominate the supply of funds in the long-term capital market.

Notes

1 Personal income less direct taxes, national insurance, etc. contributions and transfers abroad.
2 National savings comprise deposits with the National Savings Bank, savings certificates, and various savings bonds issued by the government.
3 This notion is already familiar from our discussion of saving in chapter 3.
4 Where legislative factors favour a particular category of borrower or finance for a specific purpose, there is said to be a *privileged circuit*.

8

Company financial behaviour

Companies[1] control nearly a third of the nation's physical assets, and, as we saw in chapter 2, more than half of the investment in the economy takes place in the company sector. Companies also make an important contribution to saving, much of it reflecting depreciation charges on their existing assets, and a substantial proportion of investment is financed from their own resources. But a considerable part depends on external financing – mainly short-term or long-term debt – as well as on the ability to rent property or lease assets from financial institutions. Access to external funding is particularly important for the more dynamic and rapidly growing companies, whose needs for capital usually exceed what they are able to generate internally. Companies are therefore numbered amongst the most important users of the financial system.

In this chapter we shall examine in more detail companies' financing needs and the ways in which these are met. We shall concentrate on the industrial and commercial companies sector (henceforth the company sector), not because the financial companies and institutions are any less important or because the principles governing their financing are any different, but because their balance sheets and financial transactions are dominated by the roles which they play within the financial system.

The company sector's balance sheet

At the time of writing the most up-to-date balance sheet of the company sector refers to the end of 1987. This is summarized in table 8.1, together with the data for *financial* assets and liabilities at the end of 1989. In 1987 the total tangible assets of the company sector amounted to some £480 billion, their financial assets to nearly £320 billion, and their financial liabilities to £603 billion.[2] By the

Table 8.1 Balance sheet of the industrial and commercial companies sector, 1987 and 1989 (end-years)

	(£ billion)	
	1987	*1989*
Tangible assets		
Land, buildings etc.	218	n.a.
Plant, machinery, vehicles	183	n.a.
Stock and work in progress	80	n.a.
Total	481	600[1]
Financial assets		
Liquid assets	62	84
UK company securities	51	72
Other domestic assets	95	109
Overseas assets	108	187
Total	316	452
Total assets	797	1052[1]
Financial liabilities		
UK ordinary and preference shares	310	419
Overseas liabilities	103	179
UK debenture and loan stocks	24	33
Bank lending etc.	90	160
Other domestic liabilities	104	122
Total liabilities	631	913

Sources: Blue Book, 1990, table 12.3; *Financial Statistics*, February 1991, table 14.4
[1] Author's estimates

end of 1989 the financial assets and liabilities had increased to over £450 billion and £910 billion respectively.

Nearly half of the UK tangible assets of the company sector consisted of land and buildings, ranging from agricultural land to shops, offices, warehouses and industrial premises. In addition to those included in table 8.1, premises valued at perhaps £40 billion were rented from other owners in 1987. Plant, machinery and vehicles accounted for over 35 per cent of the total, including about £10 billion leased from other sectors, with stock and work in progress making up the balance – about 15 per cent of the total value of tangible assets employed.

About 40 per cent of companies' assets in 1987 were 'financial' assets. First there were liquid assets, predominantly bank deposits, held for precautionary reasons or pending deployment of resources within the business. Liquid assets comprised about 8 per cent of total assets.[3] Secondly, there were investments in other UK companies (e.g. subsidiaries or trade investments). These do not make a net addition to the financing needs of the company sector as a whole, but they do add to those of the individual companies concerned. Other domestic assets consist mainly of trade and other credit granted to customers – at over 10 per cent of total assets they make a significant contribution to companies' financing needs. Finally, overseas assets make up over one-eighth of the total assets, consisting mainly of companies' investments abroad, whether these take the legal form of tangible assets owned in other countries, securities, loans or other assets. To the extent that they represent tangible assets, situated abroad but employed by UK-based companies in their business, their classification as 'financial' is a national accounting fiction, and the actual share of tangible assets in UK companies' operations is greater than the table suggests.

These assets have to be financed, and company financing comes in many forms. First there is share capital – the *ordinary shares* which give the holder a right to dividends which the company pays out of its profits, the size of the dividend (if any) reflecting the company's profitability, as well as the right to determine who controls the company; and sometimes also *preferred shares* which carry the entitlement to a fixed dividend out of post-tax profits, which must be paid before the ordinary shareholders receive anything. Then there are *long-term loans*, which consist most commonly of *debentures* or *unsecured loan stocks*, the former being distinguished by the fact that they are secured by some means on the assets of the company. There are many variations on these basic themes – for example participating preference shares where the return is geared in some way to profitability, and convertible debentures which carry a fixed rate of interest but which also give the holder the option of converting into ordinary shares on some future date at a predetermined price.

Share capital and long-term loans are generally regarded as the permanent capital of the company. These appear in three lines in table 8.1. UK ordinary and preference shares comprise the value of these shares held by UK residents, to which must be added practically all of the overseas liabilities, which show the value of foreign residents' equity in the UK company sector.[4] In 1987 overseas owners held about £100 billion out of a total value of just over £400 billion, or about half of total assets. Long-term loans were much less important, accounting for only 3 per cent of assets (or 4 per cent of the value of liabilities) at the time.

Companies' other liabilities consist of *bank lending* and other short-term debt and, mainly, of trade and other creditors. Many bank loans are in fact medium-term loans, usually connected with the finance of specific projects – a major investment, the purchase of a subsidiary or a property development, for example. But much of bank lending continues to be short-term, at least in the sense that facilities are reviewed and possibly renegotiated at fairly frequent (e.g. annual) intervals. Most bank loans are also at variable rates of interest; i.e. the rate is linked to the bank's base rate, which may be changed periodically, or to some other market rate. Bank lending also includes commercial bills held by banks, which are frequently used as an alternative to bank loans.[5] In 1987 bank loans were much larger than long-term loans, valued at 11 per cent of total assets or 14 per cent of total liabilities.

Over 90 per cent of the other domestic liabilities represent trade and other creditors, which account for about a sixth of total liabilities. For the sector as a whole, trade credit granted and trade credit received more or less balance, and the net demand for financing from outside the sector is very small. For individual companies, too, the net demand is often less than the gross totals – the time lag before payments are received from customers can be matched by a lag before suppliers are paid. Nevertheless, the situation varies considerably from one trade to another – major retailers receive their money from shoppers long before they pay their suppliers, whereas manufacturers generally give more credit than they receive – and from time to time, particularly when interest rates are high, companies experience delays in receipts from customers which add significantly to their financing requirements from the banks or other sources. Other domestic liabilities also include commercial paper – promissory notes issued by companies, which have not been 'accepted' by a bank, and which are usually held by other companies.[6]

The costs and obligations attached to the different components of companies' liabilities vary. Money due to creditors generally costs the company nothing, at least until bills fall due for payment; beyond that date the cost of credit may be high because discounts for prompt payment may have to be forgone. Short-term borrowing from banks or other sources is generally cheaper than long-term borrowing, though this position may be reversed· if short-term interest rates are temporarily high (see chapter 5). Properly treated, the cost of equity capital is the expected return to the company's shareholders, and, once an allowance for putative higher dividends in future is included, exceeds the cost of debt.

In terms of the other obligations which liabilities impose on a company the ranking is approximately reversed. Equity may in principle be the most expensive form of capital, but there is no obligation to repay equity or even to pay dividends on it. There is a clear obligation to repay long-term loans at specified times, and similar arrangements frequently apply to medium-term and sometimes even to short-term borrowing. Failure to make the stipulated payments will result in sanctions on the company, ranging from inability to obtain further credit to the appointment of a receiver and subsequent liquidation. The penalties for failure to pay other creditors at the appointed time may also be high. Excessive delay in paying suppliers will result in supplies being withheld, wage and salary payments cannot easily be delayed, and while there may be more leeway with tax payments, an interest penalty will be imposed.

More up-to-date figures for 1989 show some developments taking place in the company sector's balance sheet – though, as would be expected in such a short period, no dramatic changes. There are no official figures for tangible assets, but it seems likely that during 1988 and 1989 the value of companies' financial assets increased somewhat faster than that of tangible assets, owing mainly to the rise in stockmarket prices and the continuing takeover booms in the UK and USA. Liquid assets probably increased at much the same rate as total assets (i.e. by about a third) but company security holdings rose by over 40 per cent and overseas assets by over 70 per cent in this period.

Financial liabilities increased by 45 per cent overall, with overseas liabilities up by over 70 per cent, partly owing to heavy inward investment. The value of UK-held ordinary and preference share capital rose by only about a third. The increase in assets therefore depended heavily on loan financing, and bank lending rose by over 75 per cent. Debentures, loan stocks and bank lending increased from just over 14 per cent of total assets to about 18 per cent.

Gearing

The principal financial decision a firm has to take concerns the division of its liabilities between equity and debt. The aim of the firm's owners is to maximize the rate of return on the equity capital subject to taking an acceptable degree of risk. As we shall see, this risk depends on the firm's 'gearing', reflecting the relative proportions of debt and equity.

We shall define *primary gearing* as the ratio of debt to equity in a firm's balance sheet. Thus, if D stands for debt and E for equity,

$$\text{Gearing} = D/E,$$

the debt/equity ratio.

Now let us examine how the *expected* return on equity varies with a firm's gearing. Suppose that a firm expects to earn profits at a rate p on all of its assets, however financed, and that the rate of interest paid on debt is i. Then the equity return ER is given by

$$ER = \frac{p(E + D) - Di}{E}$$
$$= p + (p - i)D/E.$$

So long as $p > i$, the expected return on equity rises with D/E; but conversely, if $i > p$ (i.e. the expected rate of return is less than the cost of debt), high gearing reduces the return to equity. Normally a firm will not embark upon an investment project unless it expects that p will be greater than i, so that the expected return on equity generally increase with the firm's gearing.

But so does the risk to which the equity holder is exposed. The rate of profit which the firm will earn on its assets is uncertain, and the likelihood that it will differ from the hoped-for level has to be reckoned with. In chapter 4 we measured risk by the standard deviation of the frequency distribution of the rate of return, and we shall continue to adopt this measure here. Suppose that p is variable, that its frequency distribution has standard deviation σ_p, and that the rate of interest which the firm pays on its debt, i, is a firm commitment. Then the risk attached to the equity return, ER, is given by[7]

$$\sigma_{ER} = (1 + D/E)\sigma_p$$

which rises with the debt-equity ratio.

The effect of gearing on equity return and risk can be illustrated by means of numerical examples. Table 8.2 shows for different levels of profitability how the equity return varies with a company's primary gearing. The rate of interest on debt, i, has been taken as 10 per cent throughout, and debt/equity ratios ranging from 0.5 to 3.0 are illustrated. If the rate of profit on the company's assets is also 10 per cent, then ER is 10 per cent, irrespective of the debt/equity ratio. If p fell to 5 per cent the ER would remain positive so long as the debt/equity ratio did not exceed 1.0, but with higher gearing the

Table 8.2   The effect of primary gearing on the equity return ($i = 10$ per cent)

	Equity return ER *(per cent)*				
Debt/equity ratio	*p = 0*	*p = 5%*	*p = 10%*	*p = 15%*	*p = 20%*
0.5	−5	2.5	10	17.5	25
1.0	−10	0	10	20	30
2.0	−20	−5	10	25	40
3.0	−30	−10	10	30	50

company would make losses; and if profitability fell to nil *ER* would be negative if there was any debt to service at all. When *p* rises above 10 per cent the effect on *ER* is magnified and, as the table shows, high gearing can be associated with very high rates of return. By reading across the rows of the table it can be seen clearly that the dispersion of the rate of return on equity capital increases the higher is the company's gearing.

Another way of looking at this question is to consider a company's *income gearing*, the proportion of its profits which are absorbed by interest payments on debt. This depends both on its debt/equity ratio and on the relationship between profitability and the rate of interest charged on loans. Table 8.3 shows how income gearing varies for a company which earns 15 per cent on its assets, for debt/equity ratios ranging from 0.5 to 3.0 and for rates of interest from 5 per cent to 20 per cent.[8] Provided that the rate of interest lies well below the return on assets, income gearing remains low, even for high debt/equity ratios. But if the charge for debt approaches the

Table 8.3   Primary gearing and income gearing: the effects of varying the rate of interest ($p = 15$ per cent)

	Income gearing *(per cent)*			
Debt/equity ratio	*i = 5%*	*i = 10%*	*i = 15%*	*i = 20%*
0.5	11.1	22.2	33.3	44.4
1.0	16.7	33.3	50.0	66.7
2.0	22.2	44.4	66.7	88.9
3.0	25.0	50.0	75.0	100.0

rate of return on assets even moderately geared companies (primary gearing) find that a high proportion of their income is absorbed by interest.

Table 8.4 provides a further illustration of the dangers faced by highly geared companies. As has already been mentioned, short-term debt is frequently at variable rates of interest, and if a company is unfortunate it may well find itself hit simultaneously by a fall in profitability and a rise in the interest payable on its borrowings. Suppose that in normal circumstances a company expects to earn 15 per cent on its assets, and to pay 10 per cent as before on its debt. The first column of table 8.4 shows how the equity return rises with the company's gearing in these conditions – as gearing rises from 0.5 to 3.0, *ER* rises from 17.5 per cent to 30 per cent. But now suppose that there is a credit squeeze and profitability falls to 5 per cent, while the rate of interest on debt rises to 15 per cent. In these conditions, with gearing of 0.5, the company just breaks even after paying interest, and with higher gearing *ER* is negative. Indeed, with a debt/equity ratio of 3.0, the company's losses (after interest) would amount to as much as a quarter of its equity capital in one year.

Table 8.4   The effect of primary gearing on the equity return when profits (*p*) fall from 15 to 5 per cent and the cost of borrowing (*i*) rises from 10 to 15 per cent

	Equity return ER *(per cent)*	
Debt/equity ratio	*p = 15%, i = 10%*	*p = 5%, i = 15%*
0.5	17.5	0
1.0	20	−5
2.0	25	−15
3.0	30	−25

It will be recalled that lenders attempt to limit their exposure to risk and try to keep default risk to a low level. The effect of gearing on the risk a company faces is, of course, very familiar to lenders, and influences both the rate of interest they charge for loans and their willingness to make loans at all. In looking for protection against possible losses lenders also have regard to: the profitability of the borrower, the strength of the borrower's balance sheet, the possibility of taking security on specific assets.

In order to obtain a loan a borrower has to be able to show that there is a high probability that he will earn sufficient profit to cover the interest payments and that his business will generate sufficient cash to cover scheduled debt repayments. Lenders – particularly long-term lenders – will generally expect a considerable margin to spare to provide a cushion if things go wrong. High primary gearing eats into this margin. In deciding how much it is safe to lend, a lender will also look at the volatility of profits. As tables 8.2 and 8.4 show, when profits are volatile high gearing can easily lead to losses.

A balance sheet is said to be strong if it exhibits a low debt/equity ratio. The higher the proportion of equity in its liabilities the greater the losses a company can withstand without its viability being called in question. Equity takes the first slice of loss, so that the stronger the balance sheet the less likely it is that a lender will be unable to recover his loan.

Lenders are also influenced by the nature of a company's business and the assets it employs. If there is a high proportion of fixed assets, the lenders may take security on these assets (or a floating charge over assets) to reduce the probability of loss. Such security gives the lender a prior claim on the company's assets if it is wound up. But security is generally regarded as an added insurance against loss, rather than as sufficient justification for making a loan, and even if security is available lenders are unlikely to be willing to accept high gearing unless profits are expected to be stable.

Because default risk increases with the borrower's gearing, companies must expect to pay more for loans if their gearing rises. Unless they are able to increase their equity base companies therefore face a rising cost of debt as their borrowing expands. This is illustrated in figure 8.1, which shows how the rate of interest rises with the debt/equity ratio. It is not necessarily only the marginal

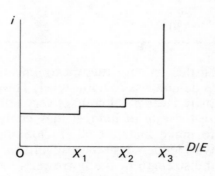

Fig. 8.1

borrowing that will cost more, because a higher debt/equity ratio makes all of a company's debt riskier. After some point, shown as X_3 in figure 8.1, the risk will become too high for lenders to entertain further loan requests. This point is, of course, dependent on the nature of the business.

The rising cost of debt capital compels us to modify our earlier conclusion that the equity return would vary positively with the level of primary gearing. That conclusion was reached on the assumption that the cost of debt would be constant. With a rising cost of debt, equity return will in fact reach a peak and then diminish, as is illustrated in figure 8.2. As a company's gearing rises it moves from one risk class to another, and this has a sharp effect on *ER*, at X_1 and X_2 in the figure. Gearing cannot rise beyond X_3, because lenders are unwilling to provide more debt at that stage, but the maximum actually occurs before this, when the debt/equity ratio is at X_2.

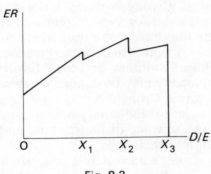

Fig. 8.2

A firm which aimed to maximize the return on its equity capital, subject to an acceptable degree of risk, would aim to prevent its gearing rising above X_2. In fact it would almost certainly stop well short of this level, partly in order to reduce its own exposure to risk and partly because the firm is concerned with the *total* cost of finance and the cost of equity finance may also increase as the equity return becomes riskier. Investors, as noted previously, have to be compensated for exposure to risk, and the higher is a company's gearing the greater the extent to which its profitability will be affected by swings in economic activity generally.

Highly geared firms are very vulnerable in bad times, not just because they make a loss on their equity capital if total profits fall and/or interest rates rise, but because companies may face further severe difficulties in the aftermath of poor profits, difficulties which may easily threaten their future independence.

A loss reduces a firm's equity base, and if it continues to employ the same capital as before its debt/equity ratio automatically rises. For example, if a firm with a debt/equity ratio of 1.0 makes a loss amounting to 20 per cent of its equity capital (or 10 per cent of assets) in some year, and if in order to continue in business its balance sheet total remains unchanged, the loss itself raises the debt/equity ratio to 1.5:1 (60:40 instead of 50:50). The burden of interest payments rises because there is more debt and less equity, and because, in view of its higher gearing and recent loss experience, the cost of new or renegotiated debt is likely to rise. It may not be easy for a company to avoid these difficulties by raising new equity capital, because investors will usually exact a high price for supplying new equity at a time that a firm is making losses.

All this assumes that lenders will be willing to increase their loans, albeit with a higher interest rate attached. In fact, if a company is making losses and its gearing is rising, lenders may be extremely reluctant to increase loans, or even to renew loans as they mature. As a result, the firm may have to contract by cutting stocks or selling parts of its business – actions which had to be taken by many firms in 1990 and 1991. If losses continue, or if the difficulty of retrenchment is too great, the company may be compelled to seek a takeover by another company with a stronger equity base or go out of business altogether. In either event the equity-holders are likely to suffer a sharp diminution in the value of their assets, and the more senior managers may well lose their jobs.

Trouble usually strikes when interest rates are high and there is a general economic slowdown; i.e. at a time when asset prices are low. What appeared to be a healthy equity base during a boom can all too easily melt away in the subsequent recession. The result is that most firms aim to keep their debt/equity ratios well below the maximum levels which lenders are likely to tolerate. By so doing they hope to be able to weather a storm without suffering permanent damage to their business and with their freedom of action intact.

Equity finance

A company's equity is its true risk capital. It is equity that enables companies to take the risks inherent in business, and it is the availability of equity that allows companies to embark upon investment programmes which increase their risk exposure. Spare equity, reflected in a level of gearing lower than the maximum which lenders think reasonable, is the key to additional borrowing, and companies with strong balance sheets and reasonable profits seldom have difficulty in borrowing.

In principle, the cost of equity capital to a company is the cost of the dividends it is expected to pay in future. As we saw in chapter 5 this cost is measured by the dividend yield plus the expected annual rate of growth of dividends.[9] This theoretical cost of equity is likely to exceed the cost of debt, partly because of the risk premium which savers demand for exposure to equity risk, and partly because UK companies are permitted to pay interest out of pre-tax profits whereas dividends are paid out of post-tax profits.

In choosing between debt and equity capital, however, companies may also be concerned with the implications for their net cash flow of raising finance by either means, and the expected cash flow cost of equity may well be less than the cost of debt. The cash flow cost of equity is the profits needed to pay dividends at whatever rate is planned in the short-run; in the case of external finance this is the planned dividend (grossed up for tax) divided by the share price. In a period of inflation when the nominal rate of interest on debt includes a substantial component to compensate lenders for the loss in real value of their capital, the initial cash flow cost of equity may be considerably lower than that of debt.

In principle companies should treat retained profits as having the same cost as external equity issues, but in practice company directors do not always see retentions in this light: they do not have to justify the use of internal funds to providers of finance, and when internal funds are available they may be more inclined to take risks or invest in relatively marginal projects.

It is important also to remember that the *committed* cost of equity is zero. There is no obligation on the company to pay dividends, and indeed, unless there are sufficient profits available, the company is not entitled to pay dividends to its shareholders. Small or rapidly growing companies often find this feature of equity particularly attractive, because it enables them to retain a very high proportion of their profits and employ them in further expansion of their business.

Large companies in the UK normally raise new equity capital by means of a rights issue to their shareholders, but small companies without a Stock Exchange quotation and larger companies in special circumstances may place shares with one or more financial institutions.

Debt finance

Debt finance is attractive to companies because it allows them to increase the scale of their business at a defined cost without giving up either a share of the profits or control of the enterprise. It is also the case that debt is often more readily available than equity, and for some firms the only practical source of increased equity capital is retained profits.

A distinction is often drawn between short-term and long-term debt, and the ratio of short- to long-term debt in a company's liabilities is known as its *secondary gearing*. Low secondary gearing is one indication of strength in a company, because long-term debt does not need to be renegotiated frequently, and the company can consequently take steps to renew its long-term capital at times of its own choosing. A company which has a high proportion of short-term debt in its liabilities is exposed to interest-rate fluctuations and runs the risk of finding the supply of funds reduced or cut off at a critical time. Most large companies try to manage the maturity structure of their debt to ensure that they are not embarrassed in this way.

Long-term loans are usually raised by issuing securities in the capital market,[10] though the possibility of direct negotiation with one or more long-term institutions or, in the case of small companies, with a specialist institution cannot be ruled out. The banking system is the dominant source of short-term loan finance.

Long-term loans generally have a life of up to 20 years, are repaid at maturity[11] and carry a fixed rate of interest. Long-term debt is particularly well suited to companies' needs for several reasons. First, it reflects the lives of many of a company's fixed assets, so that the cash generated by these assets as profit or depreciation charges can be used to service the debt. Secondly, long-term debt is usually regarded as part of the company's permanent capital, because so long as the company remains profitable it can expect to be able to refinance the debt at or around maturity. It is therefore suitable as a source of finance for both the company's fixed capital assets and the working capital which the company requires permanently. Thirdly, the rate of interest on long-term debt is usually fixed, so that the company is not at risk from swings in interest rates.

However, the supply of long-term debt to a company is not unlimited, because it needs to be able to provide adequate security to the lenders. It would be unreasonable to expect lenders to rely on profitability projections for 20 years ahead, so some alternative form of security is usually required. This may either be security over assets which are expected to retain their value, or covenants which form part of the loan agreements, specifying for example the maximum level of primary gearing which the company will be permitted to take on, and giving the lender the right to immediate repayment if the covenant is breached.

The most common form of short-term loan is the bank overdraft, under which firms are permitted to borrow up to an agreed limit, with interest charged only on the amount borrowed at any time. Commercial bills provide another important short-term debt instrument. In essence they are promises by companies to pay stated sums on an appointed day, usually three months ahead. These bills are often guaranteed ('accepted') by banks and sold ('discounted') for something less than their face value to provide the firms with cash immediately. The discount reflects prevailing short-term rates of interest.

Short-term loans are best suited to short-term needs. The archetypal short-term bank loan is an overdraft to cover the seasonal maximum in a firm's working capital. Loans of this kind are 'self-liquidating', because at the seasonal trough no part of the loan should be outstanding. Overdrafts and other short-term loans may also be used to meet a firm's financial needs due to fluctuations in profits or in investment spending. Although lenders do not usually intend their loans to be used for this purpose, some short-term loans do in practice form part of the permanent capital of a business.

Short-term loans are generally less attractive to firms than long-term because the firm cannot rely on the continued availability of the capital. Bank overdrafts, for example, are subject to regular renegotiation and review. Moreover, short-term loans are usually at variable rates of interest, with the consequence that if it is unlucky the firm may find itself paying much more than it had anticipated.

Nowadays firms also make considerable use of term loans from banks, and, to a lesser extent, issues of medium-term bonds in the capital market. These range from ordinary instalment loans, with a fixed rate of interest and a regular repayment schedule, to custom-designed forms of medium-term project finance, in which a bank makes a loan to finance a particular investment project or acquisition, and the term of the loan and the repayment schedule are linked to the expected cash flow. For example, all capital and interest payments may be deferred until after the project has begun to produce an income, with repayment over a fairly short period of years thereafter. Project loans of up to 7 years are not uncommon, and may extend to 10. Most medium-term project finance is at variable rates of interest.

The financing of acquisitions and other company reconstructions can be exceedingly complex. A range of equity and loan instruments with differing characteristics will be employed – e.g. various categories of shares, 'senior' debt (taking priority in the event of a liquidation) and 'mezzanine' finance carrying a higher rate of interest than the senior debt but with a greater risk of loss. Each of the different instruments will be syndicated amongst different groups of lenders.

Banks also provide firms (or their overseas customers) with medium-term loans to finance exports of major capital goods, for which credit extending over a period of years is required. Such loans bear a fixed rate of interest, which is below the normal market level – the subsidy being provided by the government – and the credit risk is insured with the Export Credits Guarantee Department.

On average firms must expect long-term funding to cost slightly more than short-term, reflecting the existence of liquidity premia in the market. Nevertheless, long-term loans have in the past generally been preferred for their other attributes. However, when interest rates are high firms avoid taking on new long-term debt because if rates fall subsequently a firm which had borrowed for a long period would find itself saddled with a heavy interest burden for many years. To avoid this possibility firms prefer medium-term and short-term loans from the banks at variable rates of interest, in spite of the fact that they leave firms exposed to unexpected increases in interest rates and entail more frequent renegotiation.

Provision of finance by other means

In addition to building up equity capital from retained profits or raising new equity or debt in the financial markets, industrial and commercial companies can also obtain the use of buildings and equipment by leasing them from their owners. Rental of factories, offices and warehouses is a long-established practice under which (with a long leasehold) the company takes on most of the obligations of ownership but which makes much less demand on a company's capital – the rental payment can be regarded as a substitute for interest on debt and remuneration to the providers of equity capital. In a period of inflation it may in fact be a particularly attractive means of obtaining capital assets, because rental agreements will usually make much lower demands on a company's cash flow than interest payments on debt. This is because rental agreements contain escalation clauses, so that the rent is reviewed and altered in line with general market levels periodically and can therefore approximate to the real rate of interest; whereas in a period of inflation nominal interest rates on fixed-interest debt are at much higher levels. The owner of the property – usually an insurance company, pension fund or property company – is content to hold an asset offering some protection against inflation and the prospect of income growth in future.

Leasing of plant and equipment may also be advantageous. With *finance leasing*, as opposed to the short-term hire of, say, construction plant, the user expects to employ the asset for a considerable period of time and possibly to acquire it himself at the end of the lease. For the leasing company, the acquisition of the asset is a capital expenditure, attracting the usual capital allowances for tax purposes. These represent a saving which can be passed on to the lessee company, which might not be in a position to take advantage of the allowances itself. For example a new company, or one which has been investing heavily, or one which is experiencing low profits, may not be able to absorb all the capital allowances which it has available to set against profits. But leasing is not only attractive to companies which are short of profits. Companies which are already highly geared may have difficulty in persuading their bankers to extend additional facilities; and it is very common for companies to lease, rather than buy, motor cars for their staff, frequently combined with fleet management services, thus saving both on capital and on other costs. At the end of 1989 the total initial cost of assets leased (to all sectors) was nearly £38 billion.

Government grants are another source of finance for companies, though at the end of the 1980s they formed only a small element in the total financing required. However, grants are not the main means by which the government influences the finance available to companies – policy on the structure of company taxation has extremely important implications for company retentions and the supply of internal finance.

A particular issue is the level of capital allowances which can be charged against revenue for tax purposes. In principle these allowances reflect the depreciation on the fixed assets used in a business, but by permitting companies to depreciate capital assets at a faster rate the government enables them to reduce their tax bills, thereby providing them with additional finance. With only limited exceptions for particular purposes (for example, to encourage businesses to locate in enterprise zones by allowing them to claim

100 per cent of the cost of assets in the year of investment) capital allowances in Britain are, at the time of writing, set at standard rates, with a view to avoiding any artificial distortions to investment decisions. But in the past there have been extended periods when accelerated depreciation was allowed, usually with a view to encouraging investment in specified assets,[12] and it is often suggested that accelerated depreciation should be restored for this purpose.

Government grants to industry and commerce are now associated mainly with regional policy, and take the form of Regional Selective Assistance. These are grants for investment projects which create or safeguard jobs in Assisted Areas. Some 35 per cent of the working population live in assisted areas, which are divided into two categories, Intermediate and Development Areas. Grants lie in the range of 10–30 per cent of fixed project costs, with the higher amounts payable only in Development Areas. They are by no means automatic, the intention being that they should be paid only when the project would not otherwise go ahead and additional employment can be demonstrated. Government assistance may also be made available to help to fund product development (for example, launch aid for new aircraft) which would not otherwise take place.

There are a variety of government-supported schemes to assist small and medium-sized enterprises (SMEs), some of which are discussed later in this chapter. While important qualitatively to the SME sector, they are not of great overall significance in quantitative terms.

Sources and uses of funds

Our discussion so far has concentrated upon companies' balance sheets and in particular on the structure of liabilities which companies find appropriate for their business. We turn now to examine their sources and uses of funds, which highlight the purposes for which companies have required *additional* funds in recent years and the sources from which these funds have been obtained. Table 8.5 shows figures for successive five-year periods, beginning in 1958, and for 1988 and 1989. The five-year averages bring out the trends in company financing, though there have, of course, been quite substantial year to year variations. The table includes the so-called *balancing item*, which represents the discrepancy between independent estimates of sources and uses. It is shown

Table 8.5 Sources and uses of funds of industrial and commercial companies, 1958–89

	Per cent of total sources/uses							
	1958–62	1963–67	1968–72	1973–77	1978–82	1983–87	1988	1989
Uses								
Gross domestic fixed capital formation	58	61	53	57	58	56	51	54
Value of physical increase in stocks and work in progress	7	9	4	4	–3	2	6	3
Acquisition of financial assets:								
Liquid assets	4	4	13	15	12	15	7	18
Cash purchases of subsidiaries and trade investments	8	8	6	5	5	9	15	22
Investment overseas	7	6	5	6	13	13	18	20
Other identified assets	2	4	4	10	9	3	—	–2
Balancing item	14	8	15	3	7	1	3	–16
Total uses	100	100	100	100	100	100	100	100
Sources								
Undistributed income	72	67	52	49	63	61	37	25
of which: depreciation	(28)	(30)	(28)	(34)	(46)	(44)	(31)	(31)
Capital transfers (net)	—	2	8	3	2	1	1	—
Bank borrowing	10	12	19	24	20	18	40	40
Capital issues: ordinary and preferred shares	11	3	3	5	4	12	6	2
other		9	4	—	2	8	8	17
Overseas	3	4	6	11	3	—	4	8
Other identified sources	4	3	7	8	5	3	5	8
Total sources	100	100	100	100	100	100	100	100

Sources: 1958–77, *Committee to Review the Functioning of Financial Institutions*, Report (Cmnd 7937), 1980, table 34
1978–89, *Blue Books*, 1989 and 1990; *Financial Statistics*

conventionally under uses, but could equally well reflect errors in the sources statistics. Its size acts as a warning against making too much of small changes in the percentages shown in the table, particularly in 1989 for which the data are still likely to be subject to substantial revisions as more information becomes available.

Since financing requirements derive ultimately from the uses to which companies put their funds, it is convenient to begin with uses, of which fixed investment is the most important. It can be divided between replacement and investment for expansion. The former does not involve a change in the scale of the business, and while it does entail new investment in fixed capital there is no concomitant increase in working capital requirements. In principle replacement investment should be financed out of depreciation allowances on existing equipment, either built up in previous years or derived from current operations. Unless replacement investment involves significant changes in products or processes it does not materially affect the risks a company faces. On the other hand, investment for expansion is always risky, the degree of risk depending on business conditions and upon the novelty of the product or process. A firm's ability to take these risks depends on its financial strength. This is partly a question of current profitability on its other activities, since profits derived elsewhere can be used to cover debt servicing costs and possibly initial losses on new activities, and partly on the strength of its balance sheet, which affects the extent to which the company is vulnerable to misfortune. Investment for expansion is by no means confined to the fixed capital involved, since expansion will inevitably entail some increase in working capital as well.

There has been no long-run trend in the share of fixed investment in companies' uses of funds in the last 30 years – typically it has averaged a little under 60 per cent, though it was falling towards the end of the 1980s. However, investment in stocks declined, presumably a consequence of better stock management, though there are, of course, still fluctuations in stock-building. As a result investment in fixed assets and stocks fell from 65–70 per cent of industrial and commercial companies' total uses of funds in 1958–67 to well under 60 per cent in 1978–87 and subsequently. The balance was devoted to investment in financial assets (including investment abroad).

As the value of a company's business increases its need for liquid assets grows. In part these are held for ordinary transactions purposes, such as the payment of wages and salaries and the bills for purchases of raw materials and other supplies. In part they are held for precautionary purposes, in case expenditure should run ahead of revenue: liquid assets can be regarded as an alternative to unused bank credit facilities in satisfying this need, an alternative which has the advantage of allowing the company greater discretion and flexibility. Again, part of liquid asset holdings will have been built up by companies in advance of known spending commitments. By their very nature the increase in liquid asset holdings can be expected to absorb a higher proportion of companies' funds in good years than in bad, since it is at such times that companies can afford to build them up. However, the proportion of revenues devoted to increasing liquid assets was much higher in the 20 years from 1968 than in the previous ten. This can be attributed, first to the higher level of inflation which raised the *nominal* value of companies' business and imposed considerable financing requirements on them, and secondly to a reduction in the opportunity cost of holding liquid assets – the margin between the cost of borrowing (for fixed terms) and the return on liquidity narrowed, so that the price of the security and flexibility provided by liquid assets fell.

Companies which wish to expand frequently choose to do so through a takeover or merger with another company. Takeovers and mergers occur for many reasons, including *inter alia* desires to enter related lines of business and attempts to strengthen market positions by gaining control of important suppliers or customers. Sometimes takeovers are financed by the issue of new shares, with the takeover 'raider' gaining control by offering the 'victim's' owners shares in its own company in place of those they held previously. In such cases no additional funds are required. But in others the raider pays cash for the shares of the victim company, and finance has to be obtained for this purpose. As table 8.5 shows, cash required for the purchase of subsidiaries and trade investments has typically been a significant element in companies' total uses of funds, though it fell in the 1970s, when economic conditions were generally unfavourable, and recovered strongly to historically very high levels in the boom of the second half of the 1980s.

Investment overseas has also become an increasingly important use of funds for UK companies, because a number of large multinational companies are based in the UK and many other companies have overseas subsidiaries. The figures in table 8.5 exclude investment which was financed from profits earned and retained abroad, but even after this exclusion the figure rose from an average of 6 per cent of total uses in 1958–77 to 13 per cent in 1978–87 and even more in 1988 and 1989. Until the abolition of exchange control in 1979, the bulk of this investment was financed by overseas or foreign currency borrowing, but since then companies have been free to finance this investment by whatever means they choose.

Turning now to the sources of funds, it is clear that companies' undistributed incomes form much the most important source. This category – which includes retained profits, depreciation charges, and additions to tax reserves – is known as *internal* finance. Looking at the 30-year period, the contribution of internal finance to total sources of funds was on a downward trend from 1958–62 until the mid-seventies, recovered up to the mid-eighties but fell sharply during the boom years in the second half of the decade. This was partly due to an increase in takeover activity financed, as we shall see, largely by bank and other borrowing, but partly also to a tendency for companies to pay out a higher proportion of their profits as dividends, at the expense of their own retentions. Thus the proportion of companies' retentions which represented depreciation on their existing assets increased, from about 40 per cent in the ten years from 1958 to 1967 to over 70 per cent in 1978–87; the percentage rose to over 80 in 1988 and, for what they are worth, the figures suggest that in 1989 companies' undistributed incomes were actually less than (replacement cost) depreciation. The implication is that at the end of the 1980s the contribution of internal finance to the *growth* of companies' equity had virtually disappeared.[13]

Capital transfers consist mainly of government grants for investment. Their significance as a source of funds has varied substantially over the last 20 years, though, as already noted, even when their aggregate contribution to financing has been small they may well have been a key factor in promoting investment in some instances. The high level of capital transfers in 1968–72 reflects the use of investment grants, rather than depreciation allowances, as a means of stimulating investment in that period. Subsequently the lower level of grants was matched initially by accelerated depreciation allowances, resulting in a reduction in tax payments,[14] but these too were abolished in the tax reform of 1984.

Over the entire period bank borrowing has been a significant source of *external* funds for UK companies, but it rose sharply in the mid-seventies and climbed to extraordinary levels in 1988 and 1989. Initially the increase was a consequence of inflation. Not only did inflation increase firms' working capital needs, but it also caused them to avoid raising long-term debt capital at high nominal interest rates to which they would have been committed for many years, and to turn instead to the banks for short-term and (increasingly) medium-term finance at variable rates of interest.

In the latter part of the eighties the very high level of bank borrowing was associated with the economic boom in general and the property and takeover booms in particular. Bank lending to property companies rose by nearly £20 billion in 1988 and 1989 (i.e. by almost 30 per cent of total bank lending to the company sector in this period), and bank lending played a crucial role in most of the takeovers by UK companies, both at home and overseas.

For much of the last 30 years capital issues do not appear to have been a very important source of funds for the company sector. In the first ten years, at about 11 per cent on average, they were on a par with bank borrowing, but from 1968–82 they fell to an average of only 6 per cent of total sources, with issues of long-term debt falling to a very low level owing to the generally high prevailing level of interest rates. Nevertheless, the significance of new *share* issues for industry's equity base should not be underestimated. New issues provide *additional* equity, in the same way as that part of undistributed income which does not consist of depreciation allowances provides additional equity, and it is this which enables companies to increase the real level of their business. Thus, for example, in 1973–7 new issues of ordinary shares amounting to 5 per cent of sources of funds can be compared with new equity from internal sources amounting to 15 per cent (49 minus 34 per cent); i.e. external sources provided about a quarter of the additional equity in that period.

After 1983 there was a substantial increase in new issues, first through ordinary share issues during the prolonged equity boom, and later mainly through bond issues made increasingly on the international bond market. In the 1983–7 period bank borrowing and capital issues again contributed similar amounts to external financing, and while the relatively high level of ordinary share issues was not sustained in the less buoyant stock market conditions following the crash of 1987, bond financing continued to increase in 1988 and 1989.

Just as UK companies employ funds in investing abroad, so foreign companies with operations in the UK contribute to the financing of their activities here. The substantial growth in this source of funds up to 1973–7 was due mainly to inward investment in connection with North Sea oil exploration and development. Subsequently most investment was financed from profits earned from fields which had entered production (included in undistributed income) so this source of funds fell away sharply, and in 1984 there was a substantial outflow of funds. Of course non-oil companies are also investors in the UK and inflows increased sharply in 1988 and 1989, particularly in connection with takeover activity.

Other identified sources include *inter alia* loans by long-term institutions for property development, loans from finance houses, import credit received, and, at times, loans from the government to help companies in difficulties. They were not generally of great importance in the 1980s, though substantial increases in 1988 and 1989 were associated with the boom in property development.

It is important to recognize that the composition of external financing of industrial and commercial companies often has much more to do with demand than with supply conditions. Most of those seeking funds are able to choose between alternatives available in the market, provided they are willing to pay the going price. Thus the decline in long-term debt and corresponding rise in bank loans in the mid-seventies did not reflect any *constriction* in the supply of the former – it was a result of firms' reluctance to pay the going rates of interest (which were linked to rates on gilt-edged stocks). Similarly, the increase in ordinary share issues in 1983–7 reflected companies' desire to take advantage of what they perceived as favourable market conditions, while the subsequent decline was connected with the increased cost of equity finance.

This does not, however, apply to much of the corporate takeover activity in 1988 and 1989. Some of the largest takeovers depended crucially on the availability of funds from the banking system, with no alternative source in prospect. Other activity, for example management buyouts and demergers, depends on being able to bring together an appropriate blend of equity and debt. Supply conditions are critical for this kind of activity, and it could be said that the takeover and property booms were driven as much by the supply of banking funds as by the demands of industrial and commercial companies.

Small firms

The purposes for which small firms require finance differ comparatively little from those of large firms. An analysis of the accounts of a sample of small firms carried out for the Wilson Committee[15] showed that the balance sheets of small firms contained a lower proportion of physical assets than those of large firms, suggesting that on average small firms were less capital-intensive, with correspondingly high components of trade debtors and creditors. The smallest group of firms – those with capital employed of less than £250 000 in 1975, equivalent to about £1 million in 1990 – were also more liquid than large firms, though firms in the next size group – up to £4 million at that time (say, £15 million in 1990) – relied quite heavily on bank borrowing. However, even if the composition of assets of large and small firms does not differ greatly, from the point of view of external suppliers of finance, lending or investment in small firms is appreciably riskier. Small firms typically have much more limited management resources – they are usually dependent upon at most a handful of key individuals – and since they also tend to be less diversified than their larger competitors, their fortunes are more closely linked to those of particular industries.

Small firms' access to external finance is generally much more restricted than that of their larger competitors. For equity capital most small firms depend on their own resources – the profits they are able to retain or funds which they can obtain from relatives or close friends. For debt they rely heavily on the banks, especially the clearing banks, though they can also economize on resources by leasing equipment and by 'factoring' debt – an arrangement by which the 'factor' takes on the responsibility of collecting debts and pays the company in advance (see chapter 13). Since the ability to borrow depends ultimately on an adequate supply of risk capital, small firms sometimes find that their growth is limited by their ability to generate internal funds, though other constraints (e.g. managerial resources) are more common.

The lack of external equity investment in small firms has a variety of causes, stemming both from the attitudes of the owners themselves and the needs of outside investors. Many small business owners are extremely reluctant to give up equity in their firms; they fear that outside equity shareholders might eventually try to take control, and, with their own personal standard of living at risk, they feel that the rewards of success should also be theirs. Moreover, potential investors may demand terms which seem to the owner to put much too low a valuation on the company.

From the point of view of the outside shareholder, however, the terms may be quite reasonable. Equity investment in small firms entails considerable costs of investigation before investments are made, comparatively high administrative costs to monitor investments thereafter, and a high failure rate – the returns from the successes have to pay for the failures. Some of the costs may be avoided by the private investor who is familiar with a company's business, but any such investor has to recognize that a minority shareholding in a small company generally has very poor marketability, and that he is likely to be in a weak position if he wishes to sell.

These problems are of long standing, and were identified by the Macmillan Committee[16] which reported in 1931. The committee pointed out that there was a gap, christened the 'Macmillan Gap', in the capital market provision for companies which were too small to make issues on the stock market. Since that time a number of specialized financial institutions such as Venture Capital Companies (VCCs), discussed in chapter 13, have been created and other initiatives have been taken to help to fill this gap.

Small companies depend on the clearing banks for most of their loan finance. The banks claim to be willing to provide as much finance as is reasonable, at a cost which reflects the cost of funds to them, the risk of loss, and the administrative costs inherent in retail lending. To control the risk of loss they take what security they can get. They recognize that small firms are likely to experience difficulty in raising external equity capital on acceptable terms and so, they claim, are prepared to tolerate higher levels of gearing than would be appropriate for larger companies. Competition for the business of small firms is intense and the banks argue that overcharging or an unrealistic attitude to risk on the part of any bank would lead to a loss of business.

Since the assessment of much of the risk in lending to small companies is not susceptible to precise calculation, it is hardly surprising to find that some of the banks' customers contest these claims. It is not so much the charge for loans that is at issue. Rather it is asserted that the banks are niggardly in their lending and oppressive in their demands for security. Competition between a small number of like-minded (and allegedly over-cautious) bankers does nothing to ensure that the proper needs of small firms are served.

Facts in this area are hard to come by. Some customers are certainly over-optimistic about their prospects of success, and few have full cognizance of the low risk of loss which is appropriate for institutions like banks. But on the other side, bankers' attitudes to risk vary, and the threat of taking business to a competitor may not be powerful when assessment of risk has to be based partly on a business relationship built up over many years. Nevertheless, at a time when banks are suffering severe losses on their domestic lending, paticularly to small businesses, it is difficult at present to sustain the argument that they have applied unduly severe credit criteria in the recent past.

The Wilson Committee[17] felt that there was sufficient doubt about the adequacy of the supply of loan finance to small firms to warrant the setting up of an experimental loan-guarantee scheme, under which the banks would be able to off-load on to a guarantor part of the credit risk involved in loans to small companies. This recommendation was accepted and a Loan Guarantee Scheme was set up, in the summer of 1981. Arrangements of a similar kind already existed in many other countries.

The Loan Guarantee Scheme is intended to assist small firms to obtain bank finance in excess of what would otherwise be available. Loans under the scheme have terms of from two to seven years, and the maximum is now £100 000. Loans are unsecured, and the lender receives a guarantee in respect of 70 per cent of the loan. The borrower pays an annual premium of 2.5 per cent of the amount outstanding. LGS loans usually form part of a wider financing package, and all possibility of secured borrowing must have been exhausted before a loan under the scheme is granted.

The terms of the scheme have been changed several times since it was first introduced. The peak number of loans occurred in 1982, when some 6000 were granted, but a severe tightening of terms following unacceptable failure rates (nearly 40 per cent after three years) caused a drop to under 750 in 1984. The terms were subsequently relaxed, and there were some 4000 loans in 1990, by which time the three-year failure rate had fallen to about 25 per cent.

Total lending under the scheme in 1990 was about £100 million, and an earlier study[18] concluded that about 50 per cent was truly additional to what could have been obtained otherwise. The total impact on small firm financing is not therefore very large. Nevertheless, without the guarantee, the high failure rate would clearly be unacceptable to conventional lenders, and the scheme does make some contribution to the small firm sector. Whether it makes a contribution to economic efficiency is more difficult to determine – the scheme runs at a loss. The resources devoted to it could be employed in other forms of investment, and the scheme is warranted only if productivity in the economy benefits more from the scheme than from an equivalent amount of investment generally.

In an attempt to improve the supply of equity funds for small companies, particularly in amounts that were too small to be of interest to the VCCs, the government introduced the Business Expansion Scheme (BES) in 1983. Under this scheme investors could invest up to £40 000 in BES companies in any year, and these investments could be deducted from gross income for tax purposes – that is, for an investor with a marginal tax rate of 40 per cent the tax saving is 40 per cent of the investment. The investment has to be held for a minimum of five years, after which any gain is free of both income and (since 1986) capital gains tax.

This scheme has not in fact proved effective in attracting a significant amount of high-risk funding for small companies.

Investors have generally preferred to invest in companies offering a good asset backing (for example hotels), and since schemes for residential property letting were brought into the scheme in 1988 the bulk of the funds have been invested in this relatively low-risk area.

While the development of the Unlisted Securities Market (see chapter 14) has been of value to a considerable number of relatively large SMEs, at the lower end of the range it is still difficult for these companies to obtain equity funding. VCCs have little interest in investments of less than £250 000, and are looking for rapid growth, and while government agencies such as Scottish Enterprise and the Welsh Development Agency help to fill the gap in their respective regions, SMEs seeking relatively small amounts of funds still have little alternative to the banks as their source of funds.

Notes

1 Including financial companies and institutions.
2 In principle, tangible assets are valued at current replacement cost and financial assets and liabilities at market values. The difference between total assets and total liabilities therefore represents the difference between the *market* value of companies' share capital and the imputed value of their equity when all other assets and liabilities are valued by this means.
3 A small proportion of overseas assets are also liquid, e.g. deposits with banks in other countries.
4 This equity may take the form of direct investment, of holdings of UK shares, or of inter-company loans from a parent to its subsidiary, where although legally a loan the risk effectively remains with the parent company.
5 Commercial bills are promises to pay at some future date, often issued by companies in connection with some trading transaction, and usually 'accepted' by a bank which guarantees the payment. Bills which have been accepted in this way are termed 'bank acceptances'. The linkage to particular transactions (e.g. receipts expected from an export delivery) may extend the credit which is available to a company. In addition, movements in relative interest rates on short-term financing instruments sometimes make commercial bills a less expensive form of borrowing than, for example, overdrafts.
6 A market in commercial paper developed in the second half of the eighties.
7 $ER = p(1 + D/E) - (D/E)i$. Since i is a constant it follows that:

$$\sigma_{ER} = (1 + D/E)\sigma_p.$$

8 Income gearing is

$$\frac{Di}{(D+E)p} \times 100.$$

Thus, for example, if $p = 15\%$, $i = 5\%$ and $D/E = 0.5$, we have $D/(D + E) = \frac{1}{3}$, and the income gearing is:

$$\frac{1}{3} \times \frac{5}{15} \times 100 = 11.1\%.$$

9 All grossed up for tax.

10 It is now the international, rather than the domestic, bond market which is relevant for large companies. Loans may be in currencies other than sterling and interest rates may be fixed or variable (floating), the company being able if it wishes to swap non-sterling into sterling liabilities and fixed for variable rates of interest through the banking system and financial markets.

11 Though repayment by instalments is possible, and a sinking fund is sometimes accumulated to provide the funds required for repayment at maturity.

12 100 per cent first-year allowances were also used as a crude means of adjusting for inflation, because they protected the real value of the capital allowances from erosion by inflation in later years.

13 Note that the figures for undistributed income and for the value of the physical increase in stock and work in progress in table 8.5 are net of stock appreciation. Depreciation is at replacement cost.

14 The effect was to raise the 'additions to tax reserves' component of undistributed income.

15 M. T. Jones, 'An Analysis of the Accounts of Small Companies', *Committee to Review the Functioning of Financial Institutions*, Studies of Small Firms' Financing (Research Report No. 3).

16 *Committee on Finance and Industry*, Report, Cmd 3897.

17 Interim Report, *The Financing of Small Firms*, Cmd 7503.

18 *An Evaluation of the Loan Guarantee Scheme*, Department of Employment Research Paper No. 74, 1990.

9

Public sector investment and financing

The finance of the public sector is a topic whose breadth extends far beyond the matters which concern us here. The financial arrangements between the central government on the one hand and the local authorities and public corporations on the other reflect political as well as economic considerations, and the finance of the central government is itself bound up with monetary and exchange rate policy – issues which lie beyond our remit. Instead, we focus in this chapter on how the public sector, as an important generator and user of funds, fits into the overall pattern of investment and financing in the economy.

The public sector consists of the central government, local authorities and public corporations – that is the remaining nationalized industries such as British Coal and British Rail, the Post Office, Regional Agencies such as Scottish Enterprise, New Towns and Urban Development Corporations, and bodies such as the UK Atomic Energy Authority, the Royal Mint and the Pilotage Commission. Since 1984 privatization of major public corporations, including British Telecom, British Gas, the water and the electricity companies, has brought about a considerable shift of economic activity from the public to the private sector, with a concomitant reduction in both public sector saving and investment.

The three major components of the public sector are quite distinct, and we shall consider the behaviour of each component individually. Nevertheless, in financing terms it makes sense to treat the public sector as a whole, because in formulating its financial policy the central government takes account of the overall impact of the public sector's operations on financial markets, and an increase in the financing needs of one part of the public sector may have to be accompanied by contraction elsewhere. The capital spending of all components are reviewed by the Treasury and other government departments, and are subject ultimately to a high degree of central influence and control. There are strong financial links within the public sector, with surpluses generated in some areas being channelled directly to other public sector users, and the great bulk of the sector's external financing needs (or surpluses) are raised (or deployed) centrally. The overall position of the sector determines the supply of certain categories of security, notably gilt-edged securities, and the public sector's demands on the capital market have implications for long-term interest rates and/or monetary growth.

The centralized consideration and control of public sector financing stands in sharp contrast with the dispersed decision-taking of the personal and company sectors. In these sectors economic agents take their own decisions in the light of the prices and terms prevailing in the financial markets. There is no overall control of saving or borrowing, and it is the changes in the market which maintain balance between them. For the public sector, however, there is a conscious attempt to control the overall level of borrowing to ensure that it does not impose too much pressure on the capital market, which could be relieved only by excessive monetary expansion or by driving up interest rates and contracting the supply of credit for other borrowers. Thus privatization shifts the enterprises concerned from a regime characterized by central control, and in which the individual enterprise's investment plans may have to be modified to accommodate other public sector needs (including, for example, a government's desire to cut taxation without increasing borrowing before an election), into a regime where their investment activities are subject only to the same commercial disciplines as the rest of the private sector. At certain times, however, when the private demand for funds is weak, the Treasury's normal desire to limit public spending, including investment, may give way to a desire to stimulate it in an attempt to counter recessionary forces in the economy.

We have already seen in chapter 2 how the public sector's contribution to both saving and investment in the economy has changed in the 1980s. Until the middle of the decade the general government sector (central government and local authorities) had a current account deficit amounting to about 1 per cent of GDP on average, but in the second half the deficit was eliminated and changed to a surplus of 2½ per cent of GDP in 1989. At the same time general government investment was diminishing from around 2 per cent of GDP at the start of the decade[1] to average about 1½ per cent in 1988 and 1989; this reduction was partly due to council house and other asset sales, which are counted as negative investment in the figures. Public corporations' saving fell as the sector shrank, from about 2 per cent of GDP at the beginning of the decade to 1.3 per cent in 1989, while at the same time investment fell from 2.8 per cent of GDP to only 1 per cent.[2] From the latter part of the 1970s investment in the public sector was curbed in an effort to reduce and then hold down public sector spending – the public sector financial deficit had been 5.5 per cent of GDP in the mid-seventies – efforts which continued in spite of the emergence of a financial surplus in 1988 and 1989.

At this point it is not easy to determine what levels of saving and investment in the public sector should be regarded as normal. With further privatizations since 1989 the contribution of the public corporations will continue to shrink. However, it is clear that the rise in general government saving and the emergence of a public sector financial surplus occurred at a cyclical peak and that they have already been eroded. It does not seem likely that a positive figure for general government saving will be the norm over an economic cycle as a whole, and a return to a general government financial deficit comparable to that in the mid-eighties seems probable.

The public sector's balance sheet

Table 9.1 shows the balance sheet of the public sector in 1987, together with more up-to-date figures (1989) for *financial* assets and liabilities. About 20 per cent of the nation's *tangible* assets are held in the public sector – council houses, offices and industrial buildings, all kinds of civil engineering works, and plant and machinery, especially in the public corporations. But the table shows that the public sector also holds substantial amounts of financial assets – the foreign exchange reserves, company securities, loans to the private sector and to foreigners (e.g. as part of overseas aid), and liquid assets such as bank and building society deposits. There is also credit granted to (or taken without asking by) customers and taxpayers, including very substantial amounts of tax which will be due eventually but which is not yet payable as part of the 'other' item.

To finance these assets, and sometimes simply to finance spending which does not lead to the creation of any physical or financial assets (such as wars or public sector consumption), the public sector has had to borrow in the past. The financial liabilities represent the

Table 9.1   Balance sheet of the public sector, 1987 and 1989 (end-years)

	(£ billion)	
	1987	1989
Tangible assets	379	n.a.
Financial assets		
Official reserves	27	26
Bank and building society deposits	9	12
UK company securities	18	17
Loans etc.	16	14
Trade credit	13	14
Other	21	25
Total	104	108
Financial liabilities		
Notes and coin	15	18
Treasury bills and gilt-edged securities	137	129
National savings etc.	39	38
Local authority and public corporation debt	12	7
Life assurance and pension funds	9	10
Trade credit	13	15
Miscellaneous, mainly overseas	9	8
Other	11	15
Total	245	240

Source: Blue Book, 1990, table 12.12

accumulation of past borrowing. The most important item is Treasury bills and gilt-edged securities – central government marketable debt – which accounts for over half of the total, but notes and coin are not insignificant and cost practically nothing, and national savings also make a substantial contribution. Local authority and public corporation debt other than to the central government (which is not therefore part of public sector debt) is now comparatively small and has been diminishing in recent years, the central government has substantial liabilities for future pensions to its employees, and the public sector also takes trade credit from the private sector and incurs liabilities (e.g. for interest on debt) which will be due in future but which are not payable yet. At just under £130 billion in 1989, central government marketable debt had a value of less than 20 per cent of the value of UK company securities at that time.

Government debt is often regarded as 'deadweight' in the economy, on the grounds that it makes its owners feel better off, and therefore reduces private saving, without there being any productive assets to support its value. In this it is said to differ from company securities, whose value depends ultimately on the future earning power of the company or its assets. A glance at the sector's balance sheet shows that, at least for the UK, this view is misconceived – many of the financial assets are income earning, as indeed are many of the tangible assets (e.g. the £117 billion in 1987 held by public corporations). The yield may not always be as high as would be expected in the private sector, but the privatization programme has demonstrated that the value inherent in public corporations can be released and used to extinguish public sector debt. The same goes for council house and other asset sales. Moreover, even non-marketable assets such as roads and bridges contribute to the productivity of the economy, helping to generate the tax revenue required to service debt.

Nevertheless, it probably is true that in taking their own private decisions about saving people do not take account of the income likely to be generated by public sector assets, whereas they do count the value of any national savings or gilt-edged securities in their wealth. It follows that any reduction in the level of public sector debt is likely to have a positive effect on personal saving.

Table 9.2 shows that the ratio of public sector debt to GDP in the UK more than halved, from 60 to under 30 per cent, between 1975

Table 9.2   Public sector debt to GDP ratio[1]

	Ratio (per cent)
1975	60
1980	45
1985	46
1986	44
1987	42
1988	38
1989	31
1990	28

Source: Bank of England Quarterly Bulletin,
November 1990, p. 520, table A
[1] Ratio of *net* public sector debt (i.e. consolidated total debt less liquid assets) to GDP. (Securities are at nominal values.) Figures are for end-March

and 1990. In the first five years the fall was due mainly to inflation – in nominal terms net public sector debt rose by over 70 per cent between 1975 and 1980, but nominal income increased by nearly 125 per cent. Until 1986 there was little change in the ratio, but between 1987 and 1990 the net public sector debt fell by over 12 per cent, and it is this, combined with a rise of nearly a third in nominal income, which accounts for the sharp reduction in the ratio in the second half of the 1980s. The burden of public sector debt in the UK, as measured by this ratio, is now low by international standards.

Local authorities and public corporations

Capital expenditure by local authorities now absorbs under 2 per cent of GDP, having declined from a little over 2 per cent at the end of the 1970s (table 9.3). The most important component is expenditure on housing, which accounts for about half of the total, but capital spending on education, recreation and transport are all significant items. Grants for house improvements in the personal sector also make significant calls on local authority funds. Capital funds may also be required for industrial support (by means of loans or the purchase of securities) and in connection with house

Table 9.3 Capital spending and borrowing by local authorities, 1978–89

			(Per cent of GDP)	
	1978–82 average	*1983–87 average*	*1988*	*1989*
Capital spending and grants	2.1	1.9	1.7	1.9
Acquisition of financial assets	—	−0.2	−0.1	−0.1
Total	2.0	1.7	1.6	1.8
Current surplus	0.8	0.6	0.4	0.3
Other capital receipts	0.6	0.8	1.2	1.4
Total	1.5	1.4	1.6	1.7
Balancing item	—	0.1	0.1	—
Total borrowing	0.6	0.4	0.1	0.1
of which from:				
central government	(0.2)	(1.3)	(1.0)	(0.5)
other	(0.4)	(−0.9)	(−0.9)	(−0.4)

Source: Blue Book, 1990, tables 8.3, 8.4

purchase. At one time local authorities provided a substantial part of the funding for tenants buying their council houses, but this kind of lending has now virtually ceased as tenants are able to find finance from the normal commercial sources. As a result, since 1983, repayments have substantially exceeded new lending.

The local authority sector has generally had a current account surplus out of which it could finance some of its capital spending. However, the surplus has been on a downward trend, falling from 0.8 per cent of GDP in 1978–82 to only 0.3 per cent in 1989. In place of this surplus, finance for capital spending has come increasingly from capital receipts derived from the sale of council houses and other local authority assets (such as surplus land or offices) – in 1989 over half of local authorities' capital spending could be financed in this way. There are also capital grants from the central government, principally to support investment in housing and transport.

Capital receipts from the sale of existing assets are a substitute for *public sector* borrowing, but do not obviate the need for financing in the economy as a whole. Sales of existing council houses to their tenants make just the same demands on banks and building societies for finance as sales within the private sector. Since the reduction in public sector borrowing achieved through asset sales of this kind is not matched by a corresponding reduction in total borrowing, the government's assessment of the proper level of public sector borrowing should in principle be cut accordingly. There is no evidence that this has ever happened.

Owing to the rising level of capital receipts, total borrowing had dwindled from 0.6 per cent of GDP in 1978–82 to almost nothing by the end of the eighties. However, borrowing from the central government has continued, running at over 1 per cent of GDP in the middle of the decade. Funds are made available from the Public Works Loan Board (PWLB), which in turn is funded through the National Loans Fund (NLF).[3] The interest rates charged by the PWLB are linked to current interest rates on central government debt.

In the early 1980s local authorities had access to a quota of funds which they could borrow from the PWLB, with the rest of their financing being obtained in the private market. Funds were raised mainly from banks and other financial institutions, but also from the non-bank private sector and from overseas residents; some of the debt was temporary, with a maturity of less than one year, but a substantial proportion was longer term. In 1982 the government decided to change these arrangements and encourage local authorities to obtain most of their financing from the PWLB. There were two main reasons. The first was that it was thought that funds could be obtained more cheaply by the central government, so that there would be some saving in cost. The second was connected with monetary policy, where it was felt that monetary growth could be controlled more easily if the central government obtained long-term funds from outside the banking system, rather than have the local authorities borrow from the banks. The interest rates at which local authorities could borrow from the PWLB were made more attractive, and as a result the local authorities did not renew private sector borrowing as it fell due but drew upon finance from the PWLB instead. Local authority debt held outside the public sector fell from over £16 billion at the end of 1982 to £6 billion in 1989. However, early in 1990 new measures to limit local authority borrowing from the PWLB were announced, justified in part by the changing needs of monetary policy.

Capital spending by public corporations has fallen from a little under 3 per cent of GDP at the end of the 1970s to only 1 per cent in 1988 and 1989 (table 9.4). There was a genuine reduction in the early eighties, but since 1984 the main cause of the further decline has been the privatization programme, with British Telecom, Gas,

Table 9.4 Capital spending and borrowing by public corporations, 1978–89

	1978–82 average	1983–87 average	(Per cent of GDP) 1988	1989
Capital spending	2.8	1.8	1.0	1.0
(depreciation)	(2.6)	(1.9)	(1.2)	(1.1)
Acquisition of financial assets	0.1	—	−0.2	0.2
Total	2.9	1.8	0.8	1.2
Undistributed income	1.9	1.7	1.2	1.1
Other capital receipts	0.3	0.2	0.2	0.3
Total	2.1	1.9	1.4	1.3
Balancing item	—	0.1	0.2	0.1
Total borrowing	0.8	—	−0.4	—
of which from:				
central government	(1.0)	(0.2)	(0.2)	(0.4)
other	(−0.2)	(−0.2)	(−0.6)	(−0.4)

Source: Blue Book, 1990, tables 6.3, 6.4, 14.3

Airways and Steel all accounting for the transfer of substantial investment programmes to the private sector. With the electricity and water companies now also privatized – energy and water accounted for over half of the public corporations' investment in 1989 – the share of GDP absorbed by public corporations' investment has certainly fallen further. It is noticeable, however, that from the mid-eighties on, gross investment by the public corporations has fallen short of replacement cost depreciation, suggesting that net investment has been negative.

Public corporations have been given little scope to expand by acquisition so their need for capital funds to acquire financial assets has been comparatively slight. Some funds are, however, needed for loans to the private sector, investment overseas, very limited transactions in securities, and net trade credit granted.

Part of the public corporations' investment is financed from their undistributed income and from capital grants, mainly from the central government. Undistributed income has generally fallen short of replacement cost depreciation, and in the 1978–82 period public corporations had a borrowing requirement amounting to 0.8 per cent of GDP. After 1984, however, the total borrowing requirement disappeared (British Telecom, which was privatized in 1984, had a large investment programme) and was replaced by net repayment of debt. However, the public corporations have continued to borrow from the NLF, for reasons similar to those applying to local authorities, with the opportunity being taken to reduce borrowing from other sources. This has included the repayment of substantial amounts of foreign currency debt, taken on in the 1970s at the government's behest as a means of obtaining currency for the foreign exchange reserves.

Central government

The central government is directly responsible for capital spending in the activities it controls. Typically, this capital expenditure has averaged a little under 1 per cent of GDP (table 9.5), with the health service and roads being the most important components. As we have seen, the central government also makes capital grants to local authorities and public corporations, to which must be added grants to the private sector – for example, to housing associations, universities and colleges, and companies. These capital grants, which are mainly to support investment carried out by the recipient, are of the same broad magnitude as the central government's own

Table 9.5 Capital spending and borrowing by the central government, 1978–89

	1978–82 average	1983–87 average	1988	1989
			(Per cent of GDP)	
Capital spending	0.8	1.0	0.8	1.1
Capital grants	1.0	0.9	0.8	1.1
Loans, accruals etc. to private and overseas sectors	0.4	—	0.3	0.2
Total	2.2	1.8	1.9	2.4
Current surplus	−1.4	−1.1	1.9	2.3
Taxes on capital etc.	0.5	0.6	0.8	0.8
Sales of securities and fixed assets	−0.1	0.9	1.4	1.0
Total	−0.9	0.4	4.2	4.2
Balancing item	—	—	—	−0.1
Central government own borrowing requirement	3.1	1.5	−2.2	−1.9
Net lending etc. to local authorities and public corporations	1.3	1.4	1.2	0.9
Total central government borrowing	4.3	2.9	−1.0	−1.0

Source: Blue Book, 1990, tables 7.3, 7.4

investment programme. Finally, there are loans to industry and trade, overseas aid loans channelled through international bodies, and funding needs brought about by the inevitable time lags before taxes are received. All this has added up to about 2 per cent of GDP on average, although as table 9.5 shows, the swings from one year to another (e.g. 1988 to 1989) can be considerable.

To fund this expenditure the central government can draw upon its own current surplus (if any), the proceeds of taxes on capital, the receipts from net sales of securities and fixed assets, and borrowing. As table 9.5 shows, in the course of the 1980s there were substantial changes in the contributions from each of these various sources.

Until 1988 the central government had a current account *deficit* – that is, its current spending exceeded its current tax revenue and other current account receipts. Not until 1987 did this fall below

1 per cent of GDP. However, the sharp increase in tax receipts from 1987 to 1989, combined with comparative restraint in current spending, turned this deficit into a surplus of 2.3 per cent of GDP in 1989. Subsequent events have shown that this is unlikely to be a permanent phenomenon.

Receipts from taxes on capital (mainly inheritance and capital gains tax) rose fairly steadily from 0.5 to 0.8 per cent of GDP; i.e. they were not enough to offset the current deficit in the first half of the decade. However, the trend from current deficit to surplus was complemented by receipts from privatizations together with less substantial sums from the sale of fixed assets. Prior to 1984 central government purchases of securities often exceeded realizations, but the advent of the privatization programme resulted in net sales of securities and fixed assets worth 0.9 per cent of GDP in 1983–7 and even more in 1988 and 1989. Again, it should be noted that while these asset sales reduce the *government's* need to borrow they do not reduce the calls on the nation's savings, something which needs to be borne in mind in setting a target for government borrowing.

The end result was a substantial change in the central government's *own* borrowing requirement, from an average of 3.1 per cent of GDP in 1978–82, when borrowing had to cover not only the government's capital spending but also its current deficit, to a negative borrowing requirement – that is, an ability to repay debt – of about 2 per cent of GDP in 1988 and 1989.

To this *own* borrowing requirement has to be added the substantial funding which the central government provides to the local authorities and public corporations through the NLF. This averaged 1.3 per cent of GDP in the ten years 1978–87, though it was slightly less in 1988 and 1989. Total central government borrowing has therefore ranged from an average of 4.3 per cent of GDP in 1978–82 to debt *repayment* of 1 per cent of GDP in 1988 and 1989.

As noted earlier, the government's borrowing or debt repayment programme is conducted in the context of monetary and foreign exchange policy, both of which give rise from time to time to financing requirements which can swamp those of the government itself. This is illustrated in table 9.6, which shows the financing of the central government's borrowing requirement from 1985 to 1989.[4] The first two lines of the table show flows emanating from foreign exchange and monetary policy actions.

In 1987 the government followed a policy of pegging sterling within a fairly narrow band against the deutschmark. However, interest rates in the UK were comparatively attractive and foreign

Table 9.6 Financing of the central government borrowing requirement, 1985–89

	1985	1986	1987	*(£ billion)* 1988	1989
Foreign currency and overseas financing	−0.4	−0.5	−12.4	−3.1	6.7
'Monetary policy' transactions with private sector	−1.0	−0.6	6.0	−0.4	3.7
Notes and coin	0.4	0.7	1.1	1.5	1.2
Sterling Treasury bills	0.1	0.3	2.2	1.3	2.9
Gilt-edged securities	9.6	6.9	4.6	−5.0	−18.3
National savings etc.	3.1	2.6	2.0	0.5	−1.4
Other	—	−0.9	0.6	0.5	0.1
Total borrowing requirement	11.8	8.4	4.1	−4.7	−5.0

Source: Financial Statistics, August 1990, table 3.4

exchange dealers also expected sterling to appreciate. As a result, to prevent sterling rising to an undesired level, the monetary authorities in Britain had to buy over £12 billion of foreign currency and finance this by sterling borrowing. (This can be compared with total central government borrowing of some £4 billion.) The reverse situation occurred in 1989, when action to support the pound resulted in the foreign exchange reserves falling by nearly £7 billion, with a corresponding reduction in the government's need for sterling finance.

Through much of the 1980s dealings in commercial bills played an important part in the conduct of monetary policy. In 1987, such 'monetary policy transactions with the private sector', namely a reduction in the authorities' holdings of commercial bills, released £6 billion of government funding, with a further reduction of nearly £4 billion in 1989. In 1987 the reduction in bill holdings provided some of the finance for the foreign exchange inflow, but in 1989 the two effects were additive.

The principal forms of central government liability are also set out in table 9.6. Thanks to the growth of nominal incomes the general public's demand for notes and coin also grows continually, providing each year a significant amount of additional cheap financing for the government. For monetary policy reasons the Treasury bill issue was increased from 1987 to 1989, acting as a substitute liquid asset for the declining stock of commercial bills in the financial markets. National savings provide a reliable source of funds, with the government able to vary the terms in accordance with its funding needs. Thus in 1988 and 1989, when the central government was in a position to repay debt, the terms were made relatively unattractive, resulting in only a small net inflow (1988) or outflow (1989) of funds.

Gilt-edged securities are the most important form of financing. Monetary policy considerations dictate that with the exception of national savings, recourse to other forms of financing is limited.[5] From 1985 to 1988 the decline in the central government borrowing requirement was matched broadly by a similar reduction in net issues and then a switch to repayment of gilt-edged securities,[6] but in 1989 the net repayments of gilt-edged securities rose to £18 billion, as sales of foreign exchange, the reduction in the authorities' holdings of commercial bills, the increase in Treasury bills, the usual rise in the public's holdings of notes and coin, and the central government's own surplus all came together. With the disappearance of the central government surplus and the decline which has occurred in the authorities' commercial bill holdings, such a conjunction of events is not likely to recur.

Public sector borrowing and the economy

By adding together the *own* borrowing requirement of the central government to the total borrowing requirements of the other two sectors we obtain the Public Sector Borrowing Requirement (PSBR) (table 9.7). This moved from an average of 4.5 per cent of GDP in 1978–82 to a Public Sector Debt Repayment (PSDR) of 2.5 per cent of GDP in 1988 and 1.8 per cent in 1989. The PSBR (PSDR) provides a measure of the scale of new *debt* issued (repaid) by the public sector. However, in arriving at these figures credit has already been taken for funds raised by other means (e.g. privatization issues and sales of fixed assets). It is not therefore a good measure of the public sector's impact on the saving/investment balance in the economy.

For this purpose the public sector financial deficit is superior. It omits all the financial transactions of the public sector – loans and purchases of securities on the one hand and privatization issues on the other. In so far as these financial transactions simply substitute one form of financing for another, without altering the saving and investment behaviour of the economic agents concerned, the financial deficit provides a summary measure of the public sector's impact. It is, of course, an exaggeration to imply that the public

Table 9.7 Public sector borrowing, 1978–89

	1978–82 average	1983–87 average	*(Per cent of GDP)* 1988	1989
Central government own borrowing	3.1	1.5	−2.2	−1.9
Local authority borrowing	0.6	0.4	0.1	0.1
Total general government borrowing	3.7	1.9	−2.1	−1.8
Public corporations borrowing	0.8	—	−0.4	—
Total public sector borrowing requirement	4.5	1.9	−2.5	−1.8
(Memo: Public sector financial deficit)[1]	(−3.9)	(−2.6)	(1.4)	(1.2)

Source: Tables 8.3–8.5; *Blue Book*, 1990, tables 3.5, 3.6
[1] Financial deficit (−), financial surplus (+)

sector's financial transactions have *no* impact on private saving or investment – clearly some private sector investment would not take place without government loans because private sector financing would simply not be available. But where the major privatization issues are concerned it is reasonable to suppose that the saving and investment behaviour of the newly privatized companies will be very little affected in the year in which the change of ownership takes place.

The memo items in table 9.7 show how, though still substantial, the size of the swing from deficit to surplus in the PSFD – from a deficit of 3.9 per cent of GDP in 1978–82 to a surplus of something over 1 per cent in 1988 and 1989 – has been much less than the swing in the PSBR. But the PSFD is not the end of the story because, as already noted, this takes no account of funds raised through the sales of fixed assets, which are offset against investment in the national accounts. These too have been on a rising trend, and adjusting for fixed asset sales adds 0.5 per cent to the financing requirement in 1978–82 and 1.1 per cent in 1988 and 1989. The end result is to raise financing in 1978–82 to nearly 4½ per cent of GDP, while bringing the position in 1988 and 1989 close to balance.

Since these trends have clearly been influenced by the effect of privatization in shrinking the public corporations sector in the 1980s, for long-term comparisons it is better to focus on the general government, whose functions have been subject to much less

Table 9.8   General government financial deficit, 1958–89

	(Per cent of GDP)
1958–62	−0.2
1963–67	−0.8
1968–72	0.9
1973–77	−4.0
1978–82	−3.2
1983–87	−2.7
1988	1.0
1989	0.9

Source: Committee to Review the Functioning of Financial Institutions, Report (Cmnd 7937), 1980, table 12; *Blue Book,* 1990, tables 3.5, 3.6

change. Table 9.8 shows how the general government financial deficit moved in the 30-year period from 1958. In the first half of the period, from 1958 to 1972, the deficit averaged close to zero, but there was then a sharp move into deficit in the mid-seventies, followed by a gradual return to balance.[7]

What *should* determine the government's target for the PSBR? It ought already to be clear that there is no simple answer, though a number of factors are relevant.

First, there is the scale of the public sector's commercial activities. Whether activities such as water supply, health services, electricity generation, or transport are in or out of the public sector is a matter of political choice. However, growing enterprises usually require some external finance, and the fact that an activity is carried out by a public sector body should not preclude the use of borrowing. What is important is that the investment should be justified by its likely (commercial or social) return.

Secondly, there is the level of the existing public sector debt. A high public sector debt to GDP ratio often imposes immense problems for public financing, since a high proportion of tax revenue has to be committed to servicing the debt, as well as for economic management generally. This is seen most clearly in countries with international debt problems, notably some countries in Eastern Europe and South America, where much of the debt is held externally – in these cases the problem of servicing the debt is compounded by the need to obtain foreign exchange. But a high level of debt held domestically also causes problems, because resources have to be obtained by the government and transferred to the owners of the debt. Frequently the only way the government can obtain the resources is by printing money or borrowing even more from the banking system, with obvious inflationary consequences.

The level of public sector borrowing is not the sole, or even the most important, cause of changes in the debt to GDP ratio. Inflation and real growth also play a part. This has led to the suggestion that governments need not be too concerned about the part of debt interest which reflects compensation for inflation. If this is all that is added to the outstanding debt, inflation will ensure that the debt to GDP ratio does not rise.

While technically correct, this is a dangerous argument. Public sector borrowing is often the principal reason for the monetary conditions which cause inflation, and ignoring this element in interest costs is likely to perpetuate these monetary conditions. Moreover, governments which successfully pursue policies to reduce inflation will find that the burden of servicing their debt increases, because the inflation premium in interest rates normally lags behind the actual fall in inflation.

Thirdly, there is the availability of savings generated in the private sector. If the propensity to save in the private sector is strong and there is a surplus of private saving over private investment, the government can borrow the surplus without curtailing private investment activity.[8] This raises several issues. If private investment is too low – by reference perhaps to the level achieved in other countries – the government may decide to limit its own borrowing in order to keep interest rates at a level which encourages the private sector to invest; whereas if investment is generally strong, higher government borrowing may be regarded with equanimity. Consideration has also to be given to the cyclical position, because during a boom private sector investment rises relative to saving so that an increase in the government surplus (or reduction in its deficit) will help to maintain balance in the economy. The reverse applies in a recession. To some extent this happens automatically as a result of stabilizers in the fiscal system – the natural buoyancy of tax revenue in the boom and the increase in social security payments in the recession. But it is often argued that governments should go further and alter the fiscal balance by discretionary means according to the state of the economic cycle.

Where a country's financial system is integrated with those of other countries its government will be able to alter its own level of borrowing without affecting interest rates. In some circumstances government borrowing will clearly be legitimate (e.g. when a country is undergoing rapid development and the borrowing is employed to strengthen the infrastructure and raise the country's future productive capacity). But there is a world of difference between finance for this kind of purpose and borrowing to cover a current deficit. Moreover, governments can borrow in international markets only so long as it is expected that they will be able to service and repay their debt. If debt rises to a point where this ability is called in question, the supply of funds is likely to be cut off suddenly, at considerable economic cost to the country concerned.

Very often decisions regarding the appropriate level of government borrowing boil down to decisions regarding intergenerational equity. Does the government borrow, thereby allowing the present generation to consume more? Or does it tax, thereby limiting the current generation's ability to consume? It is not difficult on equity grounds to make a case for borrowing to finance investment which will benefit future generations – though far-sighted governments may feel that the current generation can reasonably be expected to finance some improvements for its successors. The case for financing current consumption out of borrowing is much less easy to sustain – politically attractive, of course, to governments facing elections; but economically damaging.[9]

Notes

1 It had been 4.6 per cent in 1973–7.
2 Again, the figure had been higher (3.5 per cent) in the mid-seventies.
3 This is a government fund which acts as a central source for loans within the public sector.
4 Note that the table is in £ billion, not per cent of GDP.
5 It is government policy that the Public Sector Borrowing Requirement should be funded fully from outside the monetary (bank and building society) system. Changes in the foreign exchange reserves are to be funded similarly. This effectively limits the use which is made of notes and coin and Treasury bills as sources of finance, since the latter are likely to be held predominantly in the monetary system.
6 The reduction in commercial bill holdings and other forms of finance provided most of the funds for the increase in foreign exchange reserves in 1987.
7 Sales of fixed assets were very low in the 1958–72 period, and adjusting for these sales in 1988 and 1989 brings the general government financial balance close to zero.
8 In the absence of international capital flows the private surplus would, of course, be expected to lead eventually to lower interest rates, with implications for both saving and investment in the private sector.

However, if the borrowing is for public sector investment, total investment will be higher if the government takes up the surplus saving.

9 As always there are exceptions. For example, it may be reasonable to expect future generations to bear part of the cost of a war. This can be achieved through government borrowing, which gives people property rights which they can turn into consumption later.

10

The overseas sector and the UK financial system

The British economy is becoming increasingly integrated with those of its principal trading partners. The value of trade in goods and services amounts to more than 50 per cent of GDP, and capital can flow between Britain and other countries freely. As we observed in chapter 6, it is only the variability of the exchange rate for sterling that separates financial conditions in the UK from those in other countries, and which makes it sensible to draw a boundary round the UK financial system. Moreover, London's pre-eminence within the international financial system strengthens these international linkages.

We have already seen several ways in which international linkages affect financial behaviour in the UK: companies need funds for investment abroad, foreign-controlled companies in the UK obtain financing from their parents, government financing is complicated by the management of the foreign exchange reserves, and short-term interest rates have to be set with a keen eye on developments elsewhere. Other types of capital transaction are also extremely important – portfolio investment abroad by financial institutions, the purchase of securities in UK markets by overseas residents, and short-term capital movements through the banking system are all examples. Since most of the transactions with the overseas sector involve the purchase or sale of foreign currency at some stage, their effect on the economy is bound up with government policy regarding the exchange rate.

The main categories of transaction are summarized in table 10.1. At this stage, however, it is necessary to insert a health warning about the figures. The task of collecting data on international trade and payments was never easy, but has become increasingly difficult as economies have become more integrated. In particular, the abolition of exchange controls in 1979 removed an important data

Table 10.1   Financial transactions with other countries, 1978–89[1]

	1978–82 average	1983–87 average	1988	1989
			(Per cent of GDP)	
Current account surplus	1.2	0.3	−3.2	−3.7
Transactions in financial assets				
Direct investment				
Outward	−2.2	−2.7	−4.4	−3.8
Inward	1.4	1.1	2.0	3.6
Portfolio investment				
Outward	−1.4	−3.2	−2.1	−7.2
Inward	0.3	2.1	2.8	2.1
Bank deposits, loans etc.				
Outward	−11.4	−8.9	−4.7	−6.7
Inward	11.5	10.9	8.5	11.6
Reserves etc.	0.3	−0.9	−0.6	1.1
Total transactions	−1.5	−1.6	1.5	0.7
Balancing item	0.3	1.3	1.7	2.9

Source: Balance of Payments Pink Book, 1990, tables 1.1, 8.1
[1] Increase in UK assets (−), increase in UK liabilities (+)

source. When there is no good business reason to distinguish between UK and foreign customers there is no incentive for UK enterprises to record transactions separately.[1] The quality of the data is therefore generally recognized to be poor, and the balancing item representing errors and omissions in the accounts has grown in recent years.

Current account transactions

The balance of payments surplus on current account measures the difference between what the UK receives by selling goods and services abroad and what it pays for imports of goods and services. The surplus therefore shows the net amount of finance that UK residents have available to acquire foreign assets, and this will be reflected in some combination of purchases and sales of overseas assets, transactions in liabilities to foreigners, and a change in the foreign exchange reserves. Table 10.1 shows that in the ten years from 1978 to 1987 the current account of the balance of payments averaged a small surplus; but this surplus actually peaked (at over 2½ per cent of GDP) in the recession of 1981 and was on a declining trend throughout the recovery and into the boom at the end of the eighties, with deficits apparently well above 3 per cent of GDP in both 1988 and 1989. The size of the current account surplus or deficit is the result of many factors influencing the economy, including prevailing financial conditions and the sterling exchange rate. We cannot go into these further, but simply note the implications of the current account position for changes in financial assets and liabilities.

Capital transactions

Three categories of capital transaction are distinguished in table 10.1: direct investment, portfolio investment, and changes in deposits with or loans by the banks together with changes in other short-term assets. *Direct investment* refers to transactions between related organizations, for example a parent company's investment in an overseas subsidiary. It also includes property investment by individuals or companies.

Both outward investment by UK residents and inward investment by overseas residents increased in the 1980s. The figures include unremitted profits of existing subsidiaries, and in the case of outward investment this accounted for about 45 per cent of the total in the second half of the eighties, reflecting the scale of UK companies' existing overseas operations. The balance, about 2 per cent of GDP in 1989, had to be financed in other ways – by borrowing from banks in the country concerned, by borrowing in the UK or the international markets, often in foreign currency, by raising new sterling finance for the company's activities generally and deploying some of the funds in these overseas investments, by drawing on the company's liquid asset holdings, or out of the flow of current profits. Some of these sources of finance give rise to offsetting transactions under the bank deposits, loans or other short-term assets heading.

The same general considerations apply to inward investment, with unremitted profits (including those of foreign-controlled oil companies) accounting for over half the total in 1983–7. However, in 1988 and particularly 1989 other forms of inward investment rose sharply to account for about 80 per cent of the total (2.8 per cent of GDP in 1989). This was connected with European mergers activity, stimulated by the trend towards the Single Market, and continued in

1990 – further evidence of the increasing international element in the UK economy.

Portfolio investment covers investment in the securities of unrelated concerns, other than securities with a maturity of less than one year. It is carried out by banks, non-bank financial institutions and other economic agents, the motive being to secure as high a return as possible. As such it is highly sensitive to the prevailing conditions in financial markets around the world – interest rates, prospective capital gains or losses in equity markets, and expected movements in exchange rates. Prior to the abolition of exchange controls in 1979, outward portfolio investment by UK residents was severely inhibited, but since then overseas securities have made up a gradually increasing proportion of investing institutions' asset portfolios, and outward portfolio investment has represented a sizeable proportion of GDP in some years (e.g. over 7 per cent in 1989). Inward investment has also been affected by international financial market integration, and was on a rising trend in the 1980s. Year-to-year fluctuations in the net inflow or outflow of portfolio investment can be very large – for example, from a net outflow of over 3 per cent of GDP in 1986 the position changed to a net inflow of 5 per cent in 1987, and had swung back to a net outflow of 5 per cent in 1989.

Portfolio investment includes investment in securities by banks, the counterpart of which in the banks' portfolios is generally deposits. Thus holdings of US dollar floating rate notes (securities) may be funded by dollar deposits. This has accounted for a considerable part of outward portfolio investment in some years – it was about one-sixth of the total in 1989 – and does not represent a call on UK resources. Part of inward investment is similar in character – UK companies (and building societies) issue securities which are attractive to banks in the international markets, whose purchases may be funded from deposits raised in the UK. In 1989 overseas residents' purchases of UK company bonds amounted to over 80 per cent of inward portfolio investment.

After 1979 non-bank financial institutions took advantage of their freedom to invest abroad and built up their holdings of foreign shares. However, following very substantial increases in 1985 and 1986 the process was interrupted in 1987 – net sales began before the world's stock markets peaked and there was a large reduction in the fourth quarter after the crash. Purchases resumed on a more limited scale in 1988 but reached a peak of nearly 2½ per cent of GDP in 1989. Since very little of this investment is financed by borrowing it draws directly on UK financial resources. Persons and companies are also active buyers of foreign securities, with the company sector making purchases of almost 1 per cent of GDP in 1989; part or all of this may, however, have been financed by borrowing.

Until almost the end of the eighties inward investment included net purchases of gilt-edged stock every year, partly as additions to overseas monetary authorities' exchange reserves but also by other holders. The amounts involved were sometimes quite large (e.g. £4.3 billion in 1987 when sterling interest rates were attractive and the exchange rate outlook was favourable). However, these conditions were reversed in 1989 and 1990 and the net sales of gilt-edged stocks by overseas residents were substantial.

Foreign investment in UK equities is subject to the same kinds of influence as UK investment in foreign equities. It peaked at over £10 billion (2½ per cent of GDP) in 1987, when UK economic conditions appeared very favourable, but fell back to £4 billion the next year.

By comparison with the other categories of external transaction the figures for *bank deposits, loans etc.* are very large. They include UK banks' transactions with the rest of the world, which reflect London's position as an international financial centre, as well as the short-term transactions of the non-bank private sector with banks and other entities overseas. Much of the banking activity is 'entrepot' business – for example, the London offices of Japanese banks may take dollar deposits in order to lend funds to their parents in Tokyo. It is therefore the *net* position that is relevant for the UK economy. From approximate balance in 1978–82 and an average net inflow of 2 per cent of GDP in 1983–7, the net inflow increased to nearly 4 per cent of GDP in 1988 and 5 per cent in 1989.

We have already seen that some of this net inflow is directly related to the financing of direct investment and to the acquisition of overseas securities. But it may also be needed to finance a current account deficit. If the government's transactions, including changes in the reserves, netted to zero, the banking flows would have to fund the net financial requirement emanating from the current account balance together with the balances on direct and portfolio investment.[2] In practice, the change in the reserves etc. is not zero, so it is government policy regarding the exchange rate, interest rates and foreign exchange market intervention which determines the division between reserve movements and banking flows in accommodating these other transactions. Interest rates and the exchange rate have to move in whatever way is required to create the incentives in the financial markets to bring this about.

The figures for *reserves etc.* reflect the government's activities, including other external assets and liabilities of the government as well as changes in the reserves. Examples are subscriptions to international lending bodies, which require funding, and foreign currency borrowing by the central government and other government short-term liabilities (such as Treasury bills held overseas) which provide support for the reserves. As we noted in the last chapter, changes in the reserves have sometimes been substantial (e.g. in 1987, when the increase in reserves etc. amounted to 2.7 per cent of GDP). But a general policy of minimizing foreign exchange market intervention implies that this item will usually not be large.

Thanks to the balancing item it is not possible to relate the banking figures and reserve movements precisely to the changes in the other components. Nevertheless, it appears that from 1978–82 the current account surplus was sufficient to finance most of the net outward direct and portfolio investment taking place; there was a very small reduction in the reserves and little net inflow through the banks. In 1983–7 the current account surplus was smaller, net outward direct investment larger, and there was also an increase in the reserves to be financed. The result was a net inflow through the banking system.[3] In 1988 the reserves increased, in spite of a substantial current account deficit and an increase in net outward direct investment. Part of the finance came from net inward portfolio investment, much more from net borrowing through the banking system. Finally in 1989, with the current account continuing to show a large deficit there was a sharp increase in net outward portfolio investment, only partly offset by the high level of inward direct investment. The size of the balancing item obviously casts some doubt on the precise magnitudes of these figures, but it is clear that there was a substantial financing requirement. The result was weakness of sterling, a fall in the reserves, and high UK interest rates to draw in the necessary funds through the banking system.

Notes

1 Consider the problem of attempting to obtain balance of payments figures for London, when firms do not distinguish between customers in London and those elsewhere in the country and financial institutions operate over a much wider area. When trade barriers between Britain and the European Community have disappeared and there are no payments barriers, a similar situation will arise for the UK balance of payments.
2 Assuming a zero balancing item in the statistics.
3 Together with an increase in the balancing item, suggesting that the current account surplus may be underestimated or the net outward direct and portfolio investment exaggerated.

Part IV

Financial institutions and markets

Borrowers and lenders, the users of the financial system, depend upon the facilities and services provided by financial institutions and markets. The business of the main categories of institution, the nature and organization of the markets, and the factors which govern their behaviour in the UK form the subject matter of this part of the book.

Chapter 11 deals with the *banks and building societies*, the deposit-taking institutions. Banks include wide-ranging organizations whose diverse activities extend into virtually all aspects of the financial system, abroad as well as in the UK. Building societies are still much more highly specialized, confining their lending largely to the personal sector and predominantly still in the form of mortgages on owner-occupied housing, though their sources of funding have been extended to include the wholesale deposit and bond markets. In most of their business banks and building societies face keen competition, and we begin by examining the factors that constrain their activities – their need for capital and liquidity – and their sources of income. We then look in more detail at their deposit and lending business, distinguishing between each of the retail, merchant, other British and overseas groups of banks and the building societies.

The *investing institutions* – the life assurance companies and pension funds, general insurance companies, investment and unit trusts – are discussed in chapter 12. These institutions play a very significant part in the saving/investment process in Britain. They are all involved in fund management, and the life assurance and pension funds provide the main channels through which long-term saving flows into the capital market. The system of pension provision is the prime determinant of saving through life assurance and pension funds, and this and other factors influencing the flows of funds are considered. The types of business undertaken and the nature of their liabilities have a strong influence on the investing institutions' asset choices, and this in turn has implications for the working of the UK securities markets and the supply of finance in the economy.

Within the financial system a number of functions are carried out by *specialized financial institutions*, of which the finance houses and their leasing company subsidiaries are the most important. Specialized institutions are discussed in chapter 13, including also the venture capital companies which specialize in high-risk investments, factoring and invoice discounting companies serving small and medium-sized enterprises, and centralized mortgage lenders.

Practically all of the institutions make use of the organized *financial markets* to a greater or lesser extent. These are discussed in chapter 14. To begin with we outline the 'origination', 'market making' and 'distribution' functions of participants, and focus on alternative systems of market making. We then look briefly at the organization of the international securities market, before considering the workings of the securities markets in the UK in more detail. The sterling money markets and foreign exchange markets follow, and the chapter ends with a discussion of the markets in financial derivatives.

11

Banks and building societies

Of all the financial activities in an economy, one is fundamental to the working of the economic system – the provision of payments facilities. Without an adequate payments mechanism business in a modern economy could not be conducted as it is today. This key function has traditionally been carried out by banks, who provide a distribution network for the supply of cash and make both domestic and international payments on their customers' behalf. It is not something that happens automatically, and it is an activity which has been subject to rapid technological development involving heavy investment in cash machines, cheque handling equipment, and domestic and international communications networks. For the main clearing banks the provision of these facilities accounts for a substantial proportion of both capital and personnel costs.

If the provision of the payments mechanism is central to the financial system, so too are the taking of deposits and making of loans. The continual turnover of deposits and loans makes an essential contribution to economic activity. Economic agents' deposits rise or fall in the course of their ordinary business – one person reduces his deposits when he makes a payment, another adds to his when he receives it. There is an ongoing flow of new lending matched by the repayment of old – a first-time purchaser buys a house with a building society loan, and more likely than not the seller uses part of the proceeds to repay an outstanding loan. Any interruption to this process would cause significant damage to the economy.

Together with the building societies the banks are the main deposit-taking institutions and principal suppliers of loan finance in the economy. Deposits come in a variety of forms, the key characteristics being their availability to make payments, their term (i.e. the time which must elapse before they are automatically repaid or notice which must be given before they are repaid without penalty), and the rate of interest paid to the depositor. Loans are made to all kinds of borrowers and over a wide range of maturities, from the 30-year house purchase loan, through export credits and medium-term project finance, to the traditional overdraft which is technically repayable on demand but may in practice provide a more or less permanent source of working capital.

Allied to these activities, banks provide a great variety of other financial services. They have the expertise to facilitate international trade and investment; they provide sophisticated cash-management services to help customers to minimize their borrowing or maximize their interest-earning deposits; they provide 'treasury' products to enable customers to hedge foreign exchange and interest rate risks; they provide leasing and factoring facilities, usually through specialized subsidiaries, the latter enabling customers to subcontract the task of collecting payments which are due to them as well as receiving funds in advance of the customers actually paying; they advise on the raising of permanent capital, help to arrange mergers and acquisitions, and (again through subsidiaries) are involved in the supply of venture capital; and they sell investment products such as unit trusts and insurance policies and advise on investment management. Some banks (universal banks) do all of these, but most banks and all building societies specialize to a considerable extent, either in a narrower range of products or services or in the customer groups with whom they deal.

At the end of 1990 there were nearly 600 banks in Britain, belonging to about 500 separate banking groups. Under the 1987 Banking Act any institution[1] which takes deposits is regarded as a bank, and has to be authorized by the Bank of England after satisfying the Bank regarding its capital strength, standing, and the probity and competence of its management. Apart from a comparatively small number of universal banks and retail banks with branch networks, they include a large number of subsidiaries of foreign banks whose main interests centre on participation in the international financial markets, as well as finance houses specializing in providing instalment credit to both consumers and businesses, discount houses operating in the money markets, trade finance specialists and investment houses whose banking business is ancillary to investment management. At the same time there were about 100 building societies, whose principal business lies in providing mortgage finance to owner-occupiers, but who were becoming increasingly active in the provision of other personal financial services.

In this chapter we shall focus on the deposit-taking and lending activities of the banks and building societies, leaving specialist activities, whether carried out by the bank itself or through subsidiaries, for later chapters.

The role of capital

Like any other business, a bank or building society needs capital, and it needs capital for essentially the same reasons as other businesses – for premises, plant and equipment, investments in subsidiaries and associated companies, and for working capital. Thus, as in any other business, a bank's development is limited by its capital and by its ability to generate new capital by earning profits on its existing activities. Moreover, banks which are short of capital are faced with the usual choices: raise capital externally, release capital by selling subsidiaries or withdrawing from lines of business, or reduce the scale of core activities.

The distinctive feature about deposit-taking institutions is the amount of working capital required to support their balance sheets. We noted in chapter 4 how capital plays a key role in providing security for depositors – unanticipated loan losses are absorbed first by a bank's capital and only after this has been exhausted are depositors' funds at risk. The capital required for this purpose depends on the risk of loss inherent in a bank's asset portfolio,[2] but is usually large in relation to that needed for other purposes. Moreover, in the last resort capital used for other purposes, for example premises, may also be available to ensure that depositors do not lose their money.[3]

Banks' capital requirements are now governed by an international agreement, known as the Basle agreement, which stipulates the minimum level of capital in relation to assets which a bank may hold. The object behind the agreement was to ensure first that banks were properly capitalized, but secondly that banks competing in international markets did so on level terms; otherwise, banks from countries where capital ratios were low, but which enjoyed implicit government guarantees as to the security of deposits with them, would have had a competitive advantage. Essentially the same solvency regulations are incorporated in EC law.

Under these regulations banks have to hold capital amounting to at least 8 per cent of 'weighted risk assets'. Commercial loans have a weight of 1 (with the exception of mortgages on owner-occupied housing, which have a weight of 0.5) and other assets such as government securities and market loans have lower weights, the general principle being that government liabilities are regarded as less risky than private sector liabilities and that the risk attached to short-term liquid assets such as market loans is low. Account has to be taken of commitments to lend as well as of actual lending (because the commitments may lead to a loss in future) and of the risks inherent in dealing in the financial markets. Not all of the capital base needs to be equity, but at least 4 per cent must be, and the rest must be clearly subordinated to deposits in the event of the bank going into liquidation.

Attaching the same risk weight to all commercial loans is clearly a very broad-brush approach, whose principal merit is that it can be applied in practice without the need for detailed information or argument. But it is understood that the 8 per cent is a *minimum*, and it is open to the regulatory authorities in individual countries to set a higher standard where they believe it to be warranted by the nature of a particular bank's business or of its strength generally. In practice the Bank of England sets (varying) higher levels for the UK banks it supervises.

Banks normally aim to operate with capital ratios slightly higher than those set by the regulators. Large banks find it difficult to predict the exact level of their customers' demands for funds, as well as of their capital resources, and need a cushion to allow for this uncertainty. There is always the risk that profitability will fall short of expectations, or a bank may require some capital for other purposes and not wish to have its capital fully committed to supporting the balance sheet. When loan margins are narrow banks may choose to defer expanding their loan books until more favourable conditions emerge.

The relationship between capital and balance sheet size is crucial to an understanding of banking behaviour. Expanding the balance sheet by taking on more loans or buying assets is the easiest way for a bank to increase its profits in the short-run.[4] Excess capital in the banking system can therefore lead to a credit boom, with associated monetary expansion. When the banking system as a whole has excess capital banks compete strongly for lending business in an effort to expand their balance sheets, with the result that lending margins narrow. The credit expansion leads to rising asset prices (see chapter 5) and the banks are tempted to take on risky business (e.g. property loans where the developer provides little security) which in other circumstances they would not even contemplate. Rising profitability makes it easy for the banks to add to their capital bases. Even banks without spare capital are caught up in the process because, with margins on high-quality lending shrinking, they have to expand in order to maintain their profits. The end-result is monetary and credit expansion which may be extremely difficult for the authorities to control.

On the other tack, loan losses which erode the banks' capital bases may lead to a sharp curtailment of the supply of credit. It is not usually easy for banks to supplement capital from external sources in these conditions, and there is little alternative to balance sheet contraction. Lending margins increase, and the relatively risky borrowers are squeezed out. The fear that a 'credit crunch' of this kind was developing in the USA in 1990 and 1991 led the monetary authorities to ease monetary conditions in an effort to offset the contractionary forces.

Similar considerations apply to the capital needs of building societies, for whom the regulatory framework is derived from the Building Societies Act 1986. The minimum capital support required by a building society is calculated as the sum of elements reflecting the different classes of asset in its portfolio. Thus the capital support for mortgage lending varies from 1 to 6 per cent, depending on the nature of the loan, with a surcharge if payments are more than six months in arrears. Liquid assets with a term to maturity of less than a year require support of 1 or 2 per cent, while non-mortgage commercial lending (e.g. consumer credit) carries a capital requirement of 10–20 per cent, and fixed assets such as premises carry 50 per cent. There are additional requirements for small societies – 1 per cent for societies with assets up to £25 million and 0.5 per cent between £25 and £50 million. Building societies are also expected to maintain the level of their free capital[5] to total liabilities ratio – in 1989 for the large societies these ranged upwards from about 2.7 per cent for Nationwide Anglia and 3 per cent for Halifax, the two largest societies.

These capital requirements are in some respects more stringent and in other respects less stringent than those applied to banks. For mortgage lending to owner-occupiers banks require a minimum capital support of 4 per cent,[6] compared with only 1 per cent for building societies. For liquid assets the ratios do not differ greatly, but for non-mortgage lending the ratio applied to building societies is on average higher than the ratio for banks. Moreover, premises are given a specially high weight for building societies – in effect only half of their value can be used to support lending business – whereas for the banks they are treated on all fours with loans.

Differences of this kind have implications for competition between banks and building societies. They appear to leave the building societies with a competitive advantage in the mortgage market. On the other hand, the treatment of premises (and other restrictions on non-mortgage business) makes it more difficult for building societies to expand rapidly in other areas.[7] This could prove restrictive for building societies which wish to develop the scale of their non-mortgage consumer lending and other consumer financial services, and might contribute to a decision to convert to banking status.[8]

The role of liquidity

In chapter 4 we saw how financial institutions used liquidity in the maturity transformation process. By and large the maturity of a bank or building society's deposits is shorter than the maturity of its loans, so the banks and building societies have to be sure that they maintain sufficient liquidity in their balance sheets to be able to honour their obligations. For liquidity they rely both on the nature of the assets they hold and on their ability to supplement or replace liabilities in financial markets.

The liquidity of an asset derives both from its *maturity*, that is the time which must elapse before it is repaid by the borrower, and its *marketability*, that is the ease with which it can be sold for cash. The shorter the maturity and the greater the marketability the more liquid is the asset. In assessing an asset's liquidity it is the behavioural rather than the contractual characteristics which are important. Thus an overdraft, which is technically repayable on demand, is not regarded as a liquid asset because in practice repayment could not be expected without a considerable period of notice, and assets such as Treasury bills which are guaranteed to be convertible into cash, even in a crisis, are more liquid than market loans to banks or commercial bills which might have to be renewed.

The liquidity derived from the liability side of an institution's balance sheet depends on its ability to replace maturing liabilities or add to them at its discretion. Financial institutions normally fix a limit on the amount they are prepared to lend to other institutions, reflecting the size and standing of the institutions concerned. Such limits will be in place for institutions which borrow regularly in the market. In normal circumstances a bank whose borrowing falls well short of these limits will have scope to increase its borrowing if it wants to do so.[9] As noted in chapter 4, banks are also in a position to vary their need for liquidity by lengthening or shortening the maturity of their liabilities – the longer the maturity the less the need for liquidity elsewhere in their balance sheets.

Liquidity derived from the ability to issue liabilities is less certain than liquidity derived from assets. Borrowing depends on continued confidence in the institution concerned, and if a bank gets into difficulty lines of credit are liable to be cut just when they are most needed. Liquid assets – the liabilities of *other* institutions – are not subject to this drawback. Moreover, in a general financial crisis the market for bank liabilities could dry up, whereas cash would continue to be available for assets which were acceptable as security for borrowing from the Bank of England.

A bank's need for liquidity in normal circumstances depends on the volatility of its deposits and loans. The retail deposit base is generally rather stable after weekly, monthly and other seasonal factors have been taken into account. Balances held in chequing accounts depend on payments needs, notice accounts are very stable, and term deposits are often likely to be renewed if interest rates remain competitive. The trends are, of course, affected by competitive and other factors, but volatility about the trend is comparatively low. Substantial disturbances usually result from special events, such as the privatization of major companies, postal strikes etc. Retail loan demand is also fairly predictable, though the use of overdraft and credit card limits is at the individual's discretion, as often is the timing of other loans. Nevertheless, in normal circumstances there is a high degree of stability and predictability in retail business.

Banks which raise their funds in the wholesale markets and which make large lines of credit available to corporate borrowers face a different situation. Term deposits and market loans from individual lenders may or may not be renewed at maturity – for example, they may be needed in connection with a large tax payment or to purchase an overseas subsidiary. Lines of credit may be drawn upon (and others repaid) as a result of small movements in relative interest rates. Volatility can be relatively high, and in some circumstances be associated with a general shortage of funds in the market, making new deposits expensive to obtain. The need for liquidity is correspondingly high.

Nevertheless it is the risk of shocks, rather than the normal circumstances, which determine an institution's need for liquidity. Institutions need to hold enough liquidity to weather a short-term crisis. If the solvency of a bank is called in question, justifiably or not, corporate treasurers will shift their funds to safer homes and even the general public may queue up to withdraw their deposits.

With a little time, unjustified rumours can usually be laid to rest and most of the funds will return; but a bank with insufficient liquidity will not have the time to recover. It is not only the depositors who are protected by liquidity, it is the management and owners of the bank itself.

Most banks and building societies now have access to the wholesale markets, which means that their liquidity should be judged by reference to the structure of their balance sheets as a whole, but some still draw predominantly on retail deposits and expect to derive their liquidity from asset holdings. Regulatory concerns focus on asset holdings, with particular attention being paid to assets which would provide liquidity in a general financial crisis.

In Britain in 1988 the Bank of England published a consultative document suggesting that there should be a target ratio between liquid assets and deposits set for each UK bank, which that bank would be expected to maintain or exceed. Only short-term deposits would be taken into account, that is deposits (foreign currency as well as sterling) which were repayable on demand or in less than eight days, with account being taken also of loan commitments to be drawn down within this period. The target would be set by agreement with each bank and would lie in a range from 10 per cent to 25 per cent, reflecting the characteristics of the bank's business. For example, a bank with a stable retail deposit base would have a lower ratio than one which was dependent on more volatile wholesale deposits. The assets which would count as liquid for this purpose were divided into two tiers. The first tier, which included assets such as cash, Treasury bills, government securities with a maturity of 12 months or less, and secured loans to the discount market,[10] would be counted at full value. The second, with assets such as inter-bank loans of up to eight days maturity, government securities with maturities between one and five years, and other bank and building society certificates of deposit, were to be given a weight of 20 per cent of their full value. Banks would normally be expected to hold at least two-thirds of their stock of liquid assets in the form of tier-one sterling assets. Since liquidity was there to be used in abnormal circumstances, banks would be permitted to let their liquidity fall below the target level, but any shortfalls would have to be reported to the Bank of England.

These proposals were not acceptable to some of the banks (e.g. the finance houses) because they would have caused them to alter their portfolios significantly in ways which would have increased their costs and which did not seem to accord with the needs of their business. They were not, therefore, implemented. However, in regulating banks the Bank of England does take account of both the level of their liquid asset holdings in relation to their deposit liabilities and of their composition.

For building societies there are also no formal minimum liquidity holdings specified by regulation, but the Building Societies Commission, which is responsible for their supervision, discusses with individual societies the level and nature of their liquid asset holdings.

In addition to using liquidity as a buffer to absorb volatility in deposit and lending flows, and as a protection against shocks, banks and building societies may also consciously vary their liquidity in response to changes in the demand for and profitability of loans. If the demand for loans is weak and their capital base is adequate banks and building societies will choose to build up their liquid assets – better to earn a little on liquid assets than nothing. Only if the marginal cost of funds exceeds what can be earned on market loans does it make sense to contract the balance sheet. Later, when loan demand expands or lending margins rise, the loan book can be allowed to grow, with liquid assets returning to a normal level.

Sources of income

Banks and building societies have three sources of revenue: margins, position-taking, and fees and commissions. The margin is the difference between the interest earned on assets and the interest cost of funds.[11] For individual products, for example particular types of loans or deposits, the margin is normally measured as the difference between the rate of interest on the product and the bank's marginal cost of funds in the wholesale market. The contribution of margins to overall profitability is then made up of the margin on deposits plus the margin on loans. The relationship between lending margins, transactions costs and default risk was discussed in chapter 5. Margins on both deposits and loans are affected by the strength of competition in the respective markets.

Banks and building societies also derive profits from position-taking, that is successfully taking a view on the likely course of interest rates.[12] For example, if they take deposits whose interest rates are altered in line with market rates every month but make loans at rates of interest which are fixed for three years, they stand to gain if interest rates fall during the currency of the loan and to lose if interest rates rise. Since long-term rates are generally higher than the average of the expected short-term rates over the relevant period, it should on average be profitable to fix the rate of interest on loans for periods longer than those which apply to deposits. But position-taking always involves a risk – interest rates may rise when they had been expected to fall – so banks and building societies normally impose strict limits on the extent to which they leave themselves exposed to interest rate movement. Thus, for example, so-called 'fixed rate' mortgages from banks and building societies normally have the rate fixed for a maximum of three years because, in the absence of deposits with interest rates fixed for similar terms, long-term fixed-rate lending would carry too much interest rate risk.[13]

The third important source of income is fees and commissions. Fees may be charged in connection with payments transactions, there are arrangement fees for loans, advisory fees for capital markets business, fees for providing credit cards, fees for safe custody services, and so on. Commissions are earned on business introduced to others (including subsidiaries of the bank concerned), such as insurance business in connection with house purchase loans, securities transactions and sales of unit trusts. As competition has eroded margins on deposit-taking and lending business, fee and commission income has assumed increasing importance.

In managing their business banks and building societies have to be aware of all these sources of revenue. The profitability of a single product, such as trade finance, depends on both fees and the margin earned on any lending. Again, the revenue derived from any category of customer is a mixture of fees and of deposit and lending margins. The revenue of a building society branch comes from its deposits, its loans, and the commissions on insurance and other business it arranges. For the bank and building society as a whole the totality of deposit-taking and lending business may also provide the opportunity to profit from position-taking.

Competition in banking

With so many players involved, and in the absence of regulations restricting entry to particular lines of business, it is not surprising to find that competition in banking is generally keen. This has been true for many years in regard to the business of large corporate customers, and led in the 1980s to a narrowing of margins on lending business. As subsequent events, with banks experiencing severe losses on their domestic loan books, have shown these margins no longer compensated them adequately for the risks involved. The novel feature of the 1980s was the extension of intense competition into retail banking. For example, banks and building societies both now compete actively in the mortgage market, and the building societies' activities now extend into most aspects of retail banking, including the payments system. TSB, which in 1980 was essentially a savings bank, evolved into a powerful competitor engaged in a wide range of retail and corporate business, and Abbey National was transformed from a building society into a retail bank. Banks are also in competition with other providers of financial services, such as insurance and unit trust companies, in the retail market.

This upsurge in competition was driven partly by technology and partly by deregulation which enabled banks and other institutions, particularly building societies, to enter activities which had previously been closed to them. Technological developments in banking have altered the balance between the fixed and variable costs associated with banks' activities and have intensified competition for market share.

Three examples illustrate this phenomenon. First, the variable cost of withdrawing cash from a machine is much less than the cost of having it counted out and handed over by a teller, but the capital cost of providing machines is high. Whether they are worthwhile depends therefore on the volume of business, and once the break-even level of business has been reached the additional cost of extra transactions is low. Thus institutions which can secure enough business to warrant the provision of cash machines can increase their business at low marginal cost. The same goes for electronic payments systems such as SWITCH. They cost millions of pounds to develop and set up, but once in being the marginal cost of transactions is perhaps only 5 per cent of the cost of processing cheque payments by traditional means. To realize the economies of scale a large market share is needed.

The application of information technology to marketing has had a similar effect. It has cut the cost of selling financial products to customers (e.g. house purchase loans, car loans, insurance, new types of deposit). Instead of waiting for customers to come into a branch and take the initiative in enquiring about these products banks can now process the information they possess about their customers and their financial affairs and market their products to those customers who are most likely to be interested. Again, the systems required are costly, giving rise to economies of scope as well as economies of scale. Once the information is available it makes sense to use it to sell a wide range of products – narrow product specialists are at a disadvantage.

Credit assessment of retail borrowers is a third area in which technology has cut costs and placed a premium on market share. Most retail credit is now granted on the basis of a 'score', calculated from objective information provided by the customer. The credit is granted if the score exceeds some critical level, with the scoring model generated by past lending experience. Clearly a large number of loans is needed to provide the relevant information, but once the system is in place the marginal cost of assessing additional customers is relatively low. The information still has to be verified, but this is certainly much cheaper than the cost of investigating in some depth the circumstances of individual potential customers. Once more there is a premium on market share.

If technology has driven banks to seek to expand their market shares and extend the range of products supplied to their customers, deregulation has permitted them to do so. Until the early 1980s banks in Britain were discouraged from providing mortgage finance, leaving the building societies with a protected market. Building societies for their part were not permitted to lend for other purposes. Nevertheless, strong demand for mortgage finance, together with a regulatory system which discouraged price competition amongst building societies, enabled the societies to pay rates for deposits well above those offered by the banks, whilst at the same time earning a substantial margin on their business and expanding their branch activities rapidly. These margins were eroded by the entry of the banks into the mortgage business and by a gradual move to the payment of more competitive interest rates by the banks. As one-product companies with a restricted source of funding the societies would have been at a competitive disadvantage, so they in turn were given access to the wholesale market for funds and permitted to engage in some other forms of banking business. The result has been an across-the-board intensification of competition.

Banks and building societies sector

To examine the relationships of banks and building societies with the other sectors of the economy we must consolidate the figures for individual institutions to eliminate intra-sector assets and liabilities. The result for the end of 1989 is revealed in table 11.1, which shows the sector distribution of the banks' and building societies' deposits and loans. At that time other sectors held deposits amounting to

Table 11.1 Sector distribution of bank and building society deposits and lending, end-1989

| | Sterling | | | | | | Foreign currency | Total |
| | Domestic | | | | Overseas | Total | | (£ billion) |
	Public	OFI	I & C companies	Personal				
Deposits	12	59	66	284	74	495	585	1080
Lending	21	69	125	310	45	569	602	1171
Net deposits (+) or lending (−)	−8	−9	−59	−26	29	−74	−18	−91

Source: Financial Statistics, February 1991, tables 6.1, 6.2, 6.8, 6.9 (partly estimated)

£1080 billion (more than double the level of GDP in 1989) and had borrowed through loans or securities over £1170 billion from these institutions. The excess of lending over deposits is an indication of the capital resources which banks and building societies employed to support their lending. Over half of the deposits were in foreign currency, with sterling deposits falling just short of £500 billion. Sterling loans exceeded sterling deposits by a margin of 15 per cent, while the margin was much smaller in the case of foreign currency loans.

In the UK the public sector is neither a large depositor with the banks and building societies nor a large borrower from them, although overall it is a net borrower. For reasons already discussed in chapter 9, public sector borrowing from banks and building societies was declining in the second half of the 1980s. However, since public sector liabilities play an important part in the first tier of liquidity the central government is likely to continue to borrow significant amounts through Treasury bills and short-dated gilt-edged stocks.

Other financial institutions make considerable use of the banks' and building societies' deposit-taking and lending facilities, with both growing rapidly in the second half of the eighties; overall they too are net borrowers. Lending to leasing companies is one element which has increased, to account for over 20 per cent of total sterling lending to the other financial institutions sector in 1989, but much of the growth has reflected business with securities dealers and the 'other financial' group.

As is to be expected, industrial and commercial companies were substantial net borrowers from the banks, with the amount trebling in the five years up to the end of 1989 – a reflection of the credit boom and the company sector's large financial deficit towards the end of this period. To find that the personal sector was also a net borrower is, however, more surprising, because in most countries one of the functions of the deposit-taking institutions is to channel surplus household saving to other sectors. Until 1986 that was the case in the UK too, but very heavy personal borrowing in later years caused the normal position to be reversed.[14] Over half of both sterling deposits and lending involve the personal sector.

The overseas sector appears as a net supplier of sterling funds through the banking system, the implication being that part of the banks' domestic sterling lending is funded by borrowing sterling deposits overseas. This was not a new phenomenon, but its extent was rising rapidly towards the end of the eighties (see chapter 10). The overseas sector also accounts for the lion's share of the foreign currency deposits and lending – over 90 per cent of the deposits and over 85 per cent of the lending – reflecting London's position as an international financial centre. There was, however, also a net transfer of foreign currency from the overseas to the domestic sectors (largely industrial and commercial companies, but also other financial institutions). Some of this will have been connected with overseas and international financial markets business, but it is also likely that some foreign currency loans were swapped into sterling for use in the UK.

Balance sheet structures of banks and building societies

In examining the balance sheet structures of any individual bank or group of banks, account has to be taken of deposits with and claims on other banks, since these deposits are an important source of resources for some banks and play a significant part in the liquidity of the banking system. Table 11.2 shows the *sterling* liabilities and assets of UK banks at the end of 1989. Total sterling liabilities amounted to £537 billion, with assets slightly greater at £542 billion,

Table 11.2 Banks in the UK: sterling assets and liabilities, December 1989

			(£ billion)
Liabilities		**Assets**	
Notes and deposits		Cash, market loans and bills[1,2]	154
Sight deposits and notes	158	Advances	335
Time deposits	271		
Certificates of deposit	43	Investments	
		Public sector investments[3]	7
Items in suspense and transmission	10	Other	19
Capital and other funds	56	Items in suspense and collection	15
		Other miscellaneous assets	11
Total sterling liabilities	537	Total sterling assets	542

Source: Financial Statistics, February 1991, table 6.4
[1] Notes and coin, balances with the Bank of England, market loans, bills.
[2] Of which loans to other banks, and UK banks' certificates of deposit, £97 billion.
[3] Including Banking Department lending to central government (net)

reflecting the fact that some sterling lending was funded by foreign currency liabilities.[15]

Sight deposits and notes[16] made up almost exactly a third of total deposits, with time deposits (which may be very short-term) comprising nearly 60 per cent and certificates of deposit (9 per cent) making up the balance; these are marketable instruments and consequently more liquid than deposits of an equivalent term, which makes them attractive to potential depositors. Items in suspense accounts and in transmission are mainly a result of the payments system – for example bank giro credits which have been debited to the payer's account but not yet credited to the payee's.[17] Capital and other funds amounted to just over 10 per cent of the total.

Banks held nearly 30 per cent of their assets in a highly liquid form – cash, market loans and bills – and of this about 5 per cent of total assets came in the first tier of liquidity. Some of the public sector investments, namely gilt-edged securities with less than 12 months to maturity, would also come in this category. However, inter-bank lending amounted to nearly £100 billion, approaching 20 per cent of total assets. Advances accounted for over 60 per cent of total assets, to which must be added a further sum for non-public sector securities, making 65 per cent in all. The latter have been affected by a trend towards securitization of loans. There are some banks which have customer relationships sufficient to enable them to make more loans than their capital can easily support, while others have the capital but not the contacts to be able to add to their loan books. Securitization enables the former to satisfy their customers and retain any fees and some of the margin, whilst the latter are able to acquire assets which are more profitable to them than market loans or other liquid assets. Items in suspense and collection arise mainly from the time which elapses before a cheque which has been credited to a depositor's account is debited to the payee's.

The composition of the banks' sterling loans and acceptances at the end of November 1989 is shown in table 11.3. Lending for primary production – agriculture etc., energy and water supply – accounted for under 3 per cent of the total, while at 10 per cent manufacturing also seems comparatively low. (Manufacturing made up 22 per cent of GDP in 1989.) However, the low figure is misleading, because over a third of bank lending went direct to the personal sector, and lending to the financial sector included finance for leasing to manufacturing companies. Making the necessary adjustments raises manufacturing's share of lending for industrial and commercial activity to over 18 per cent – still less than its share

Table 11.3   Bank sterling lending to UK residents, November 1989

	£ billion	Per cent
Agriculture, energy and water supply	8.9	2.7
Manufacturing	35.2	10.5
Construction	13.7	4.1
Financial services	64.0	19.1
Property companies	30.0	9.0
All other services	66.0	19.8
Persons		
House purchase	78.1	23.4
Other	38.2	11.4
Total	334.1	100.0

Source: Bank of England, *Analysis of bank lending to UK residents, November 1989–November 1990*

of GDP, but not by very much. In contrast, lending to property and construction companies absorbed 13 per cent of the total, reflecting the very high level of property development activity at the time. Financial services took nearly 20 per cent (of which leasing was over 4 per cent) and all other services also 20 per cent. Within the lending to the personal sector, two-thirds was mortgage lending, at least ostensibly for house purchase, and one-third was other lending – overdrafts, personal loans, and credit card credit.

Table 11.4 shows the balance sheet structures of the various categories of bank and of the building societies at the end of 1989. In terms of their aggregate balance sheet size (£391 billion) and their importance in the economy the retail banks are much the most significant. They include almost all the banks with extensive branch networks in the UK – for example, Barclays, National Westminster, Bank of Scotland, Northern Bank and Abbey National. At the end of 1990 banks from 14 distinct groups were included in this category. Though they share some common characteristics they are, of course, by no means uniform in their size or in the range of their business. Some – for example, Barclays and National Westminster – are universal banks operating on an international scale, whilst others – for example Abbey National – concentrate mainly on retail business in the UK. The retail banks were responsible for 63 per cent of total bank sterling lending to UK residents in November 1989, of which nearly half was lending to the personal sector. They accounted for 90 per cent of the lending for house purchase and 75 per cent of other lending to the personal sector.

Table 11.4   Banks and building societies: balance sheets, end-1989

	Retail banks	British merchant banks	Other British banks	Overseas banks	(Per cent) Building societies
Liabilities					
Sterling deposits and notes					
UK non-banks	52	29	27	5	75[1]
Other	16	28	37	14	14[2]
Foreign currency deposits	16	30	18	79	1[3]
Other liabilities	15	14	18	3	10
Total liabilities	100	100	100	100	100
Assets					
Sterling					
Cash, market loans and bills	16	34	20	8	13
Advances					
UK non-banks	53	22	53	10	82
Other	1	2	—	1	—
Investments					
Gilt-edged stocks	1	—	1	—	2
Other	2	4	3	1	1
Total sterling	74	63	77	20	98
Foreign currency					
Market loans, advances and investments	20	33	20	80	—
Sterling and foreign currency					
Miscellaneous assets	6	4	3	1	2
Total assets	100	100	100	100	100
Total assets (£ billion)	391	59	54	729	190

Sources: Bank of England Quarterly Bulletin, February 1991, tables 3.1–3.7; *Financial Statistics*, tables 6.8, 6.9
[1] Retail shares and deposits
[2] Sterling wholesale liabilities
[3] Foreign wholesale liabilities

Sterling deposits accounted for over two-thirds of total liabilities, with foreign currency deposits only a sixth. Within sterling deposits 52 per cent of total liabilities were deposits by UK non-banks, from overseas or were certificates of deposit (whose holders cannot be identified). Cash, sterling market loans and bills made up a sixth of total assets, and advances to UK non-banks accounted for over half. Foreign currency assets were only 20 per cent of the total. The preponderance of sterling assets and liabilities reflects the size of their domestic business, whilst the relatively low level of liquidity is warranted by the size and stability of their retail deposit base.

The British merchant banks comprise banks which are British-owned and whose business is primarily concerned with corporate finance and mergers. At the end of 1990 there were 26 distinct groups, including banks such as Barclays de Zoete Wedd, Baring Brothers, Samuel Montagu, and S. G. Warburg. In their deposit-taking and lending business they focus less heavily on domestic business than the retail banks and they are much more dependent on the wholesale markets for deposits. Their balance sheet total (end-1989) was £59 billion, some 15 per cent of that of the retail banks. In view of the nature of their operations their profits depend at least as much on fee income as on the margins earned on their deposit-taking and lending business.

Sterling deposits accounted for 57 per cent of total liabilities, divided equally between deposits from UK non-banks and others, with other UK banks providing a third of total sterling deposits. Foreign currency deposits made up 30 per cent of total liabilities. The composition of their deposit base was reflected in a high level of liquid assets, at 34 per cent more than double the level held by the retail banks. Sterling assets and investments accounted for under 30 per cent of total assets, with foreign currency lending comprising most of the rest. In November 1989 nearly 90 per cent of their lending to UK residents was in sterling, but in total it amounted to only 7 per cent of that of the retail banks.

All other British-controlled banks are classified to the rather heterogeneous 'other British banks' group. They include international banks such as Standard Chartered, finance houses such as Forward Trust and Lloyds Bowmaker, development capital companies such as 3i, small banks associated with investment houses such as Foreign and Colonial Management and Scottish Amicable Money Managers, as well as a large number of small finance companies. At the end of 1990 there were about 150 banks in this category; the end-1989 balance sheet total was about £54 billion.

With such a varied group it is not easy to interpret the aggregate balance sheet in table 11.4. Nearly 80 per cent of their business (and over 90 per cent of lending to UK residents) was in sterling, and within sterling advances about 80 per cent consisted of consumer and other instalment lending to the personal sector and to companies (as well as some associated loans, such as stocking loans to motor dealers) by finance house and other specialist grantors of consumer credit. The largest finance houses are subsidiaries of major retail banks, and obtain their finance in the wholesale markets. At the end of 1989 deposits from other UK banks (which includes short-term loans from their parents) made up 40 per cent of sterling deposits. Sterling deposits from UK non-banks accounted for only a little over a quarter of total liabilities, and most of the foreign currency deposits were from overseas. Sterling liquidity accounted for 20 per cent of total assets, but 70 per cent of foreign currency assets took the form of market loans.

The overseas banks form the largest group, nearly 350 in all, with an end-1989 balance sheet total of £729 billion. Of this the American banks accounted for £119 billion and the Japanese for £282 billion.

The overseas banks' emphasis on international financial markets emerges clearly from the balance sheet, with foreign currency deposits and loans accounting for some 80 per cent of the total. Sterling deposits from non-banks made up only 5 per cent, with other sterling deposits from UK banks, overseas, and certificates of deposit adding another 14 per cent. Sterling advances to UK non-banks were twice the level of the corresponding deposits, demonstrating a degree of dependence on professional market funding for customer lending. This dependence was also reflected in a high level of sterling liquidity – only 8 per cent of total assets but over 40 per cent of sterling deposits.

The overseas banks were responsible for 23 per cent of sterling and 80 per cent of foreign currency lending to UK residents. They were particularly heavily involved in lending to the oil and natural gas companies, providing two-thirds of total bank lending to this sector, to the financial sector (60 per cent overall and 90 per cent of lending to securities companies), and to property companies. Most of the lending to property companies was in sterling, and the overseas banks' lending amounted to over 40 per cent of total bank lending to the sector, illustrating the important part played by the overseas banks in financing the property boom. Some overseas banks also had a significant involvement in personal sector lending, which accounted for 10 per cent of their total sterling advances.

Next to the retail banks, the building societies are the most important group of deposit-taking institutions dealing with the personal sector. Their balance sheet total at the end of 1989 was £190 billion, and their personal sector deposits fell only just short of those of the banks, whose share had been boosted by the conversion of Abbey National from a building society to a bank earlier that year. With mortgages outstanding nearly twice the level of those of the banks, the building societies were still dominant in the provision of housing finance, but they had begun to undertake other personal lending as well as providing payments services. At the beginning of the 1980s there had been about 250 building societies, but under the pressure of competition this was reduced to just over 100 by the end of the decade. The five largest societies accounted for over half of the total assets, with the largest, Halifax, itself responsible for over 20 per cent.

At the end of 1989 nearly 90 per cent of total liabilities consisted of sterling retail shares and deposits and liabilities issued in the wholesale markets. The retail element was the traditional source of funds, and made up five-sixths of the whole, but non-traditional borrowing through wholesale markets had contributed the other sixth (table 11.5). This wholesale market borrowing involved a variety of financial instruments – deposits, commercial paper, certificates of deposit, other bank borrowing and building society bonds (including some foreign currency bonds swapped into sterling) issued in the international bond market.

Table 11.5 Building societies: selected liabilities, level end-1989 and increase 1985–89

	1985–89 increase	(%)	*(£ billion)* 1989 level	(%)
Retail shares and deposits	78.1	(65)	143	(75)
Wholesale liabilities				
Certificates of deposit	4.8	(4)	6	(3)
Deposits and commercial paper	9.5	(8)	10	(5)
Bank borrowing	1.7	(1)	2	(1)
Bonds	10.9	(9)	10	(5)
Total	26.9	(22)	28	(15)
Other	14.9	(12)	19	(10)
Total	120.0	(100)	190	(100)

Source: Financial Statistics, February 1991, table 6.8

During the second half of the eighties building societies had encountered much stronger competition from the banks in the retail deposit market. At the same time they were under pressure to meet the very buoyant demand for mortgage finance and had turned to the wholesale markets to raise the necessary funds; the regulations which had impeded access to these funds previously were eased progressively to enable them to do so. As a result, in the five years 1985–9 about a quarter of the increase in their external funding was obtained through the wholesale markets.

In comparison with the banks, at 13 per cent of total assets (table 11.4), the liquid asset holdings of the building societies were not high. The bulk now consists of deposits with the banks, holdings of gilt-edged securities having been run down in the second half of the eighties (thanks to a tax change which made them less attractive). The stability of the retail deposit base provides some justification for the overall level, but holdings of assets which would count in the first tier of liquidity for banks were significantly less than retail banks engaged in similar business would have needed.

Table 11.6 Building societies: commercial assets, level end-1989 and increase 1985–89

			(£ billion)	
	Change	*(%)*	*Level*	*(%)*
Commercial assets				
Class 1	22.4	(85)	149.8	(96)
Class 2	2.6	(10)	4.6	(3)
Class 3	1.4	(5)	1.8	(1)
Total	26.5	(100)	156.2	(100)

Source: Financial Statistics, February 1991, table 6.9

At the end of 1989 over 80 per cent of building societies' assets consisted of advances to the private sector, predominantly first mortgages on owner-occupied houses (class 1 assets in table 11.6). But other lending was becoming increasingly important, and represented 15 per cent of the increase in assets in 1989. Class 2 lending includes lending to companies (usually house-builders) and housing associations which is secured on land, while class 3 is other lending including consumer credit. Building societies are not permitted to hold more than 10 per cent of their assets in class 2 and 5 per cent in class 3.

It seems likely that commercial pressures will compel the building societies to continue to broaden the range of services they provide to the personal sector. As a result the number of small societies will decline further, and the differences between the business of the larger societies and the personal banking activities of the retail banks will diminish. The limits on class 2 and class 3 lending by building societies may soon restrict their freedom to compete and propel them towards seeking banking status. Moreover, the differing regulatory requirements regarding capital and differing practices regarding liquidity are liable to become a cause of increasing tension. Pressure for a common set of rules, which permits all the institutions to compete on level terms, seems likely to grow.

Notes

1 Other than a building society or credit union.
2 It also depends on the risk of failure by the banks which is tolerable. The larger the capital support for any asset portfolio the lower the risk of outright failure.
3 Capital invested in subsidiaries is not regarded as being available for this purpose.
4 Though the risks taken on in the process may lead to losses later.
5 Reserves, general bad debt provisions (i.e. provisions not allocated to individual loans from which known losses are expected) and designated external capital which ranks below building society shares and deposits in the event of a liquidation, less fixed assets.
6 With a risk-asset weight of 0.5 per cent and a capital adequacy ratio at the minimum level of 8 per cent.
7 This is not just an unintended side-effect – the relatively high weight on non-mortgage lending was designed to encourage building societies to enter this activity cautiously, in the hope that they would not get their fingers burned.
8 Following the lead of Abbey National in 1989.
9 Building societies are subject to additional regulatory limits on the extent of their borrowing in wholesale markets.
10 See chapter 14.
11 Banks also earn margins on foreign exchange business, namely the difference between the exchange rates employed in dealing with customers and the exchange rates at which the bank itself deals in the wholesale foreign exchange markets.
12 Or of exchange rates in the foreign exchange market.
13 Note that the maturity for *repricing* of interest rates is quite distinct from the maturity for *liquidity* purposes. A three-year loan whose interest rate is altered at three-monthly intervals is matched by similar three-month deposits for interest rate repricing purposes but by three-year deposits for liquidity purposes.
14 The trend towards endowment mortgages also played a part. With repayment mortgages the bank or building society lender receives repayments of capital by instalments during the currency of the loan,

whereas with an endowment mortgage the capital repayments are held by a life assurance company until the policy matures or is surrendered.
15 This does not necessarily mean that the banks were exposed to exchange rate risk, because the position may have been hedged in the foreign exchange market.
16 The Scottish banks issue their own notes but are obliged to maintain matching holdings of Bank of England notes in their asset portfolios.
17 The figures in table 11.1 have been adjusted to eliminate these items.

12

Investing institutions

The *investing institutions* facilitate long-term saving, provide funds for long-term investment in the property and capital markets, and manage existing asset portfolios. Their common characteristic is their involvement in fund management – funds which may be derived from investment in a variety of financial instruments such as life assurance contracts, pension arrangements, and investment and unit trusts, which may result from general insurance business, or which may be entrusted to them by private individuals or charities. The fund managers may be found in insurance companies, self-administered pension funds, stockbrokers, or independent fund management groups. The historical divisions into specialist life assurance companies, specialist pension fund managers, specialist investment trust managers, and so on, has now given way to overlapping fund management activities, and all the major groups now provide fund management services to more than one type of client. Thus the major independent fund managers commonly manage funds for investment trusts, unit trusts, pension funds, charities and private clients, while the insurance companies usually provide special funds for pension schemes and often engage in unit trust business. The funds controlled by the largest groups are substantial with several, such as Prudential and Standard Life amongst the insurance companies and Mercury Asset Management and Robert Fleming Holdings amongst the fund managers, having more than £15 billion under management.

No figures for the total funds under management are available, but table 12.1 shows the most important categories of institutional funds in the UK. At the end of 1989 the life assurance companies' and pension funds' asset portfolios amounted to nearly £500 billion, general insurance companies held about £40 billion, and the unit and investment trusts £57 billion and £24 billion respectively. There

Table 12.1 Investing institutions: assets and net inflows, 1989

	Assets (end-year)	(£ billion) Net inflow
Life insurance and pension funds	498	28
General insurance funds	40	2
Unit trusts[1]	57	4
Investment trusts[1]	24	—

Source: Financial Statistics, various editions
[1] Includes holdings by other funds

is, however, an element of overlap, in that unit and investment trusts are held by other institutional investors – probably to the tune of nearly £50 billion at the end of 1989.

Active fund management plays an important part in the financial system. Fund managers seeking to maximize the return on asset portfolios (subject to constraints reflecting the nature of their liabilities) direct resources to where the return is expected to be highest. As a result, the managers of firms with good growth prospects, enjoying high share prices, find it relatively cheap to raise new equity capital, while those with poor prospects find it more expensive. This helps to direct investment in the economy into the most profitable channels.

This, in essence, is the role of an efficient capital market, on which more will be said later. Of greater concern here is the role of the investing institutions in encouraging and facilitating saving on the one hand, and in providing funds for *risky* investment on the other. The key players are the life assurance and pension funds, each with nearly £250 billion of assets under management, and with a net inflow of new funds adding up to £28 billion in 1989. Pension arrangements and life assurance policies connected with house purchase, are much the most important vehicles for contractual saving in the economy. By comparison the net inflow to the capital market from general insurance companies was only £2 billion. In 1989 the £4 billion shown for unit trusts was not in fact an additional contribution to saving at all, because these units were taken up by life assurance companies on behalf of their policyholders, and the contribution from investment trusts was negligible.

The fundamental principle governing the operation of fund managers is that of matching – the nature of the assets they hold for each fund reflects the characteristics of their liabilities. Thus the majority of the liabilities of life assurance and pension funds do not fall due for many years, and are therefore properly matched by long-term assets. Again, the majority of life assurance and pension fund liabilities are not fixed in money terms but are linked to real incomes or to the performance of ordinary shares, so these institutions have a strong demand for ordinary shares in their portfolios. In contrast, the claims on general insurance funds are liable to arise much sooner, so general funds have a greater need for liquid assets in their portfolios, although they too invest a considerable part in long-term assets. Investors in investment trust shares or unit trusts expect their funds to be held largely in ordinary shares, often with a stipulated regional or sectoral bias, so the funds controlled by these institutions are employed mainly in the world's equity markets.

The great majority of investments are made by purchasing securities in the financial markets at home or abroad. Where the objectives for a fund permit it, the institutions take a view on the prospective returns to be earned from investments in different regions (e.g. UK, North America, Japan, Continental Europe), and adjust the balance of their portfolios accordingly.[1] Within each market particular shares have to be selected and, once selected, monitored. Fund managers are subjected to a continuous flood of analysis and recommendations from stockbrokers and other invest- ment advisers, and in each market they are always on the lookout for companies in whose shares they might hope to invest profitably or add to an existing holding, or where they would prefer to reduce their holding or sell it altogether. By holding a well diversified portfolio the institution can virtually eliminate the specific risk attached to the shares of individual companies, as well as part of the specific risk attached to particular markets.[2]

Many of the funds have several hundred distinct security holdings, whose values range from, say, £100 000 or even less in very small funds to tens of millions in large funds. They normally limit the maximum size of a holding by reference to the scale of the total portfolio – say 3 per cent – and the value of the company's share capital available in the market – say 2 per cent. Any larger holdings are treated as exceptional, requiring special justification. The larger the holding, both in absolute terms and as a proportion of the ordinary shares outstanding, the more difficult it becomes to dispose of it, should the institution wish to do so; the institutions set considerable store by the marketability of their assets. At the other end of the scale, few of the larger fund managements would seek to invest less than £2 million in a company (with the holding possibly spread amongst several funds) because deciding on acquisitions and sales and monitoring the performance of companies whose shares are held are time-consuming and costly activities.

The institutions do not have any preference for new issues (or rights issues) of securities over purchases of existing securities in the market, though a rights issue frequently presents them with a good opportunity to obtain a significant holding in a company or to acquire a large block of shares at one time without driving up the price. Otherwise the minimum size of holding which is of interest to the larger funds may be difficult to acquire, unless some other large institutions are willing sellers.

In normal circumstances the institutions do not seek to influence the policy or management of the companies whose shares they hold. However, large institutions do expect to be kept informed, and when the holding is abnormally large, or strategic in character, the institution will try to maintain particularly close contact with the company's management, extending in rare cases to representation on the company's board. The scope and scale of the institutions' holdings of assets have implications for the capital market, which we shall return to in chapter 13.

Life assurance and pension funds

Death is certain, but its timing is not. The essence of life assurance is that it provides some protection against the financial consequences of this unpredictability. Life assurance policies are designed to provide security for a policyholder's dependants or creditors in the event of his or her premature death; pension arrangements and annuities provide security for the policyholder in the event of unexpectedly long life. Of course the security has to be paid for. But the price reflects *average* experience, not that of each individual concerned. The premiums of policyholders who survive until a policy has matured help to pay for the unfortunate ones who die early, and the annuitants who die relatively young help to pay for those who live to a grand old age.

Nowadays, however, the life assurance companies are best viewed in the context of the personal savings market. They are competing for savings, and while the products they offer contain an element of insurance, other features may carry more weight with their potential customers. Thus the ability to save for retirement out of untaxed income, their investment record, the flexibility and convenience of their savings schemes are important, and it is their performance as portfolio managers rather than the security provided by life cover which is stressed in many of their products. In 1990 nearly half of the new annual premiums from individuals and over half of the single premiums were for policies whose values were linked to the performance of particular investment portfolios. Pension provision has also become increasingly important, stimulated by the tax provisions for personal pensions after the Social Security Act 1986.

Life assurance business can be divided into four broad categories; whole of life and endowment assurance, pension business, term assurance and annuities.

Whole-of-life and endowment policies constitute a form of saving with the added advantage of life cover. The premiums paid, less expenses, contribute to a fund which the insurance company manages, and build up over the term of the policy to provide a capital sum payable when it matures. With a whole-of-life policy the sum assured (or maturity value) is paid when the policyholder dies, but the policy may be surrendered earlier for its value at the time. With an endowment policy the maturity date is fixed, and the value of the policy is paid out at that time or on the policyholder's death if earlier. Again, surrender before the final maturity date is possible. Policies may be 'without profits', in which case the sum assured is fixed in advance, 'with profits' in which case a minimum sum is guaranteed but bonuses are added periodically reflecting the profitability of the insurance company concerned, or 'linked' in which case the payout reflects the performance of a particular investment portfolio managed by the insurance company. In many cases the companies have set up unit trust subsidiaries, for which they have provided in-house portfolio management, and have invested these linked funds in the relevant unit trusts.

Most endowment policies at present are taken out in connection with house purchase finance. Banks and building societies make loans on an interest-only basis; i.e. there are no capital repayments to the bank or building society while the loan is outstanding, and it is repaid in full when the property is sold or at the end of some fixed term (which can be as long as 30 years). The borrower takes out an endowment policy with a life assurance company for the same term, in order to build up a capital sum sufficient to repay the loan at that time (or earlier if he dies earlier). At present about 80 per cent of house purchase loans take this general form. The advantage for the borrower is that tax relief is available on the first £30 000 of borrowing for house purchase, and by deferring any loan repayments this tax-relieved borrowing can be kept at its maximum level.

Whole-of-life policies have become popular as a means of saving through 'linked' funds. As already noted, these policies can be surrendered at any time, for a value determined by the value of the fund into which the premiums have been paid. It is therefore a convenient form of saving, and the tax treatment of life assurance companies' income and expenses means that it is also tax-effective for some savers.

The pension business of life assurance companies can be divided between group business and individual business. The former consists of occupational pension schemes run for employers by the life companies. They are akin to the self-administered occupational pension schemes considered below. Until the 1986 Social Security Act these formed much the more important part of the life companies' pension business. Since that Act, however, individual pension business has grown rapidly, and in 1990 personal pensions accounted for nearly 40 per cent of life companies' new individual premium income.

Before the 1986 Act life offices had provided personal pension policies for the self-employed, under tax arrangements intended to be comparable with those available to members of occupational pension schemes. The 1986 Act extended these arrangements to employees, who thus became able to make contributions out of pre-tax income and accumulate income free of tax within the fund. The Act also gave employees the option of making their own pension arrangements rather than joining a company's pension scheme; employees who do so and contract out of the earnings-related element of the state scheme (see below) receive a temporary 'bounty' of 2 per cent of income towards their contributions. Opting out of company pension schemes may well be attractive to younger employees, particularly to those who expect to work for several employers during their careers.

The 1986 Act has thus given the life companies access to a new source of business, enhancing their importance as gatherers of savings in the financial system. By the spring of 1991 some four million people had taken out personal pensions. The life companies have also developed new products such as pension mortgages, in which the pension policy is used as a substitute for the endowment policy in more conventional arrangements – part of a personal pension may be converted into a lump sum at retirement, which can be used at that time to repay a mortgage loan.

Under a term insurance policy the life company pays benefits (a capital sum or an annuity) if the insured person dies within the specified period, but no benefit is paid if the person survives beyond the end of the term. These policies are often used in conjunction with conventional mortgage loans from banks or building societies, with the term insurance covering the element of capital still outstanding at any time during the currency of the loan. They may also be used in conjunction with endowment and pension mortgages where the loan outstanding may for many years exceed the guaranteed value of the endowment or pension policy. Other uses are to provide annuities while families are growing up, or to cover other costs which would arise if the insured person were to die suddenly.[3] This is classic life insurance with no element of saving involved, and since most people do survive to the end of the term the annual premiums are low relative to the sums assured.

Annuities provide the policyholder with a regular income for some defined period, usually the annuitant's remaining life, but often with a guarantee that a minimum number of payments will be made even if the annuitant dies earlier. They protect the annuitant from the financial consequences of undue longevity, and are often used in connection with personal pensions, where part of the capital sum accumulated at retirement *must* be used to purchase an annuity (not necessarily from the same company that issued the personal pensions policy), and in connection with inheritance tax planning. Annuities may be purchased either by payments of premiums over a period of years (which is effectively what happens with pensions policies) or by means of a single premium before the annuity starts. In any event the life assurance company accumulates and holds a capital fund, which is gradually run down as the annuity is paid.

The most important form of saving for retirement is still the occupational pension scheme, with some 15 million of the working population now covered. These schemes are run by employers for their workforces, with responsibility vested in trustees for each scheme. The larger schemes are usually self-administered (i.e. run by the employers concerned) but medium-sized and smaller schemes are insured with life companies and run by them. Occupational pension schemes involve the creation of a pension fund, and the task of managing the fund may be delegated by the scheme's trustees to independent fund managers – for whom it represents a very important source of business.

The pension funds are built up from contributions made by individuals and their employers during the employees' working lives. These contributions are invested and, with the earnings on the investments, accumulated until the employees retire. After retirement each employee is entitled to a regular pension, part of which may be commuted into a capital sum. In principle the pension, like an annuity, is paid out of the capital fund and the income derived from it. In practice, however, pension schemes normally contain both contributing and retired members, so that the pensions can be paid partly or wholly out of current contributions. In most schemes the contributions and benefits are treated as a whole, with no direct link between an individual's pension and the size of his own contributions. The most common practice is to calculate a person's pension by reference to his years of service and to his final wage or salary, while contributions are fixed as a percentage of the wage or salary earned. Since the contributions to occupational pension schemes are made out of pre-tax income and the return on the investments is free of both income tax and capital gains tax the schemes have to conform to certain Inland Revenue rules, which limit the benefits provided. Pensions now have to contain an element of index-linking for inflation, including a guarantee of uprating for inflation of up to 3 per cent in any year.

A life assurance company's asset portfolio reflects the nature of its liabilities. Annuities, guaranteeing fixed future payments, are best matched by fixed-interest securities. The same goes for term insurance and for non-linked whole-of-life policies. Non-linked with-profits policyholders enjoy a guaranteed minimum sum assured but are also looking for growth of value through bonus payments. This leads companies to hold a mixture of fixed interest securities, with an eye on the guarantee, and of equities and property, with an eye on growth. For linked business the appropriate portfolio is obviously that specified in the link – normally equities or property.

The long-term nature of a life company's liabilities creates a corresponding demand for long-term assets, including equities – companies are generally in a position to withstand any short-term reductions in market values. Moreover, while matching of assets and liabilities determines the portfolio composition which minimizes risk, companies are prepared to depart from this position when they expect by so doing to increase the return on their funds. Their investment performance, as reflected in the bonuses they have been able to pay in the past, has a crucial influence on their competitive position in the market for new business. Nevertheless, the minimum-risk portfolio continues to exert a considerable influence on their investment policies.

Similar considerations govern investment by pension funds. In this case their liabilities are not fixed in money terms – they are linked to final salaries up to the date of retirement, and partially or fully linked to inflation thereafter. Structural considerations therefore point to holding assets which are likely in the long run at least to maintain their real value – equities, property, and index-linked securities. Since the cost of a pension scheme's benefits depends also on the return earned on its investments – the higher the return the lower the level of contributions required to finance the scheme – the funds generally aim to earn as high a return as possible, consistent with prudence, on their funds. Again, they have a preference for long-term investments, principally equities and property, with fixed-interest securities held for reasons of diversification against the risk of falls in other asset prices or when the returns on such securities seem unusually favourable.

The composition of the assets held by life assurance and pension funds at the end of 1989 is shown in table 12.2. Neither category has much need of liquidity, though at that time the pension funds had built up their short-term assets in view of the uncertainty concerning future share price trends. The funds' holdings of fixed-interest securities are mainly government securities – substantially more, as is to be expected, in the life assurance than in pension funds. However, the stock of government securities had been contracting in the second half of the 1980s, and the life companies also held significant amounts of 'other' company securities (mainly fixed-interest) and loans and mortgages. So far as these institutions are concerned, with the exception of index-linked securities, there is

Table 12.2 Life assurance and pension funds: composition of asset portfolios, end-1989

	Life assurance	*(Per cent)* *Pension funds*
Short-term assets (net)	3	6
Government securities	14	8
UK Company securities		
Ordinary shares	36	53
Other	5	2
Overseas securities	12	17
Unit trust units	10	1
Loans and mortgages	3	—
Land and property	16	10
Other	2	2
Total assets	100	100

Source: Business Monitor, MQ–5, Q3–1990

little to choose between the different types of fixed-interest security, provided that the interest received on mortgages and loans and on company fixed-interest securities allows an adequate margin over gilt-edged securities to compensate for their poorer marketability and greater default risk.[4]

Ordinary shares in UK companies account for about a third of the life companies' and over half of the pension funds' portfolios. To this must be added almost all the overseas securities, again more important for the pension funds than the life offices, and most of the life offices' unit trust units held in connection with their linked liabilities. Both categories had built up their overseas holdings during the 1980s – until 1979 such holdings had been impeded by exchange controls, and life offices held less than 3 per cent (pension funds 5.5 per cent) of their funds in overseas securities at the end of 1979. Over half of the life offices' portfolios and two-thirds of the pension funds' were held in equity assets.

The last major type of asset is direct investment in land and property. This accounted for 16 per cent of the life offices' portfolios but only 10 per cent of pension funds' at the end of 1989. Both these figures are well down on those of ten years previously (by nearly a quarter and a fifth respectively). The equity price boom of the mid-eighties had resulted in equities yielding much higher returns than property, reducing the latter's popularity as an investment. The higher ratio for life offices than for pension funds reflects the size of their portfolios. The expertise required for direct investment in property differs from that which is needed for managing a securities portfolio, and comparatively few pension funds are of a size to make this worthwhile.

The distribution of the asset portfolio at the end of 1989 results from the combined effects of past purchases of securities and property and of changes in the capital values of these assets. Since ordinary shares and property are more likely than fixed-interest securities to show capital gains consistently, the proportionate distribution of new investment is rather different. This is illustrated in table 12.3 which shows the distribution of the life assurance and pension funds' net purchases of the different kinds of assets from 1985 to 1989. Within this period the pattern of investment differed quite sharply from one year to the next as investors' perceptions of the capital market outlook changed.

Over the five-year period as a whole the life assurance companies put 7 per cent of new money into short-term assets and the pension funds as much as 18 per cent. These were abnormally high levels, particularly for the pension funds, and reflected the continuing

Table 12.3 Life assurance and pension funds: investment, 1985–89

	Life assurance	*(Per cent)* *Pension funds*
Short-term assets	7	18
Government securities	4	−5
UK Company securities		
Ordinary shares	25	42
Other	13	6
Overseas securities	13	32
Unit trust units	21	2
Loans and mortgages	5	—
Land and property	9	1
Other	3	4
Total assets	100	100

Source: Financial Statistics, January 1991, table 7.3

uncertainty in capital markets following the crash of 1987. From 1987 on, the pension funds shifted their portfolios more firmly towards equity investments and sold government securities, while the life offices continued to add to their holdings until 1989. In that year, however, the diminishing supply of government securities led to net sales in both categories, and helped to create a demand for 'other' company securities and, in the case of the life offices, loans and mortgages as alternative fixed-interest instruments. Altogether the life offices purchased fixed-interest instruments amounting to over 20 per cent of their new money, compared with practically nothing for the pension funds.

Aside from investment by linked funds in unit trusts (which accounted for 21 per cent of the life offices' new money), the life funds put a quarter and the pension funds over 40 per cent into UK ordinary shares. The life funds' purchases were fairly stable from year to year, but the pension funds ranged from purchases of nearly £8 billion in 1987 to under £400 million in 1989. Purchases of overseas securities (of which ordinary shares made up over 90 per cent) were even less stable. Both categories of fund sold heavily after the crash, resulting in negligible purchases by life funds and net sales of over £600 million by the pension funds in 1987. In 1989, however, life funds purchased over £4 billion and pension funds over £8 billion, in the latter case absorbing over 80 per cent of the funds' new money in the year. For the five-year period as a whole the proportion of new funds devoted to overseas investment was in both cases substantially higher than the proportions in their existing portfolios, reflecting a general trend toward increasing the foreign weighting in investment portfolios.

The concentration on equity investment in this period was reflected also in relatively little money being invested in the property market. The pension funds sold almost as much property as they bought and the life offices allocated only 9 per cent of new funds. In both cases this contributed to the decline in the share of property in their portfolios.

Pension provision

All societies have to make some arrangements for supporting their old people, and there is no general rule about the methods which are employed. Individualistic societies put the emphasis on people providing for themselves, others place greater weight on social provision. The balance is often a matter for political debate, and may shift from time to time as political conditions change. However, the choice of arrangements does have important economic consequences, and in particular the level of voluntary saving in a society is likely to be affected.

At one time most people in Britain depended on their families for support in old age. Some, including businessmen and members of the professions, aimed to save enough from their incomes to provide a capital sum sufficient to keep them in retirement, but they were very much in the minority. Others, who did not have families or former employers to support them, relied on the communities in which they lived. But nowadays the system is quite different. Practically everyone is covered to some degree by the state Retirement Pension Scheme; as already noted, some 15 million people are included in occupational pension schemes which will provide additional pensions when they retire and four million have personal pension arrangements; and many people build up some savings of their own to provide themselves with a measure of extra security. Since much of the current annual saving through life assurance and pension funds results from pension schemes and personal pension arrangements, their importance for saving in the UK is clear.

Most state pension schemes run on a pay-as-you-go basis, in which current pensions are financed from current contributions. With this kind of scheme the notion that people are saving up during their working lives to build a capital sum from which their pensions will be paid in due course is abandoned. Instead, the scheme depends on an implicit social contract between generations: the working population of today pay the pensions of their predecessors, in the hope that the next generation will do the same for them. Rather than relying on the ownership of property (an accumulated fund) for their pensions, people rely on the political process to ensure they get a fair deal.

In the United Kingdom the state scheme is in two tiers. The lower tier provides a flat-rate pension, while the upper tier – the State Earnings-Related Pension Scheme (SERPS) – provides an earnings-related supplement. Participation in the lower tier is compulsory for everyone with more than a minimum level of earnings, but members of occupational pension schemes and, since 1988, employees who take out personal pensions are able to contract out of the upper tier. To be entitled to the full flat-rate pension employees must make contributions of at least a specified minimum amount throughout most of their working lives – failure to do so results in a lower pension – but there is no precise relationship between the individual's contributions and benefits. However, the scheme as a whole works on the principle that total contributions and total benefits in any period will balance.

Pay-as-you-go schemes have the great advantage that they are not undermined by inflation, because wage and salary inflation leads automatically to higher contributions, which provide the revenue from which higher pensions can be paid. They may also appear attractive to the current working generation when, as used to be the case in Britain, the pensions paid to the retired generation are less than those which the working generation expects to receive itself. However, such schemes become burdensome if there is a decline in the size of the working relative to the retired generation, or if the future pension entitlements under the scheme would entail higher contributions than people now would willingly pay. Considerations of this kind led the government to alter the British scheme in 1986, reducing the entitlements under SERPS and encouraging people to make their own (funded) personal pension arrangements in place of the earnings-related element in the state scheme. Moreover, pay-as-you-go schemes are not really desirable on an enterprise basis, because the continuity of an enterprise cannot be guaranteed and the pension entitlement of the scheme's members is therefore insecure. In practice, in countries such as France where pay-as-you-go schemes are the general rule, they are operated on a very wide basis – so wide that they can effectively rely on the state for support.

The alternative is to have *funded* pension schemes operated on the principles already described. Contributions are made by employers and, usually, employees,[5] with the general level depending on the typical career patterns and the expected mortality experience of the scheme's members. The fund is valued actuarially at regular intervals to test whether it is sufficient to cover the scheme's liabilities, and to help to determine the level of contributions which will be required in future to ensure the solvency of the scheme. Unless there is a surplus in the fund any improvement in benefits for the members has to be paid for out of higher contributions by either the employer or employees. Final salary schemes provide members with a high degree of protection against inflation during their working lives, and approved[6] pension schemes must also adjust pensions annually for inflation up to a maximum of 3 per cent[7] in any year.

Funded pension schemes make a contribution to saving so long as the contributions together with the income earned by the fund exceed the benefits paid out. The level of contributions depends on the number of working members in the scheme and upon the level of their earnings; it will also be affected by any deficiency in the existing fund, which has to be made good, or any surplus which can be run down. The benefits depend on the number of retired members, their earnings at the time they retired, and the number of years of service on which their pensions are based. While pensions may now be fully or partially adjusted for inflation, they are seldom adjusted to take account of increases in the real earnings of the working population, so contributions will generally be calculated by reference to salary levels greater than those of the retired members. Moreover, since the coverage of occupational schemes spread rapidly in the sixties and seventies, retired members at present generally have considerably less service than their counterparts will expect to have in future. For both these reasons the funds as a whole can be expected to grow for many years to come. However, not all funds are in this position, and in firms or industries where employment has contracted sharply there are instances of funds which are running down.

The level of surpluses or deficiencies in existing funds also has a very important influence on saving through pension schemes. In the early 1980s, thanks to earnings inflation which was not matched by a rise in the funds' incomes, many funds had deficiencies, which necessitated an increase in the level of contributions with a view to restoring balance over a period of years. However, later in the decade the strong performance of the stock market and rapid rise in dividends created substantial surpluses in many funds. To some extent these were employed in improving the schemes' benefits, but to a considerable degree they enabled firms to reduce their contributions to their pension schemes and in some cases to cease them altogether for some years.

Pension funds thus provide an example of 'target' saving leading to an inverse relationship between saving and the yield on assets. High realized yields lead to pension fund surpluses, which translate into lower future contributions; low yields have the opposite effect. The same principle applies to the level of *expected* yields in future. The higher is the expected yield on investments the lower is the level of contributions required to provide any given level of pension benefits. Thus any sustained rise (or fall) in yields which causes actuaries to revise their assumptions about what can be expected in future has an inverse effect on the required contribution levels.

Role in the saving/investment process

Reporting in 1980, the Wilson Committee[8] showed that in the previous two decades saving through life assurance and pension funds had risen from some 3 per cent of GDP to nearly 5 per cent. The main cause was the rapid extension of the coverage of pension schemes to include a broader cross-section of the population, coupled with improvements in the benefits provided. Contributions increased accordingly, but the rising nominal yield on the funds' holdings of short-term assets and fixed-interest securities due to rising inflation also played a part. Inflation had an even larger effect on the personal sector's acquisitions of liquid assets, so that as a proportion of financial saving by the personal sector, the share of life assurance and pension funds fell from 50 per cent in the 1960s to nearer 40 per cent in the second half of the 1970s.

Table 12.4 shows that saving through life assurance and pension funds continued to grow as a share of GDP in the first half of the 1980s, averaging 5.7 per cent from 1980 to 1984, but then fell back to only 5 per cent in 1988 before jumping to 5.8 per cent in 1989. Structural factors accounted for much of the growth in the previous two decades, and they also accounted for the jump in 1989 – the introduction of personal pensions in 1988 led to a substantial increase in pension business, including transfer payments in respect of employees who moved out of SERPS and the 2 per cent bounty paid by the government towards new personal pensions.

The trend in the mid-eighties was affected by two partially offsetting legislative factors. Until 1984 most individual life assurance

Table 12.4   Saving through life assurance and pension funds, 1980–89

	1980–84 average	1985	1986	1987	1988	1989
Per cent of GDP	5.7	5.7	5.6	5.3	5.0	5.8
Per cent of financial saving[1] by the personal sector	50	53	49	49	47	58

Source: Blue Book, 1990, table 11.2
[1] Comprising liquid assets, securities, life assurance and pension funds, miscellaneous domestic assets

premiums received a subsidy through the tax system, but this was abolished in the 1984 Budget for policies taken out after that time. This made saving through life assurance policies less attractive. However, this was offset by the growing practice of using endowment mortgages in conjunction with house purchase loans, to maximize the tax relief on mortgage interest, and this business grew rapidly in the housing boom which peaked in 1988. Most of the saving towards the repayment of house purchase loans is now made through life assurance companies. Mortgage-related business peaked in 1988, and regular individual premiums for life policies actually fell in 1989, but this was more than compensated by the growth of personal pension business.

Market factors have also been extremely important. We have already noted the effect of the high rates of return in the mid-eighties which led to pension fund surpluses and a decline in employers' contributions – the main reason for the falling share of GDP from 1985 to 1989. Market factors – the poorer stock market prospects after the crash of 1987 – also led to a reduction in single-premium business. And market factors, in the form of marketing, help to account for the life offices' powerful position in the savings market. Life offices generally pay higher commissions than unit trusts for the introduction of new business, the introductory commissions for endowment insurance policies are much higher than for term policies, and the rewards for selling personal pensions are also high.

Table 12.4 also shows that the proportion of the personal sector's financial saving passing through life assurance and pension funds averaged about 50 per cent in the 1980s. In fact there was a rise in the first half to a peak of 55 per cent in 1984, followed by a decline to 1988 and sharp rise in 1989 for the reasons already mentioned.

The life assurance and pension funds are the central institutions concerned with mobilizing long-term saving in the economy. They gather together the savings of millions of individuals and make that saving available for long-term investment through the capital market. The size of some of the individual institutions, as well as the total volume of funds available, ensures that very large sums of money can be provided to borrowers when they are required. Examples are privatization issues, where the institutions have invested billions of pounds in a short period, and rights issues of around £1 billion.

In doing this they also play an important part in asset transformation in the economy, though it is the transformation of risk rather than of liquidity which is their concern. In contrast with the building societies, for example, they have no need to convert short-term liabilities into long-term assets, because their liabilities are by and large already long-term. But risk transformation remains an important function. People expect their savings through life assurance and pension funds to be safe, they expect commitments to be honoured, and even when that commitment is linked to the value of a securities portfolio, as in linked life business, they expect that portfolio to be diversified to eliminate much of the specific risk involved. The provision of security and reduction of risk exposure is therefore central to the operations of life and pension funds.

General insurance

General insurance companies hold funds (or *reserves*) to enable them to meet claims on the policies they have issued. Since most policies run for a year and most claims are made very soon after the event giving rise to the claim occurs, the liabilities are mostly short-term. But in some instances claims may be delayed or a settlement may not be reached until several years after the event, during which time a reserve has to be retained to cover possible payments. In addition to the specific (technical) reserves which an insurance company maintains to meet the claims it expects, companies also hold general reserves in case their loss experience is worse than they have anticipated. The largest general insurance companies in the UK have substantial overseas operations, particularly in North America, and most of the funds held in connection with this business are invested and managed overseas. However, at the end of 1989 the total assets managed in the UK amounted to about £40 billion.

A significant proportion of the assets of general insurance companies are held in a liquid form, because substantial claims can arise with little warning (e.g. storm damage over a wide area) and there is also a chance that underwriting experience will deteriorate quite quickly; e.g. the cost of repairing motor cars may rise faster than had been forecast when premiums were set, so that claims turn out to be higher than expected. Most of their longer-term assets are also readily marketable. But liquidity is not the sole consideration: they also seek to protect the real value of their reserves from the effects of inflation, and therefore invest part of their assets in ordinary shares and property, and they are naturally concerned with the yield they earn on their funds – competitive conditions often compel them to accept an underwriting loss, to be recovered out of earnings on investments. Thus a balance has to be struck between liquidity, real value certainty, and return.

The composition of general insurance funds at the end of 1989 is shown in the first column of table 12.5. At that time short-term assets amounted to 8 per cent of the total, but these could easily be supplemented from government securities (15 per cent of assets) of which a third were short-dated and most of the balance medium-dated. Ordinary shares of UK and overseas companies made up just over a third of the total portfolio, and other (mostly fixed-interest) company securities, mortgages and loans amounted to under 10 per cent. Overseas government securities accounted for 6 per cent –

Table 12.5   General insurance funds: assets, end-1989 and investment, 1985–89

	Assets end-1989	(Per cent) Investment 1985–89
Short-term assets (net)	8	20
Government securities	15	12
UK company securities		
Ordinary shares	23	6
Other	5	10
Overseas securities	18	15
Loans and mortgages	4	10
Land and property	9	5
Other	17	21
Total	100	100

Source: Financial Statistics, April 1991, table 7.10

most of which can be linked to overseas business supported by funds managed from the UK. Property and land comprised 9 per cent, having declined slightly from 10 per cent a decade earlier, and other assets amounted to about a sixth – these include investments in overseas subsidiaries and items such as premiums collected by brokers or other agents, which had not yet been paid over to the companies.

Net investment by general insurance companies averaged some £2.3 billion a year in the period 1985–9. Compared with the life assurance and pension funds, whose assets grew by ten times as much in the same period, their impact on the capital market is not very large. Most of the additional funds were generated by higher premium income (partly due to inflation) and from retained profits, but a small amount was raised through capital issues in the market.

The second column of table 12.5 shows how the additional funds were invested. Short-term assets took 20 per cent, and a further 12 per cent were added to government securities. In this case too, however, the declining supply of government securities appears to have led to compensating purchases of 'other' company securities (and possibly of short-term, liquid assets). Only a small proportion of funds went into ordinary shares – 6 per cent in the UK and less overseas, where the 15 per cent includes a majority of fixed-interest securities. Loans and mortgages took 10 per cent of new funds, and property 5 per cent. Other assets continued to absorb a substantial proportion of funds, including further direct investment overseas.

Though they are responsible for substantial investment portfolios, general insurance funds should not be regarded as a reliable source of funds in the capital market in the future. If inflation falls the growth of premium income will decline correspondingly, and the growth of domestic business is linked to the growth of the economy generally. So the inflow of new funds is likely to be small on average, and in bad years could turn negative.

Investment and unit trusts

Investment and unit trusts are the other important groups of investing institutions. The values of their funds at the end of 1989 amounted to £24 billion and £57 billion respectively. The principal services provided are portfolio diversification to spread risk, and professional management of funds. In addition, many of the fund management groups which manage the funds or trusts operate regular savings schemes or offer PEPs (see chapter 7) to encourage individuals to build up savings in these forms.

Investment trusts are companies set up for the purpose of collective investment in shares and other securities. At the end of 1990 the members of the Association of Investment Trust Companies managed over 200 trusts, accounting for over 95 per cent of total investment trust funds. Many fund management groups are responsible for manging several trusts, and the top ten groups accounted for over 50 per cent of the total funds.

Shares in investment trusts can be bought or sold in the same way as any other shares, at whatever price prevails in the market. The share price is influenced by the value of the trust's assets and by the past success of its management, but it will not generally be the same as the value of the underlying assets – in recent years the shares have generally stood at a discount to the underlying asset values.[9,10]

An investment trust shareholder obtains, in effect, a proportion of a diversified asset portfolio. He is protected from the extremes of risk associated with holding shares in only a small number of companies, and he benefits from the relatively low transactions costs which apply to purchases or sales of large blocks of shares. This is particularly true of holdings in overseas shares, where the construction of an adequately diversified portfolio is frequently not a practical proposition for the individual private investor. He also hopes that, thanks to its investment expertise, the trust's management will be successful in earning an above-average return on the trust's assets. Investment trusts have the additional advantage that they can borrow to augment their asset portfolio if they wish (which would usually be more expensive or difficult for the individual shareholder). For these benefits the shareholder has to bear the costs of remunerating the trust's management.

Originally most investment trusts were general, investing overseas – particularly in North America – as well as in the UK. During the period of exchange control up to 1979, when overseas portfolio investments were subject to restrictions, they maintained a high level of expertise. After the abolition of exchange controls in 1979 access to overseas investment was freely available, eroding one of their attractions. Part of their response was to alter their investment policies to provide a clearer focus so that investors could choose to hold trusts which better suited their precise needs or investment preferences. Thus there has been increasing regional specialization, giving investors the opportunity of backing their own judgements about regional investment prospects while leaving it to others to select a portfolio of shares, and a clearer division between current income and future growth as objectives. There are also a limited number of trusts specializing in high technology companies or other sectors.

While they provide services to savers the investment trusts have not in recent years been a significant source of new funds for the capital market. With their shares generally at a discount issues of new equity have been small, and at the end of 1989 medium and long-term borrowing amounted to less than 10 per cent of their equity capital. Their total holdings in ordinary shares were almost equally divided between the UK and overseas, both a little over £10 billion.

Unit trusts fulfil similar functions. Their liabilities, unit trust units, are sold by the trust's managers to the public. The value of each unit is calculated regularly, usually daily, as a fraction of the value of the fund's assets, and the managers undertake to buy or sell units on request, at prices which lie within a prescribed margin of the unit's value. The extent of any discount to the value of the underlying assets is therefore limited. Since regular valuations are required, unit trusts are not permitted to invest any substantial proportion of their funds in unlisted securities, whose true value may not be easy to establish.

At the end of 1989 there were about 170 unit trust management groups in the UK, managing a total of £57 billion. The top ten management groups account for over 40 per cent by value of the funds. About 60 per cent of the value was held by other financial institutions, namely life offices holding linked assets in this form, with direct holdings by the personal sector amounting to £23 billion.

Unit trusts have a variety of objectives – income, growth, or regional specialization, for example – and most management groups operate several trusts. There are frequently arrangements to allow holders to shift between trusts within a single management group on comparatively favourable terms. Unit trust units are often held by individuals with relatively small sums to invest – there are nearly five million holdings – though many individuals have holdings in more than one trust. The cost of dealing is determined by the spread between the manager's bid and offer prices (usually 5 or 6 per cent), though there are also annual management charges deducted from the trust's income. Out of this spread the managers normally pay a fee to intermediaries who introduce business to them, putting them at a marketing advantage in comparison with investment trusts.[11]

There was a strong demand for unit trusts during the rapidly rising equity market in the middle of the 1980s, with net sales peaking at over £6 billion in 1987 (of which sales to the public were

£3.7 billion). But after the crash in October 1987 demand fell away and the total number of individual holdings declined slightly in 1988 and 1989. Net sales in these years were due entirely to purchases connected with the life offices' linked business, and there were net repurchases from the public.

The 1990 Budget altered the basis of life office taxation in ways which make the holding of unit trust units much less attractive to life offices, and it seems likely that their holdings will decline. Direct sales to the public may prove attractive in the next upswing in the equity market, but sales through intermediaries are likely to remain inhibited by the superior commissions payable on broadly comparable linked insurance policies.

At the end of 1989 unit trusts held nearly £30 billion of UK ordinary shares and nearly £20 billion of overseas ordinary shares. Like the investment trusts, they provide a medium through which the private investor can invest in overseas securities. Their portfolios show a high level of turnover – about 100 per cent for UK equities and 170 per cent for overseas equities in 1989. These levels are considerably higher than those of equivalent investment trusts, and there is no evidence that the additional turnover is justified by superior investment performance. In fact, the reverse is true, and in the latter part of the eighties the average investment trust outperformed the average unit trust.

Investing institutions and the capital market

We are now in a position to consider some of the implications of the investing institutions' behaviour for the capital market. On the investment side of their activities these institutions have very similar objectives, and seek to attain their objectives by very similar means. Thus they all attempt to maximize the return on their portfolios, subject to certain constraints determined by the nature of their liabilities, which influence the optimum (risk-minimizing) structure of each institution's portfolio. Departures from the optimum, which expose the institution to extra risk, have to be justified by the prospect of additional return.

The institutions all hold portfolios of financial assets, and sometimes also property, and buy or sell at the margin when they believe that conditions are favourable. The portfolio managers are bound to act prudently: they are under fiduciary obligations to their liability-holders, and cannot take unreasonable risks with their clients' money. Prudence demands that they hold a diversified portfolio, and that they have regard to the nature of their liabilities, but subject to these considerations they are free to vary the proportions of the various categories of financial instruments – e.g. equity or debt – in their portfolios in favour of those on which they expect the return to be relatively high. Within each category they select stocks on which they hope the return will be above average. Since investment overseas can offer the prospect of as high or a higher return than investment in UK securities, and since international diversification adds to the stability of a portfolio, pension funds whose liabilities are entirely in sterling are entitled to invest some of their funds abroad. How much of a single institution's portfolio can reasonably be invested abroad, whilst still discharging its fiduciary responsibilities, can only be judged by reference to the practices of other institutions.

All the investing institutions attach considerable importance to the marketability of their assets. They put a premium on being able to dispose of at least part of holdings which they regard as over-priced, and on being able to buy new holdings or add to holdings which seem under-priced. Poor marketability has to be compensated by a higher expected yield. They are not unwilling to take risks – risk-taking is inherent in investment – but they are unwilling to take *unnecessary* risks or to purchase a risky asset if their expectation of the rate of return falls short of what is available on other investments. High risk does not in itself rule out an investment if the return is adequate – as investment in North Sea oil and certain other activities has demonstrated. Nevertheless, since investment managers must be able to show that they are behaving in a responsible fashion, the proportion of their assets devoted to abnormally risky investment is seldom high.

The effects of the institutions on the securities market will be considered in more detail in chapter 14. At this stage it is only necessary to point to some of the effects of the very large size of their holdings of securities, both in aggregate and in terms of individual stocks, and of the annual flow of saving which passes through their hands. First, when one of the large institutions wishes to deal, substantial volumes of stock and large sums of money are involved; the market organization and arrangements for dealing have to be able to cope with their requirements. Secondly, the flow of saving through the institutions makes it comparatively easy for public sector bodies or large companies to raise the capital funds they require, provided they can satisfy the risk criteria applied by the institutions. Finally, while many of the institutions are too large to wish to hold shares in smaller or unlisted companies, this need not imply that such companies will find difficulty in obtaining funds, provided that there are institutions which specialize in catering for them. The specialized institutions will be able to attract funds from the larger institutions if they offer a superior return.

Notes

1 The assessment for each region has to take account not only of the region's economic prospects, but also of any expected exchange rate movements and of any special factors affecting investment in the region.

2 That is, the risk of general share price movements affecting a particular market, but which are independent of worldwide share price trends.

3 For example, the parties in complicated civil legal actions may insure the judge's life. If the judge were to die in the course of the action it would have to be started again, giving rise to substantial additional legal costs.

4 The proportions of fixed-interest securities had fallen very substantially in the preceding decade – at the end of 1979 they were nearly 40 per cent and over 25 per cent for the life assurance and pension funds respectively.

5 In any event the contributions are regarded as part of the employees' total remuneration.

6 Inland Revenue approval is required before a scheme can enjoy tax benefits.

7 This figure is due to be increased to 5 per cent, but the change has not yet (1991) been implemented.

8 *Committee to Review the Functioning of Financial Institutions* (Cmnd 7937), 1980.

9 That is, the share price has been less than the value of the trust's assets (less liabilities) divided by the number of shares.

10 There are a number of contributory factors. A significant proportion of the trust shares are held by other institutional investors who can obtain diversification cheaply in other ways and who therefore value the benefits of diversification at less than the trusts' management costs. They would sell their shares if the discount narrowed sufficiently. Liquidating trusts does not provide an alternative solution because the value on liquidation falls short of the underlying asset value. There have, however, been takeovers of trusts by other institutions (e.g. pension funds), which have found it a convenient way of acquiring new equity assets.

11 Investment trusts now often pay fees when intermediaries introduce clients for their PEPs and sometimes also for their savings plans.

13

Specialized financial institutions

While the major categories of deposit-taking and investing institutions discussed in chapters 11 and 12 deal with the broad spectrum of financing needs in the economy, there are a number of gaps or niches remaining to be filled by specialized institutions. In many instances these specialized institutions are subsidiaries of deposit-taking or (less commonly) investing institutions, and represent the most cost-effective means for the parent company to provide the service in question.

The finance houses and related leasing and consumer credit companies will be the first category considered: these supply finance to companies of all sizes, to some public sector organizations, and to consumers, handling very substantial volumes of funds. Next are the venture and development capital companies, which are particularly important to small companies and new ventures. Then there are the factoring and invoice discounting companies, providing a service mainly to small enterprises. Lastly the personal sector is served not only by specialized consumer credit companies but also by a number of centralized mortgage lenders.

Finance houses

Finance houses engage in industrial credit, consumer credit and leasing business. They are the major source of instalment finance in the economy, and at the end of 1989 held leased assets with a written-down value amounting to some £20 billion, provided hire purchase and other credit to business amounting to £11 billion, and were responsible for some £15 billion of 'bank' lending to consumers. In addition non-bank consumer credit companies had outstanding loans to consumers of more than £5 billion. As noted in chapter 11, most of the finance houses are subsidiaries of banks and are also included in their own right in the banking sector.

The finance house 'banks' obtain their funding in the wholesale deposit markets, by issuing bills and by other borrowing from the banks. Since they are not banks, non-bank credit companies do not rely on deposits for their funding. Instead they rely very heavily on the banks for both short-term and longer-term funds, as well as making some use of the commercial bill markets (10 per cent of total funds at the end of 1989) and of other borrowing (5 per cent). Capital funds amounted to 11 per cent of total liabilities.

Finance houses and other credit companies represent a major source of funds for capital investment in the economy, especially for investment in vehicles, plant and equipment. Many of these capital assets are provided through 'finance leasing' contracts, and the finance lease is now the most important form of instalment lending for industrial and commercial companies. Strictly speaking it is not lending at all, because the lessor retains ownership of the assets – the user chooses the equipment, the rental over an agreed period covers its full cost, but the user does not actually own it. It is a substitute for credit, rather than being a form of credit itself.

In comparison with direct ownership, financed by credit, finance leasing offers several advantages to the lessee. The leasing company provides 100 per cent of the cost, whereas otherwise users might be expected to put up part themselves. The term of the implied loan matches the expected life of the asset, and the rental cost is generally fixed in advance regardless of changes in interest rates.[1] The financing element in the rental cost takes account of the lessor's security from owning the asset, and there is scope for negotiating rental terms which reflect the projected cash flows of the lessee. Lastly, and by no means least important, the rental will reflect the capital allowances for tax purposes which are available to the lessor, at a time when the lessee may not have enough taxable profits to take full advantage of them.

While the rental in a finance lease is intended to cover the full cost of the equipment over its useful life, companies can also obtain the use of equipment by means of operating leases. The lessee has the use of the equipment for a defined period, but it is expected that the equipment will retain some residual value at the end of this period, and that it will then be sold or leased to a third party for their use subsequently. Finance leases often run for 4 or 5 years,[2] whereas operating leases are more likely to be for shorter periods. (Operating leases are often used for computers, vehicles and aircraft, for which there is a viable secondhand market – albeit with substantial uncertainty regarding future secondhand prices.) Under the version of operating leases known as contract hire the lessor may go further and take some responsibility for the management and maintenance of the equipment – leases of car fleets often incorporate this feature.

Finance houses also provide credit to companies through traditional hire purchase contracts, under which the hirer becomes the owner at the end of the rental period. Any capital allowances are available to the hirer from the outset, so that for companies which are in a position to use these allowances fully leasing does not offer tax advantages. Finance houses also provide stocking finance to companies, notably to motor dealers from whom they obtain other business, and they 'block discount' consumer credit agreements made by retailers who prefer to offer customers their own finance facilities.

Lessors' capital expenditure on assets for leasing amounted to £9.8 billion in 1989 – that is nearly 20 per cent of total capital expenditure on vehicles, plant and equipment in the UK – and new hire purchase and other credit to business amounted to £6.9 billion. The corresponding figures for the increase in the value of assets were about £4 billion and £1.6 billion respectively. As with the non-bank credit companies, leasing companies rely heavily on bank finance for their funding – sterling bank lending to leasing companies in November 1989 was £20.7 billion.

According to Bank of England figures about 40 per cent of lessors' capital expenditure in 1989 was for vehicles and 60 per cent for plant and machinery. The Equipment Leasing Association, whose members are responsible for a very high proportion of all leasing business, provides a more detailed breakdown, for both leasing and non-leasing business (table 13.1). Within leasing business, computers and office equipment accounted for 24 per cent, and other plant and equipment for 29 per cent – making over 50 per cent in all. Cars took 21 per cent, commercial vehicles 12 per cent, and ships and aircraft 8 per cent. The high proportion in the computers and office equipment category reflects the use of leasing as a sales aid – along with the product the manufacturers offered the customer an apparently attractive financing arrangement, in which some of the risks attached to obsolescence remained with the leasing company.[3] For non-leasing business the proportions were quite different, with cars and commercial vehicles between them accounting for over two-thirds of the business. Computers and office equipment were only 5 per cent, and other plant and machinery 18 per cent.

Table 13.1   Leasing and non-leasing business, 1989

	Leasing	*(Per cent)* *Non-leasing*
Computer and office equipment	24	5
Other plant and machinery	29	18
Cars	21	54
Commercial vehicles	12	14
Aircraft and ships	8	2
Other	7	7
Total	100	100

Source: Equipment Leasing Association

Typical rental periods also differ between leasing and non-leasing business. Motor car business has a shorter duration than much of the business in computers and other plant and machinery.[4] Thus nearly two-thirds of the leasing was for periods over three years, with a mean duration of over five years and 13 per cent over ten years; whereas for the non-leasing business over two-thirds was for periods up to three years, the mean was three years and only 2 per cent was for more than ten years.

Finance houses and other specialized consumer credit companies accounted for 40 per cent of the nearly £50 billion of total consumer credit outstanding at the end of 1989. Consumer lending by finance houses takes a variety of forms. Most common is the simple unsecured personal loan repayable by equal instalments over a fixed period, which is usually connected with the purchase of particular goods such as a car, consumer durable goods – for example washing machines, furniture, photographic or audio equipment – or home improvements. (Retail banks, building societies and sometimes retailers themselves are also important providers of consumer instalment loans for these purposes.) However, loans are not necessarily connected with particular purchases. Sometimes the loan will be secured by a first or second mortgage on property owned by the borrower, particularly when it is unconnected with the purchase of specific goods or services or when larger sums are involved. Loans may also take the form of a revolving credit, where the consumer normally makes a fixed monthly payment and can borrow up to a prescribed multiple of this payment, an arrangement often used in connection with the purchase of clothing. There is hire purchase, where ownership of the goods remains with the finance house until the final payment has been made, credit sales where a retailer accepts payment by instalment over an agreed period, and credit cards which enable holders to buy goods from particular stores up to their credit limits.[5]

Most finance house lending is arranged at the point of sale. The period over which the loan has to be repaid is related to its purpose – perhaps 12 months for photographic equipment, three years for a car and seven years for a home improvement loan. The average period is between two and three years. In 1990 the major finance houses[6] made new loans amounting to £11 billion, divided as shown in table 13.2. Cars accounted for just over a third, goods purchased in stores for 30 per cent, home improvements and property lending for 15 per cent, and other lending for 20 per cent. This last category includes items such as boats, holidays and loans which are not related to the purchase of particular goods and services.

Table 13.2   Finance houses: personal lending, 1990

	(Per cent)
Cars	35
Store goods	30
Home improvements and property	15
Other	20
Total	100

Source: Finance Houses Association, Annual Report 1991

The emphasis on point-of-sale lending by finance houses and specialized consumer credit companies contrasts with lending for similar purposes by the retail banks. Point-of-sale lending is viewed as a sales aid by the vendor, and one on which he may be able to earn a commission; this is an important source of income in some trades, for example the used-car business. Finance houses are dependent on the vendors for the introduction of much of their new business, and commission payments to vendors play a significant part in competition between them. Retail banks, by contrast, have their connections with their customers and aim to provide instalment lending as one element in a range of banking services. New business for the retail banks depends therefore on the strength of these connections, their ability to target potential borrowers amongst their customers, and the terms they offer.

Venture and development capital companies

As noted in chapter 8, access to equity capital has long been recognized as a problem for certain categories of company: young companies, rapidly growing companies which are too small to have a Stock Exchange listing, companies which offer the prospects of high profits if they are successful but for which there is a correspondingly high risk of failure. Compared with quoted securities, managing investments in such companies is costly for the investor, often involving not only special monitoring but also active assistance to the company's management. It is a task for which the major investing institutions discussed in chapter 12 are not well equipped, and which is now carried out by specialist institutions, the venture and development capital companies (VCCs).

The common characteristic of all the categories of company in which VCCs invest is that they have an abnormally high risk of failure. This is especially true of start-ups or very young companies without a track record, but applies also when companies undergo major change – whether through rapid expansion or for other reasons – or when gearing reaches abnormally high levels, such as can occur in a management buy-out or buy-in (discussed below). Companies may require seed-corn capital to help to develop an apparently good idea into a potentially marketable product with an appropriate business plan – many projects of this kind fail. Or funds may be needed to help to implement a business plan by starting a new company or assisting it in its early stages – again the risk of failure is high. Moreover, at this stage companies are unlikely to be completely self-sufficient in all the management skills required, and the investor may need to help to remedy any deficiencies, providing management support as well as financing for the company. A similar situation exists when an established company attempts to grow very rapidly or to branch out into new activities.

VCCs also provide capital to facilitate a change in the ownership or management of quite substantial existing companies. Management buy-outs provide the prime example. A major company may decide to dispose of some non-core parts of its business and sell the business to its existing management. These, however, do not normally have sufficient capital of their own to provide more than a small proportion of the equity capital that is required, but with the help of VCCs (which take the lion's share) a financing package can be put together, comprising a combination of equity and debt appropriate to the business concerned. Provided there is sufficient equity in place, the banks are normally prepared to supply the debt finance. Similar situations occur when companies go into liquidation and viable parts of the business are sold to their existing managements.

In a management buy-out control of the business remains with the existing management but ownership changes. In a management buy-in there is generally a change in both ownership and control. This often occurs when the existing owners and managers want to sell their business, but instead of selling it to another established company sell it to another group of managers who want to take it on. Again, their own limited capital resources have to be supplemented by external equity provided by VCCs.

Not all of VCCs' financing goes on such high-risk activities; part is devoted to providing additional capital to firms in which they have already invested and part merely facilitates a change in ownership of existing firms, as for example when a major shareholder in an unlisted company wishes to retire and withdraw part or all of his capital from the firm, without there being any additional development or change of management team. In these cases the VCCs are providing development, or even just permanent, capital rather than strictly venture capital, but it is nonetheless capital which cannot be obtained readily from other sources.

There are about 130 VCCs in Britain, which invested nearly £1.4 billion in over 1500 companies in 1990. Over half was for management buy-outs and buy-ins, with only 12 per cent for early-stage financing and the balance being made up by finance for expansion and secondary purchases. The VCCs obtain their funds from a variety of sources. Some are captive funds which form part of larger financial services groups (e.g. universal banks) and which derive most of their funds from them. However, the majority are independent funds, set up and run by professional venture fund managers, which obtain their funds from other long-term investors seeking to invest indirectly in this area. Thus their funds come from pension funds, insurance companies, conventional fund management groups, other UK investors and overseas investors – the last group accounting for over 40 per cent of their funds in 1989 and 1990. The independent funds often have specific objectives, reflecting the objectives of their own investors, such as participating in management buy-outs.

With the notable exceptions of 3i, discussed below, and of the development agencies in Scotland and Wales, the VCCs do not regard themselves as permanent investors in the companies they support. Their aim is to develop the companies over a limited period of years – five years would be typical with ten a maximum – to the point where they can realize their capital either by floating the company on the market or by selling an on-going business. By and large their return takes the form of capital gain, since few of the companies they support are in a position to pay large dividends. Investors in VCCs are looking for a compound annual rate of return of 20–25 per cent, which means that the managers of VCCs have to aim higher in order to cover their own costs and earn a profit – they are generally remunerated through annual fees and a share in any capital profits realized.

Much the largest VCC is 3i, with an investment portfolio exceeding £2.5 billion and new investment of nearly £600 million in 1990. The origins of 3i go back to 1945 to institutions set up at the government's instigation by the Bank of England and the major commercial banks (who are still the shareholders in 3i) to fill gaps which the Macmillan Committee (1931)[7] had identified in the financial system. These gaps involved in particular the supply of capital to small firms and the supply in some circumstances of long-term loan finance to industry. It is now primarily a venture and development capital company, which operates from about 25 branches throughout the UK as well as having subsidiaries and associated companies abroad. Unlike most of the VCCs, 3i regards itself as a permanent investor with no particular need to turn over its portfolio of investments. It obtains the greater part of its revenue from interest and dividends on its investments and does not rely mainly on realizing capital gains, with the financing for new investment being provided by a combination of retained profits and borrowing in the international capital markets.

The remits of Scottish Enterprise[8] and the Welsh Development Agency are to promote economic development and employment in their respective regions, and both are able to operate as VCCs on a limited scale. The intention is that their publicly-funded investment should be additional to what can be raised from the private sector, and the emphasis is on investments which are too small to attract private equity funding or which, while in industries of strategic importance, are at the high-risk end of the spectrum. A limited contribution to equity investment by these agencies may also form part of a package to attract inward investment from abroad. The sums involved are not large in the context of VCCs as a whole – for example, new equity investment by the Scottish Development Agency (the predecessor of Scottish Enterprise) amounted to only £5 million in 1990/91 – but do improve the availability of funds for small enterprises in Scotland and Wales.

At one time it was hoped that the Business Expansion Scheme

might become a significant source of funds for VCCs. This seemed likely at the outset – over £100 million was subscribed in the first year – but, as noted in chapter 8, BES investment has been channelled increasingly into asset-backed, relatively low-risk investments rather than genuine venture capital, because the risk/reward ratio for the former is generally superior.

Another source of funds for VCCs is corporate venturing, a practice under which a major industrial company makes seed-corn and early-stage financing available for new ventures, generally also providing more practical assistance as well. This is done in the expectation that successful developments may ultimately be taken over and incorporated in the company itself; that is it is seen as a way of promoting innovation in fields of interest to the company. This practice is quite common in North America, but as yet it is rare in the UK.

Whether the supply of equity capital to small companies is adequate remains a matter of debate. In 1988 less than 5 per cent of the total funds invested by VCCs was for sums of under £200 000, and while in 1990 half of 3i's investments were for under this sum they accounted for under 10 per cent of new investment. Moreover, while it does act as a permanent investor 3i does not have many competitors. The VCCs generally are undoubtedly prepared to take risks but they do not have a strong appetite for companies which have a prospect of moderate but sustained growth – the nature of the VCCs' own funding ensures that they cannot be an important source of patient money for small companies. To have a chance of earning the rate of return they seek they have to look for the prospect of a flotation or trade sale within their time horizon, and investments where this is unlikely are of little interest.

In spite of the large number of VCCs it continues to be difficult for companies to obtain seed-corn and early-stage capital. For proposals to be subject to very careful scrutiny before funding is provided is desirable – the risks are always high, and usually underestimated by a project's proposers. Nevertheless, it does seem that the hurdles are set too high. At a later stage of development there is no shortage of funds for companies with a prospect of rapid and profitable growth, and there is no shortage for management buy-outs or buy-ins in profitable businesses. It seems likely, however, that the general run of unlisted companies are liable to find their growth constrained by their limited ability to generate additional equity internally. At the very least, these companies would benefit from greater diversity in the sources of development capital, as opposed to true venture capital.

Factoring and invoice discounting

Factoring and invoice discounting companies perform a specialized task for small and medium-sized enterprises. The average time that businesses have to wait for invoices to be paid is 75 days. Under invoice discounting the firm receives immediate finance for up to 80 per cent of the value of invoices sent out, with the balance (less charges) paid later. Under factoring, the factor will in addition assume responsibility for sending out invoices and collecting debts, and may also provide insurance against bad debts. This may be done without disclosing to the firm's clients that a factor has been employed.

The main clearing and Scottish banks all have subsidiaries which offer factoring and invoice discounting services. In 1989 total turnover exceeded £11 billion, for 7500 client companies, and the net balance advanced to clients was £1 billion. A third of the clients had annual turnovers under £250 000 and nearly 70 per cent under £1 million.

The services provided by factors are valuable to SMEs for three reasons. First, they free them of the administrative hassle of sending out invoices and collecting debts, and provide them with a professional service. This allows the firm's managers to concentrate on other, more important aspects of their business. Secondly, they provide working capital at a cost which is comparable to a bank overdraft. This is not all additional funds because the fact that the firm's debts are being factored will reduce the overdraft limit it can negotiate, though probably not on a one-for-one basis. But invoice discounting has the advantage that the finance made available rises automatically with turnover, whereas any increase in an overdraft limit has to be negotiated. Rapidly growing firms find this automaticity valuable, and may take advantage of invoice discounting even if they are of a size to administer their invoices efficiently themselves. Lastly, factors provide credit insurance if it is required. Insurance could generally be obtained from other sources, but probably at greater cost. The factor, who is responsible for collecting debts, is in a position to minimize the incidence of losses.

Centralized mortgage lenders

Until the early 1980s lending for house purchase in Britain was dominated by the building societies. We have already noted in chapter 11 that deregulation in the eighties brought the banks in as major competitors, and during the housing boom in the second half of the decade they were joined by centralized mortgage lenders. In the main these companies sought business through mortgage brokers and other agents, though some banks have also chosen to manage their mortgage lending through non-bank subsidiaries, having obtained the business in the usual way through their branch networks.

At the end of 1989 financial institutions other than banks, building societies and insurance companies had house purchase loans outstanding amounting to £15 billion – 6 per cent of total loans for house purchase – of which a little under half was held by bank subsidiaries. However, about 90 per cent of this lending had been done in the previous four years, during which the centralized lenders took over 10 per cent of the market. The demand for mortgages was very strong until 1989, and the non-bank centralized lenders, who raise their funds in the wholesale markets, were able to raise funds more cheaply than building societies which depended more heavily on retail funds. Mortgage interest rates linked to money market rates seemed attractive, and the centralized lenders also took a leading part in pushing out the limits of mortgage lending.

In 1990, when the housing market was in recession and mortgage margins were slim (at the beginning of the year typical mortgage rates lay below the cost of wholesale funds) the position was reversed. The centralized lenders found it difficult to offer competitive terms and net lending was very low. The relatively high rates charged in this period may lead to a loss of goodwill in future. Moreover, innovative financing arrangements brought in during the boom were leading to losses for some lenders. As a result there has been a tendency for non-traditional lenders, including some overseas banks, to withdraw from the mortgage market. While it seems likely that there will be a continuing role for the more efficient of the centralized lenders, the experience in the recession suggests that they will not rebuild the market share of the boom years unless mortgage lending by building societies and banks is artificially constrained.

Notes

1 Leasing contracts in which the rental is adjusted in line with changes in financing costs can also be negotiated.

2 Though they can be anything from two to ten years.
3 The bankruptcy of a computer leasing company subsequently called the attractiveness of some of these arrangements into question.
4 There is also a small amount of property leasing in the Equipment Leasing Association's figures.
5 Unlike banks, finance houses do not provide general overdraft lending, and credit card lending is restricted to cards which can be used only in particular stores or in a narrow geographical area, whereas bank credit cards can be used very widely.
6 Members of the Finance Houses Association.
7 Committee on Finance and Industry, Report (Cmnd 3897), 1931.
8 Also Highland and Islands Enterprise within its part of Scotland.

14

Financial markets

In this chapter we shall consider the contributions made by the major financial markets to the working of the financial system. These markets can be divided into the *securities* markets in which new capital is raised and trading in existing bonds and shares takes place, the *money* markets where highly liquid financial instruments are traded, the *foreign exchange* markets where currencies are bought and sold, and the *derivatives* markets in which standardized contracts derived from the more basic financial instruments are traded; these can be used to hedge or speculate on future interest rate, exchange rate, or security price movements. They are *organized* markets, in the sense that they are either regulated or subject to well-established custom and practice, and that direct access to them is limited to professional participants who are usually members of some organization, for example the International Securities Market Association (ISMA), the International Stock Exchange (ISE) and the London International Financial Futures Exchange (LIFFE). End-investors and ultimate borrowers normally gain access to the markets through intermediaries.

It is useful to distinguish three functions which have to be performed in financial markets: origination, market making and distribution. *Origination* is the function of creating financial instruments in order (in the securities markets) to provide funds to ultimate borrowers or intermediary institutions. The markets in which funds are raised are known as *primary* markets and the securities in question may, for example, be shares, bonds, commercial bills or commercial paper. Normally banks and other corporate financial specialists make the necessary arrangements for their clients and issue the securities on their behalf. To carry out this function successfully a financial institution has to maintain a substantial list of prospective clients, and competition for origination business is generally keen.

Market making is the key function in the *secondary* markets where existing securities are traded. The market makers' tasks are to determine the securities' prices, and to ensure that those who wish to buy or sell are able to do so without influencing prices unduly. An efficient market making system will avoid sharp and erratic price movements in response to individual buying and selling orders, and make it possible to deal on a substantial scale. It will also ensure that the actual transactions costs are not unnecessarily high. The prices which prevail in the secondary market are a key determinant of the prices at which new securities can be issued in the primary market.

There are a number of possible market making systems. For example in some foreign securities markets all the buying and selling orders in some period are collected together and the price which equates purchases and sales is then found. This task is assigned to specialist market makers. Market making in this way has the disadvantage that there may be some delay before a transaction can be completed, and it is a system which is much better suited to comparatively small than to large deals – to complete a sale of a large amount of stock it is necessary either to find a substantial number of potential buyers, each of whom will buy a comparatively small amount, or for there to be investors who are prepared to hold an inventory temporarily, neither of which can be guaranteed.

The traditional method in the UK stock market was to bring all the professional traders together in a single location where they could do business with each other face-to-face and openly, that is by 'open outcry'. Since everyone knew the price at which business was being done it was easy to seek out the best price for any deal. Prices changed as the balance between supply and demand altered or in response to news which led traders to expect that prices would react. For this system to work effectively there had to be some professional dealers who held an inventory of stock and were prepared to be either buyers or sellers, depending on the price available. As dealers they hoped to profit by buying cheaply and building up their inventory when there was a temporary excess of sellers in the market, with a view to selling at a higher price when buyers predominated subsequently, or vice versa when there was a temporary excess of buyers. Prior to Big Bang in 1986, when the practices in the Stock Exchange were changed, these *jobbers* did not deal directly with end-investors, but quoted prices to the *brokers* who brought the buying and selling orders to them.

More modern variants of this technique use the telephone network or the dealer's screen in place of the dealing floor, with market participants keeping in continuous contact. In such markets there are normally some dealers who act as market makers by quoting buying and selling prices and being prepared (within limits) to deal at these prices. Other participants are either buyers or sellers on any particular occasion and are seeking the best price at which to carry out the transaction. For example, in the foreign exchange market, a bank may wish to sell French francs on its own account or on behalf of a client, and will do so by contacting the market-making banks to find the best price. Alternatively it may employ a foreign exchange broker to obtain the best price for it. Prices change because if, as a result of successive deals, the market maker finds that it is steadily acquiring French francs, it will reduce the price it offers in an effort to attract buyers and reduce its French franc holdings, or attempt to sell francs to other market makers. Competition between market makers then ensures that the overall balance of supply and demand in the market is reflected in the price of francs. In a similar fashion participants in the stock market can call up market makers' prices on their screens and find the best price at which to deal.

Distribution is the function of distributing securities, either to ultimate lenders or to financial institutions which are prepared to hold them in their asset portfolios. As with origination, the financial institutions engaged in distribution need to have a network of contacts who are prepared to hold the relevant securities. In many markets there are specialist brokers who carry out this function, though it is by no means confined to brokers.

Sometimes a single institution carries out all three functions – for example a merchant bank may arrange a commercial paper programme for a corporate borrower, distribute the paper to other corporate clients, and be prepared to act as a market maker should they wish to dispose of the paper before maturity. In other cases several institutions with different specialisms cooperate to complete a deal – a merchant bank may arrange a share issue for a corporate customer in association with a firm of Stock Exchange brokers, who undertake to find buyers for the shares, and with market makers who take on the responsibility of making the market subsequently. In some markets the ability to carry out all three functions provides a competitive advantage. It may be simpler and quicker if the client has to deal with only one set of advisors, or the market maker which deals regularly with a large number of substantial clients can contemplate taking larger positions than its more specialized competitor simply because it can expect to trade out of a position quickly. In other markets there is a clear role for the specialist, which can hope to achieve a very high level of expertise in its chosen area. The balance between specialization and complete coverage varies from one market to another, and also within markets as changing conditions alter the balance of competitive advantage.

International securities market

Securities markets do not observe national boundaries. Borrowers in one country issue securities denominated in the currency of another, which are sold to investors in third countries by banks and securities houses situated in any of the world's major financial centres. The funds raised may be held in the currency borrowed, converted into the currency of the issuer's own country, or deployed in some other currency altogether, and the future contractual interest payments in the borrowed currency may be swapped[1] into equivalent payments in another. It is no longer possible to analyse supply and demand for funds in terms of domestic capital markets alone.

We start therefore by looking briefly at the international capital markets, whose three principal centres are London, New York and Tokyo. In 1989 borrowers raised nearly US$175 billion (net of redemptions) in the international capital markets through the issue of bonds and US$15 billion through the issue of equities – so-called eurobonds and euroequities respectively.[2] The principal currencies for 'straight', that is fixed interest-rate, bonds were the US dollar, yen, ECU, sterling, Canadian dollar and deutschmark. The minimum normal size of issue is about US$100 million, or the equivalent in other currencies. The majority of bonds issued in 1989 were straights, but about a third contained some sort of equity element, and around 10 per cent had floating rates of interest. Issuers borrow in the currency and form in which it is cheapest for them to do so and use the swap markets to convert into the currency and interest-rate terms which best suit their business – it is estimated that 80 per cent of eurobond issues are the subject of swaps.[3] There are also international markets in euronotes (i.e. short- and medium-term notes) and eurocommercial paper, though in overall terms they are much less important as a source of funds, supplying only US$7 billion (net) in 1989.

In these international markets origination, market making and distribution are all carried out by major international banks and securities houses. The issuer gives a mandate to one or more lead banks to manage the issue. The lead bank recruits a syndicate of other banks to underwrite the issue and to distribute it to their investment clients – the end-investors; these comprise financial institutions and wealthy investors throughout the world. Sometimes the issue will be pre-placed with clients, while on other occasions the banking syndicate will take it on to their own balance sheets and sell it on to clients subsequently. When the issue has been made the lead bank normally acts as market maker in the secondary market, though other banks and securities houses may also trade actively in particular bonds. The size and timing of issues can be decided at short notice in the light of market conditions, and pricing is normally measured in terms of basis points (i.e. hundredths of one per cent) over government securities of an equivalent term.

In 1989 there were 116 banks and securities houses which acted as lead banks in the eurobond markets, though the top five accounted for over 40 per cent of the new issues. The banks that participate in new issues receive their remuneration by means of fees for managing and underwriting the issue and from any profit they can earn by placing the issue with clients at a price higher than they have paid.[4]

UK issuers are no strangers to these markets. Table 14.1 shows that of over £26 billion raised through capital issues by UK companies and building societies in 1989, less than £8 billion was raised through securities listed in the Stock Exchange or the 'unlisted' securities market (discussed below). While the total figures in table 14.1 include relatively small amounts of funds raised through unquoted securities, it is clear that in 1989 the banks and building societies relied almost exclusively on the international

Table 14.1 Capital issues by UK companies, 1989

Issues by	Total	*(£ billion)* Raised through UK Stock Exchange
Industrial and commercial companies	12.5	5.3
Banks and building societies	8.7	—
Other financial institutions	4.9	2.3
Total	26.1	7.6

Sources: Bank of England Quarterly Bulletin, tables 19.3, 19.7, 19.8; *Financial Statistics*, tables 12.1, 12.2

market for new capital funds, whilst industrial and commercial companies and other financial institutions obtained over half of their new external capital from this source. However, the international markets are still much more important as suppliers of fixed- and variable-interest rate funds than of equity capital, and in the UK the Stock Exchange remains the principal source of new share capital for companies.

UK securities markets

The main domestic securities market is the International Stock Exchange (ISE) which, as its name suggests, also provides facilities for trading in foreign securities. Companies and other bodies whose securities are listed on the stock exchange have to meet certain requirements (i.e. regarding the content and timeliness of accounts, and publication of information) to ensure that the market in the security is fair. Table 14.2 shows the value of securities listed on the ISE at the end of 1990. While the ISE is the principal market for the UK securities listed, the same cannot be said in general for the foreign securities, which are also of course traded on their own domestic markets.

Since for historical reasons the ISE is also the principal market for Irish securities it is convenient to consider UK and Irish securities together. Within the government securities section of the list they account for all but £4 billion, with UK public sector securities at £116 billion. Listed eurobonds amounted to over £120 billion, of which some 70 per cent were denominated in foreign currency. Of the UK companies' issues, two-thirds were in sterling and one-third in foreign currency. The relative popularity of eurobonds is shown by the comparatively low figure for loan capital – only £13 billion. Preference shares of UK companies amounted to £16 billion and ordinary and deferred shares to £450 billion, demonstrating the fact that listed company securities consist predominantly of equity capital. The value of foreign companies' shares listed on the ISE is very large, but does not of course rank nearly so highly in terms of business transacted.

ISE turnover figures are shown in table 14.3. The total figures include intra-market trading as well as business with customers. Turnover in government securities in 1990 was more than three times the value of securities outstanding, though less than half was customer business: trading in other fixed-interest securities was much less active – less than 20 per cent of the end-year value. The

Table 14.2 Securities listed on the ISE, end-1990

	(£ billion)
Government securities	
UK and Irish	128
Other	4
Total	132
Eurobonds	
UK companies	46
Overseas companies and international institutions	76
Total	122
Company securities	
Loan capital – UK	13
Loan capital – Other	1
Preference shares – UK	16
Preference shares – Other	15
Ordinary and deferred shares – UK and Irish	450
Ordinary and deferred shares – Other	1124
Total	1620
Total	1874

Source: ISE, *Quality of Markets Review*, winter 1990

Table 14.3 Turnover[1] on the ISE, 1990

	Total	*(£ billion)* Customer
British and Irish government securities	497	242
Other fixed-interest	25	13
Equities		
UK and Irish	158	103
Other	148	n.a.

Sources: ISE, *Quality of Markets Review*, winter 1990; *Stock Exchange Fact Sheet*, January 1991
[1] Purchase and sale counted as one transaction

corresponding figures for UK and foreign equities were about 33 per cent (about two-thirds customer business) and 13 per cent respectively. Though comparatively small as a proportion of the value of the securities listed, the latter represents a high proportion of trading outside the domestic markets concerned, much more than in any other centre. Low transactions costs and good liquidity are probably the main reasons for the ISE's success – in 1990 ISE turnover in Dutch and Swedish equities amounted to about 50 per cent of domestic trading, and for French and German equities the corresponding figures were about 25 per cent and 12 per cent respectively.

Prior to Big Bang the jobbers and brokers in the Stock Exchange operated in a *single capacity* – the jobbers as market makers who did not deal directly with customers, and the brokers having the customer contacts but refraining from dealing with clients for their own accounts. This single capacity system provided an important element of protection for investors – the broker's duty to his client was to seek out the best price for his transaction and there was no question of a broker selling shares to his clients from his own book at a price higher than the market price. During market hours trading took place on the floor of the Stock Exchange, avoiding any fragmentation of the market.

However, the system had a number of important weaknesses. The Stock Exchange operated as a cartel with agreed minimum commission levels, which were held at levels which seemed likely to be higher than could be expected in a freely competitive market. Member firms were partnerships, with only limited access to capital, which constrained the jobbers' ability to take positions (thus reducing the liquidity in the market) and inhibited both the brokers and the jobbers from investing in modern technology. The lack of jobbing capital hindered large transactions by institutional investors, which came to be 'put through' the market by brokers, who used their client bases to find counterparts for large deals, with the jobbers merely certifying that the price was fair. Moreover, jobbing was not very profitable, and the number of jobbers had been declining steadily, to the point where the competitiveness of the jobbing system was being called into question. The lack of capital more generally made it difficult to introduce modern screen-based trading in place of the obsolescent trading floor.

Big Bang introduced radical changes to the system. First, single capacity was no longer required, with some firms becoming market makers who dealt with clients as well as with brokers. Brokers no longer had to offer business to the market makers but could match trades between clients if they wished. Fixed minimum commissions were abolished – each firm was free to set its own scale, or negotiate with individual clients. Secondly, outside capital was brought into the market, with banks vying with each other to purchase existing firms of brokers and jobbers in order to gain an established position in the market. Overnight, the shortage of capital was turned into a surfeit.[5] Thirdly, the Stock Exchange automated quotation system (SEAQ) was brought in, with each market maker quoting buying and selling prices for the stocks in which it dealt and making these available to other participants in the market through a screen-based trading system. Brokers or direct clients of the market makers could call up the relevant screens and telephone orders to the market makers, who were bound to deal at the quoted prices for orders up to a specified size. Very soon trading on the floor of the Stock Exchange was abandoned. Information on trades is made available quickly – trades in most stocks of up to three times the normal size (for the stock in question) have to be reported immediately with short delays permitted only for large deals and particularly illiquid stocks, where the market maker's position would be liable to be prejudiced by immediate dissemination.[6]

The current system is able to handle large transactions much better than its predecessor, because the market makers have sufficient capital to be able to take substantial positions in individual shares. This is one of the major strengths of the ISE, and one of the reasons why it has been so successful in attracting international business. It serves the institutional investor well. Market makers have also engaged in 'bought deals', in which they purchase a portfolio of securities at a small discount to the market price, with a view to selling them on immediately through their client networks – competition amongst major market makers for this business ensures that the prices are keen. Moreover the abolition of minimum commissions resulted in substantial reductions for the larger transactions.

The system depends, however, on active competition between market makers to hold down the margins between buying and selling prices and active competition amongst brokers to keep down commission levels on brokered business. Immediately after Big Bang there were 33 market makers,[7] but by the end of 1990 this had declined to 24 as a result of the withdrawal of some unprofitable firms from the market, partly offset by the entry of new firms. Competition at the top end of the market remained strong – for the top tier of securities (nearly 200) quoted on SEAQ there was still an average of twelve market makers quoting prices, and for the middle tier (over 550 securities) the average was five. But for the third tier – over 1400 securities from smaller companies or which were lightly traded – the average was only three, and for 150 securities there was only one. A competitive market making system with only one market maker in a stock is clearly unsatisfactory, and from early January 1991 the Stock Exchange agreed with six market makers that they would ensure that there were at least two market makers in these relatively illiquid stocks.

The number of market makers has declined because business has not proved profitable. Market makers' margins (the 'touch') fell sharply after Big Bang, and prior to the crash of 1987 ranged from 1 per cent for the top tier of companies to 3 per cent for the third tier. They widened gradually in 1988 and 1989 and more sharply in 1990, so that by the end of 1990 for the three tiers they were over 1½ per cent, 5 per cent and 10 per cent respectively. At these levels the system seems to be operating satisfactorily for the most actively traded and liquid securities, but if the margin for the third tier – the majority of companies – remains at this level the verdict as regards less liquid stocks must be less favourable.

Brokers continue to play important roles within the stock market. In competition with market makers they provide research to institutional and other substantial clients, for which they are remunerated by means of commissions on business placed through them.[8] They also provide access to the market for retail clients, at a cost which reflects the range of services supplied. Thus some brokers provide only dealing services with no frills, at a relatively low cost, while others provide advice on particular transactions, on the composition of portfolios, and on related tax matters, charging rates of commission and fees which reflect the services rendered.

In financial terms the retail investor has benefited little, if at all, from the changed arrangements. Under the old system, minimum commissions were set at a level which resulted in some cross-subsidization of small-scale by large investors. This no longer exists. But the new system has led to specialization and the development of dealing-only services through, for example, the branch banking system, which enable the retail investor who does not seek advice to deal quickly and economically.

The ISE is also a vital component of the primary market for new capital in the UK. Table 14.4 shows capital raised through securities listed on the ISE in 1989. The figures only cover issues which raised new money, and exclude shares issued in connection with takeovers and mergers as well as sales of existing securities such as privatization issues.

Table 14.4 Capital issues of listed securities in the UK, 1989

	(£ billion)
Gross issues	11.0
Less Redemptions	3.1
Net issues	7.9
Of which:	
UK companies	
Ordinary shares	3.3
Preference shares	0.9
Convertible debentures	1.1
Other loan capital	1.5
Total	6.8
Overseas companies	1.0

Source: *Financial Statistics*, February 1991, table 12.1

Gross issues amounted to £11 billion, but were partly offset by redemptions and repurchases of existing securities in excess of £3 billion, so net issues were just under £8 billion. UK companies accounted for the greater part, with just under half consisting of ordinary shares and nearly 80 per cent having some element of equity.[9] About a third of the £1 billion raised by overseas companies also comprised ordinary shares. Both the level and composition of new issues do, however, vary from year to year – in the period from 1986 to 1990 net issues ranged from over £15 billion in 1987 to under £3 billion in 1990.

When a company wants to raise new share or loan capital it normally approaches an issuing house (usually a merchant bank) for advice and assistance, and a sponsoring broker which is a member of the ISE. Together these perform the origination function. The former advises on the terms on which the company should seek to raise capital and on the mechanics of the issue, while the latter is responsible for seeing that the necessary documentation is provided to the Stock Exchange and that the shares are distributed amongst end-investors – the distribution function. Sometimes the issuing house and sponsoring broker are part of the same group, sometimes they are independent.

New issues of shares entail the preparation and publication of a prospectus, setting out information about the company and its affairs in considerable detail to satisfy both legal requirements and the regulations of the ISE. The purposes of these regulations include giving potential investors the opportunity to acquire shares, and ensuring that ownership is sufficiently widely spread to facilitate an adequate trading market subsequently. Shares in a company which does not already have an ISE listing may be issued through an *offer for sale*, usually at a fixed price, though tender issues in which the public are invited to tender for shares at prices no less than a stated minimum are also possible.[10] The issuing house underwrites the whole issue – that is it agrees to subscribe itself for any shares remaining at the end of the offer period – though much of the risk is usually passed on to sub-underwriters recruited by the sponsoring broker.

The share offer is publicized widely, usually by advertisement in national newspapers. Under ISE regulations issues in excess of £15 million must employ the offer-for-sale technique.

For smaller issues, when public interest in the shares is likely to be more limited, the technique known as a *placing* may be employed – the issuing house buys the whole issue from the issuing company and then places the bulk of the shares at a negotiated price with institutional or other large investors selected by the issuing house and sponsoring broker. With the exception of very small issues, part of the issue must still be made available to the public at large.

From 1985 to 1989 there were 105 offers for sale (including tender offers) and 120 placings. The mean size of placings was £6 million. Over half of the offers for sale were for under £12 million, but the mean size was nearly £60 million.[11]

Issuing houses generally price issues by reference to the prevailing prices of similar securities which are already traded on the ISE. Normally the issuing house aims to set the issue price a little below the price at which the shares will trade subsequently, in order to encourage applications for the shares.[12] Issues therefore involve both direct costs – fees to the advisers, underwriting commissions, advertising costs etc. – and the indirect cost associated with the discount to the market price of comparable shares.

In the period 1985–9 the average direct cost of small (less than £5 million) offers for sale was nearly 14 per cent of the proceeds, compared with under 12 per cent for placings. In the £5–10 million range the corresponding figures were 10 per cent and 7½ per cent respectively. After 1987 there were no offers for sale of less than £10 million. For offers for sale over £10 million the average direct cost was 7 per cent. The indirect costs averaged a further 12 per cent, though this figure was affected by experience during 1987, a 'hot issue' period when share prices were rising rapidly and under-pricing averaged nearly 25 per cent. Excluding 1987 the average indirect cost was 8 per cent, with the average discount on placings being slightly higher than that on offers for sale.

Under ISE regulations the normal method by which a company already listed on the exchange raises new equity capital is the *rights* issue, and in 1989 companies raised £4.3 billion through rights issues. With only limited exceptions existing shareholders have the right to subscribe for new equity in preference to sales to third parties, the new shares being allocated pro rata to existing shareholdings. The price asked is usually set at a discount of some 15 to 20 per cent below the share price at the time of the announcement. Shareholders who do not wish to take up their allocation of new shares can sell their rights in the market and so avoid any financial loss which might otherwise result from setting the rights issue price below the prevailing market price. To ensure that the issuing company raises the capital it needs, rights issues are usually underwritten, with the underwriters taking up the shares if the share price falls below the rights issue price before the issue closes. Normally there is a period of some three weeks between announcement and subscription date, during which the share price is vulnerable to any unexpected events affecting the company as well as to influences affecting share prices generally. However, as an alternative to having the issue underwritten, companies sometimes make rights issues at a deeper discount to the prevailing market price, thus making it virtually certain that the shares will be taken up.

A takeover or merger situation is one occasion when shareholders often waive their pre-emption rights on new share issues. It is quite common for the buying company in a takeover to finance its operations by the issue of new shares to the vendors of the company being taken over – in 1989 £3.5 billion of shares were issued for this purpose – and these new shares have also to be listed on the ISE. Though no new money may be involved, the deal may be dependent on the vendors being able to sell the shares they receive at a known price, and this involves a *vendor placing*. The buying company's merchant bank or stockbroker places the shares with clients in the market, calling upon the distribution capacity of the stock market. A similar situation may arise when shareholders in the company being taken over are given the option of receiving either shares in the buying company or cash. To the extent that they opt for cash the buying company may wish to place new shares in the market.

Strictly speaking privatization issues involve a transfer of ownership of existing shares from the government to the private (and overseas) sector; therefore they do not raise *new* capital. However, like other issues which do raise new capital, they make demands on the private sector's funds, and they have in practice done so on a scale which entailed novel issue methods. In 1989 privatization issues raised £5.2 billion for the government.

In privatization issues the techniques of the placing and the offer for sale have been combined, and have involved capital markets abroad as well as the ISE in the UK. Part of the issues have been placed with financial institutions in the UK or distributed to overseas investors through securities dealers in other countries. The balance of the issues have been the subject of offers for sale to the public, with this portion being underwritten in the market. Provision has been made for a proportion of the placing to be clawed back for issue through the offer for sale in the event of public demand for shares being sufficiently strong.

In most cases all the shares were issued at a price fixed in advance in the usual way. But in some an element of tendering has been involved, with the institutions being invited to indicate how much they would wish to take up at different prices. This information has then been used to determine the price for the offer for sale, as well as influencing the amounts placed with individual institutions. As with other new issues there has been a significant degree of under-pricing relative to the price in the market subsequently – the average in 1985–9 was almost 20 per cent.

The unlisted securities market

There are certain minimum requirements which companies have to satisfy in order to have their securities included in the ISE's Official List. For example, a company must now (1991) provide full financial information on its trading record for a minimum of three years, and at least 25 per cent of its capital must be available to the public. As a result the Official List is unsuitable for many new or smaller companies which cannot or may not wish to meet these conditions.

Some of these companies would, however, benefit from a stock market listing which can provide access to capital on more favourable terms than would otherwise be available and can also provide a means by which the existing owners can dispose of some of their shares. In an attempt to meet this need the Stock Exchange has, since 1980, maintained the so-called Unlisted Securities Market (USM) for companies which want the benefit of a listing on some market and are prepared to satisfy a set of less demanding rules. Originally the minimum length of trading record was three years (at a time when the Official List required five), which was reduced to two years in January 1991. At least 10 per cent of the shares must be available to the public.[13]

The USM is a valuable adjunct to the Official List. At the end of 1990 over 400 companies had securities listed with a market value of £5.5 billion. Issues during 1989 amounted to £767 million, of which rights issues by companies which were already listed raised £296 million. Over 80 per cent of the funds were raised by issues of ordinary shares.

The gilt-edged market

The market in British government securities, the gilt-edged market, is a significant component of the UK securities market. At the end of 1990 the nominal value of gilt-edged stock outstanding was £122 billion, involving 84 actively traded stocks. Some 20 per cent of the value consisted of index-linked stocks, whose average maturity was more than 15 years, whilst the 80 per cent of conventional stocks had an average maturity of about eight years. Thanks to the substantial PSDR in 1989 and 1990 (see chapter 9) there was no need to issue new stocks in these years, even in order to replace maturing stock, though new issues were resumed in 1991. In spite of the lack of new issues the secondary market remained very active, with customer turnover in 1990 double the value of the securities outstanding.[14]

The key participants in the market are the Gilt-Edged Market Makers (GEMMs), which carry out the trading and sales functions in a single operation. Twenty-seven GEMMs were created at the time of Big Bang, whose target market shares added to no less than 175 per cent of the potential market! Not surprisingly this excess capacity led to severe losses and subsequent withdrawals from the market – between Big Bang in October 1986 and the end of 1989 about a third of the capital initially committed to the market was lost and the number of GEMMs fell to nineteen. The position stabilized in 1990, and the GEMMs as a whole were profitable, though still not at a level which provided a reasonable return on capital employed. The largest six GEMMs accounted for more than 60 per cent of the turnover, with the bottom six taking only 10 per cent.

In relation to the scale of dealings in the gilt-edged market the

GEMMs operate on a comparatively narow capital base. At the end of 1990 this fell just short of £400 million, to support daily turnover with customers approaching £2 billion on average. Other institutions in the market help to make this possible.

Inter-Dealer Brokers (IDBs) are employed to help individual GEMMs to lay off their positions in the market. For example, if a GEMM buys a large line of stock from an institution and wants to reduce its holding it will attempt to sell to other GEMMs. They could, of course, trade directly, but at the risk of revealing their position and driving the price against themselves. By operating through an IDB they are able to deal anonymously, and so on more favourable terms. In turn, this facility enables them to offer a better price for the stock to their own customer.

When the new trading system was introduced at the time of Big Bang there were six IDBs – again, more than the volume of business could support. Subsequent withdrawals from the market reduced the number to two, but a new entrant created a third in 1990.

Trading would also be restricted if GEMMs could only sell stock which they already held and if they were unable to build up overall positions in excess of their capital resources. To avoid these difficulties they use the services of Stock Exchange Money Brokers (SEMBs), of whom there were nine at the end of 1990. Their functions are to arrange for GEMMs to borrow stock temporarily from large institutional investors to enable them to complete their deals, and to lend the GEMMs funds to finance their holdings of stock. Stock lending is done on a secured basis and in exchange for a small fee, and the GEMM does not know from which institution the stock has been borrowed. Again, anonymity is preserved.

When a GEMM has a substantial holding of an individual stock it is exposed to two kinds of risk: the risk that interest rates generally will change and the risk that the price of the stock will move relative to the market as a whole. The former is the greater risk and GEMMs make considerable use of the long gilts futures market (see the derivatives market below) to hedge against it. In effect they are able to offset the risk inherent in a holding of long-dated gilts by entering into a commitment to sell an equivalent amount at a fixed price in future, thus insulating themselves from general market movements. The consequence is that they can safely take large positions in the gilts market without exposing their capital to undue risk, thereby increasing the liquidity of the market.

Most of the business for large investors is carried out directly by the GEMMs without the intervention of agency brokers. However, these continue to provide advisory and dealing services, particularly for retail investors, and about 10 per cent of the turnover in 1990 passed through their hands.

New issues of gilt-edged securities are handled by the Bank of England, which arranges the issue on behalf of the government and employs a variety of techniques to distribute the stock to investors. The traditional method of issuing a new gilt-edged stock is the public issue, in which the stock is offered for sale at a fixed price and the Bank England acts as underwriter. In practice the Bank has often ended up holding most of the stock, which it then sold in the market in response to bids from GEMMs or brokers, the Bank of course being free to accept or reject any of these bids.

Rather than issuing new stocks the government can also issue additional tranches of existing stocks. This has the advantage that the new stock will be traded in a liquid market; indeed, by increasing the size of the issue it enhances the liquidity of the existing stock. Again, the Bank holds the stock initially and distributes it gradually through the market when opportunities arise.

A third technique is to make a tender issue. The government stipulates a minimum tender price which it expects to be below the price at which the stock will trade in the market and invites bids at the minimum or higher prices. The issue is underwritten by the Bank of England. Investors (including GEMMs on their own accounts as well as on behalf of clients) bid for the stock. The minimum price at which all the stock will be sold is found, and this is the price paid by all investors. Allocations are made in full for bids at prices higher than the minimum accepted price and the balance is distributed pro rata to bidders at this price. In normal circumstances a tender is likely to result in the whole issue being distributed to investors, but there is always the risk of price movements between the announcement of the issue and the tender date leading to a shortfall of bids, with the Bank of England having to take up the balance.

The fourth technique, the auction, resembles the tender, but differs in two respects. First, there is no minimum tender price, and the issue is not underwritten, though the government does reserve the right to reduce the size of the issue in exceptional circumstances. Secondly, bidders all have to pay the price they bid – they do not receive stock at the minimum accepted price. This increases the bidder's risk – he is liable to pay significantly more than other investors and find that the stock trades immediately at a discount to what he has paid. To limit this risk and assist the market in formulating bids the Bank has permitted trading in the stock to take place shortly before it is issued, thus giving investors an indication of the probable price level. The auction technique has the advantage that the government can be quite sure that the whole issue will be sold, even in unfavourable market conditions.[15]

Lastly, instead of waiting for bids from the market for relatively small amounts of stock the Bank of England may negotiate a price with the GEMMs for them to buy a substantial amount. (This can be compared with bought deals in the equity market.) The GEMMs are then left to distribute stock to their clients subsequently.

The Bank of England is able to choose whichever method seems most likely to be successful in the prevailing market conditions. This will depend both on the amount of stock the government wants to sell – for example, successive small tranches of existing stocks are well suited to relatively light funding programmes – and the market's appetite for gilt-edged stocks at the time. Auctions and sales to GEMMs seem likely to prove robust even in difficult conditions.

Sterling money markets

The sterling money markets are wholesale, professional markets in which sterling deposits and various kinds of money-market paper are traded. The principal financial instruments are: unsecured deposits with banks, secured money placed with the discount market or other money-market dealers, certificates of deposit issued by banks and building societies, Treasury bills, bank bills and commercial paper. The main participants in the money markets are the banks, other issuers of money-market paper, the discount houses (see below) who act as market makers for the negotiable instruments, and the money-market brokers. The money market's prime function is to assist banks and building societies (and to a much lesser extent local authorities and other companies) in their treasury operations – that is the management of their cash, short-term assets and short-term liabilities.

The amounts of money-market instruments outstanding at the end of September 1989 are shown in table 14.5. The largest element is unsecured market loans – deposits placed by banks with other banks in the inter-bank market. This is a telephone market, with direct links between the major participants, and brokers playing only a relatively minor part. The deposits cover a wide range of maturities, with a strong bias towards the short end of the spectrum, and banks use the market to manage both the level and maturity

Table 14.5 Money-market instruments, September 1990

	(£ billion)
Unsecured market loans (deposits)[1]	88.5
Secured loans to discount houses	12.1
CDs issued by banks	51.1
CDs issued by building societies	7.6
Treasury bills	13.8
Bank bills	21.2
Commercial paper	5.7
Total	200.0

Sources: Bank of England Quarterly Bulletin, November 1990,
p. 516; *Financial Statistics*, table 6.4
[1] Market loans to other UK banks and discount houses

structure of their assets and liabilities. For example, a bank which wanted to add to its liquidity might take three-month deposits and place the same amount in seven-day deposits with other banks.[16] The significance of this inter-bank deposit market for liquidity and interest-rate management was explained in chapter 11, but it is important to note also that it is the principal source of resources for the lending activities of banks which are short of customer deposits.

Bank and building society CDs fulfil a similar function, but because they are marketable they provide an added degree of flexibility in asset portfolios – marketability is assured by the discount houses and certain other market makers. Secured loans to the discount houses provide them with the necessary resources. Most of these loans are callable (that is, repayment can be demanded without notice) or overnight, ensuring that they rank only just behind cash in terms of liquidity. Like Treasury bills and bank bills,[17] which are eligible for rediscount at the Bank of England, they represent tier-one liquidity for the banks as a whole – a reliable source of cash in a crisis. The stock of Treasury bills and bank bills is strongly influenced by Bank of England operations, both in their management of government debt and in their day-to-day conduct of monetary policy.

Commercial paper is a much less important asset and, as noted earlier, it is mainly held outside the banking system. Companies of high standing do not need the cachet of a bank's guarantee to make their paper acceptable. Even if it trades on a slightly higher yield than bank acceptances, it is less costly to the borrower once the bank's acceptance fee is taken into account. For the bank there is a lower limit to the fee it can afford to charge determined by the bank's need for capital support for all its business, regardless of the quality of the company's credit. Compared with bank bills, commercial paper may also have advantages of flexibility regarding the period of issue or other characteristics. Commercial paper programmes are normally managed by banks for the companies concerned, with the bank taking responsibility for distributing the paper to suitable investors.

Turnover in the money markets is assisted by the money-market brokers, of whom there were fourteen in May 1990. While they play a much more significant role in the foreign exchange market and in the market for foreign currency deposits than in the sterling markets, the brokers nevertheless had daily turnover in sterling money market instruments of over £200 million in the first quarter of 1990. Their role is strictly that of brokers – they bring clients together – and they do not act as principals in any transactions. In May 1990 the Bank of England estimated that the brokers' share of the sterling money markets was certainly not more than 25 per cent, and was probably significantly less in instruments such as bank bills, CDs, and commercial paper.

Discount houses

The discount houses fulfil three distinct economic functions: they act as the key market makers in the sterling money markets, their principal liabilities form the nearest asset to cash in the banks' portfolios, and they have a relationship with the Bank of England which is central to the implementation of monetary policy in the UK. Each of these functions has a bearing on their balance sheets (table 14.6).

Their sterling assets consist of Treasury bills, other bills, bank CDs, market loans to banks and time deposits with building societies, building society CDs and other lending to UK companies. With the possible exception of the last (which includes commercial paper), these are all low-risk assets and most are assets in which the discount houses make the markets. Indeed, to qualify as a discount house they have to accept the obligation to act as a market maker in the bill markets, and this extends to ensuring that the bids at any Treasury bill tender cover the amount of bills on offer. In practice the houses are also expected to fill a similar role in the CD markets. Turnover in the bill and CD markets is substantial – almost 50 per

Table 14.6 Discount houses: balance sheets, end-1989

	(£ billion)
Liabilities	
Borrowed funds, sterling	
Bank of England	0.1
Other UK banks	10.2
Other	4.2
Total	14.5
Borrowed funds, other currencies	0.4
Other liabilities	0.4
Total	15.3
Assets	
Sterling	
Treasury bills	0.9
Other bills	6.0
Bank certificates of deposit	4.3
Other	3.6
Total	14.9
Foreign currency	0.4
Total	15.3

Source: Financial Statistics, February, 1991, table 6.5

cent of the outstanding stock each month in the third quarter of 1990.

Discount houses also accept the obligation to take callable (secured) deposits from banks. Of the £14.4 billion of borrowed funds (other than from the Bank of England) at the end of 1989, £12.4 billion was at call or overnight. These funds are immediately available to any bank which is short of funds the next day, and there is no risk of capital loss due to changes in market interest rates, such as exists with marketable instruments.

Discount houses are able to accept these obligations by virtue of their relationship with the Bank of England. If they run short of funds, either because the funds are withdrawn or because they are honouring their obligation to purchase other money-market instruments, they have access to funding from the Bank of England. In the normal course of events the Bank will 'take out' any shortage by purchasing bills, but failing this they are able to borrow from the Bank.

It is through this arrangement that the Bank of England manages interest rates in the UK. The Bank itself deals actively in the bill markets, and is in a position to create a shortage of cash when it wishes to do so. In that case the discount houses have no option but to go to the Bank for funds, and the terms on which these funds are provided indicates to the market the level of short-term interest rates of which the Bank approves. Market rates tend to remain close to this level.[18]

In view of the nature of their business the discount houses can safely operate with much lower capital ratios than is appropriate for other banks. They are therefore subject to different regulations. Assets are put into seven risk categories, of which six add various multiples to the basic risk attributed to the lowest category. The basic risk plus additions for the higher risk categories must not exceed 80 times the discount house's eligible capital.

Foreign exchange market

London is the home of the world's largest foreign exchange market. A survey in April 1989[19] showed estimated daily turnover of US$187 billion, compared with $129 billion in New York, $115 billion in Tokyo and $57 billion in Switzerland. The survey covered 356 organizations which act as principals in the market, together with nine foreign exchange brokers (whose intermediation in transactions between overseas principals added another $12 billion of daily turnover).

The market consists of principals – market makers who buy or sell currencies on their own account, dealing with customers and with other principals – and brokers. The principals are mostly banks, including a majority of the overseas banks in London. The major banks in the market, and some non-bank market makers, deal actively in a wide range of currencies, whilst others are concerned primarily in carrying out transactions involving their own currencies. Brokers carry out the classic function of finding counterparties to deals for their clients, who may not have direct links with principals or who may not wish to reveal their transactions to other principals in the market. The foreign exchange market is a telephone market, with the market makers having direct links to other major participants in the UK and abroad, and the brokers having a similar range of contacts with their clients.

The transactions in the market fall into four categories: spot contracts for settlement within two days, forward contracts for settlement further in the future, and standardized futures and options contracts. The forward contracts may involve the outright purchase or sale of one currency against another for some specified future date, but also include swaps (e.g. a spot purchase matched by an offsetting outright forward sale) and 'forward/forwards' (e.g. a forward purchase at one date matched by a forward sale further in the future). In the 1989 survey 64 per cent of business involved spot contracts, 35 per cent forwards, and only 1 per cent futures and options.[20]

Over 90 per cent of the transactions involve the US dollar, which acts as the key currency in the market. The volume of transactions between most pairs of currencies is comparatively small, and by using the dollar as an intermediary a high proportion of the transactions involving any other currency are brought together. For example, transactions between Dutch florins and, say, sterling, yen, French francs, and deutschmarks are carried out by exchanging Dutch florins for US dollars and then exchanging the dollars into sterling, yen etc. The effect is to improve the depth and liquidity of the market for florins, making it easier to carry out large transactions without affecting the price significantly. However, business involving other major currencies is sometimes sufficient to warrant direct conversion, and so-called 'cross-currency' business not involving the US dollar rose from 3 per cent in 1986 to 9 per cent in 1989. Short of full monetary union, this proportion can be expected to increase further as monetary integration proceeds within the ERM.

The international nature of the London foreign exchange market can be seen from a breakdown of its business. Eighty per cent of the turnover by principals is carried out by foreign banks in London, while 34 per cent of direct business and nearly 60 per cent of the business transacted by UK principals through brokers (38 per cent of principals' business) involves a non-UK bank as the counterparty. Adding in the 15 per cent of brokers' business in which neither party is resident in the UK brings the total in which at least one principal is a non-UK bank to almost 60 per cent.

The principals' ultimate customers are non-financial companies and other financial institutions. These provide the counterparties in only 15 per cent of transactions, but they are the driving force for a much higher proportion of the business in the market. The reason is that several transactions are frequently required to carry out one customer order. For example, where the customer's order does not involve the US dollar, using the dollar as an intermediary doubles the number of transactions, and where the order is for forward delivery additional swap transactions will be required for the principal to hedge its own foreign exchange exposure. A customer order can thus easily give rise to four other transactions in the market. Much, though by no means all, of the activity in the market is generated by customers' requirements.

Markets in financial derivatives

Financial derivatives take two basic forms. They may be contracts which commit the parties to buy or sell financial instruments, such as long-dated gilts, at set prices on some agreed future date. These are known as *forward* or *futures* contracts. Alternatively, they may be *options* contracts which given one party the right, but not the obligation, to buy (or sell) at a set price on an agreed future date, while the other party takes on the obligation to sell (or buy) if the first party chooses to exercise his option. The contracts may be on financial instruments themselves (e.g. a company's shares) or on a statistical index such as the FT-SE 100 index of share prices, or even on another financial derivative (e.g. an option on interest rate futures). They may also be tailor-made by financial institutions to suit the requirements of particular clients, or they may be standardized and traded on organized markets such as LIFFE.

To take one example, the long gilts contract traded on LIFFE is a contract to buy £50 000 of a notional 9% 20-year gilt-edged stock, on specified dates in the current and following quarters. Contracts can be settled by delivering certain actual gilt-edged stocks on the relevant date, but normally they are 'closed-out' beforehand by reversing the initial purchase or sale. Profit or loss is determined by the difference in price between the initial and closing-out contracts.

LIFFE's 3-month sterling contract provides a second example. This is a contract on the interest on a £500 000 three-month deposit on specified (quarterly) future dates. Again, contracts are often closed-out in advance of these settlement dates, but those that do run to maturity are settled in cash, the amount being calculated from the difference between the interest rate inherent in the contract and the three-month rate prevailing at the settlement date.

A third example is the option contract on the FT-SE 100 index traded on the London Traded Options Market (LTOM). These option contracts are for specified levels of the index on particular future (quarterly) settlement dates, at which time the holder of the option can exercise his right to buy (or sell) at that level. Settlement is by means of cash payments, reflecting the difference between the actual level of the index and the level specified in the contract.

The markets in derivatives are used for three purposes: hedging, speculation and arbitrage – hedging being the most important economic function. For example, by entering into a 'forward rate agreement' a company treasurer can fix the cost of borrowing which will be required on some future date, thus avoiding the risk of interest rates changing in the intervening period. The treasurer of a bank can use interest rate futures contracts to match the interest rate characteristics of the bank's asset and liability portfolio. Or, as we have already noted, market makers can hedge the risk arising from substantial positions in equities or bonds by purchasing offsetting contracts in equity or interest rate futures. Hedging provides the basic motivation for a high proportion of business in the financial derivatives markets.

Speculation is driven by the profit motive, but performs the valuable function of providing liquidity in the markets, thus enabling them to operate efficiently. Speculative positions are required to offset any imbalance which may arise from hedging transactions, and active speculation in response to small price movements ensures that any such temporary imbalances will not lead to substantial price changes. Active dealing by speculators helps the market to absorb other transactions without disturbance.

The function of arbitrage is to ensure that the derivatives and cash markets move in tandem. For example, if the long gilts future rises but the prices of the gilts stocks which are deliverable against the contract do not rise correspondingly, it will be profitable for arbitrageurs to buy the actual stocks and sell futures, with a view to delivering the stocks in settlement in due course.[21] The consequence is that movements in either the cash markets or the futures markets are transmitted rapidly to the other.

Futures contracts are a means of avoiding risk, but they do this at the cost of eliminating opportunity. The purchaser of an interest rate futures contract cannot lose if interest rates rise unexpectedly, but does not gain if interest rates fall. Options preserve the possibility of gain.

An investor who expects that share prices will rise but wants to protect his portfolio against the possibility that they may fall can do so by purchasing options to sell the shares in his portfolio at the current price. If share prices do in fact fall the options will be exercised and his capital will be preserved. If, however, share prices rise the option is allowed to lapse and the investor enjoys the benefit of the capital gain. Of course, the protection against loss has to be paid for through the option 'premium'. This will reflect the volatility of share prices – the greater the volatility the larger the insurance premium against loss. By accepting some risk of loss, that is by purchasing an option to sell at prices which lie some way below the current prices, the premium can be reduced.

The cost of an option is, of course, much higher than the cost of a futures contract, where the risks are evenly balanced. Corresponding to the purchaser of the option there has to be a seller (or 'writer') who is prepared to accept the increased exposure to risk, and the premium has to be large enough to compensate the writer of the option for the risk taken on.[22]

Standardized financial derivatives are traded on organized markets, such as LIFFE. The most important contracts on LIFFE are the three-month sterling and deutschmark interest rate contracts, the long gilts contract, and the so-called 'bund' contract, namely the contract in German government bonds. There are also futures contracts in US dollar, yen, ECU and Swiss franc interest rates, in the FT-SE 100 index, and in options on some of the futures contracts. During working hours trading is by 'open outcry' on the dealing floor; this accounts for some 95 per cent of business. After hours a screen-based trading system operates. Standardized contracts, which are cleared through the exchange,[23] help to produce liquid markets in the major contracts. Dealing is on a very large scale – for example in 1990 the value of contracts in the long gilt was approximately half the level of turnover in the gilt-edged market.

Options on individual company shares and on the FT-SE 100 index are traded on the LTOM, which employs a screen-based trading system. Taking LIFFE and LTOM together the value of equity-related futures and options derivatives almost equalled that in the cash market in 1990. LIFFE and LTOM are expected to merge in 1991.

Financial derivatives are also available over the counter (OTC) from banks and other financial institutions. These are often tailor-made to suit the needs of the client. For example, forward rate agreements (FRAs) are similar to interest rate futures, but are available for non-standard dates and in non-standard amounts. More complex option-based derivatives are also offered – the 'collar' which sets upper and lower limits on interest rates being one example. As already noted, in the foreign exchange market banks provide currency options, which are valuable to firms tendering for foreign contracts which they cannot be certain of winning.

Providing these products exposes the banks to risk. In part they can offset this by matching contracts for other customers, but to a considerable extent they rely on the organized market to hedge their positions. The matching, for example of dates, is likely to be less than perfect, so that some residual risk remains. Nevertheless, much the greater part can be eliminated.

Notes

1 A swap is an agreement between two parties to exchange streams of payments, for example fixed-interest payments on a loan of a given size for payments linked to a variable market rate of interest (an interest rate swap) or payments in one currency for payments in another (a currency swap).
2 Originally these were all US dollar denominated securities issued outside the USA, in practice in Europe.
3 If, for example, investors have a stronger appetite for deutschmark than for US dollar securities it may be cheaper for an issuer to borrow in deutschmarks and swap into dollars than to borrow the dollars directly.
4 When competition for business is particularly strong, banks may find that they have to sell to clients at a lower price than they have paid for the issue, in effect forgoing part or all of their fees.
5 In their rush to enter this business the banks paid far too much for the Stock Exchange firms they acquired, and the inevitable result of the excess capital was substantial losses in the ensuing years.
6 For example, other market makers with whom the market maker might want to deal would know that it had acquired a large line of stock and would reduce their buying prices accordingly.
7 Compared with eighteen jobbers in the Stock Exchange prior to Big Bang.
8 The market makers' spread between buying and selling prices is somewhat higher for direct client business than for brokered business, the difference corresponding to the broker's commission for research and dealing services.
9 Convertible debentures are issued in the expectation that they will be converted into equity in due course, though these expectations are not always realized.
10 Issues by tender were common in the eighties, but became less popular subsequently – there were none at all in 1987–9.
11 The mean was affected by flotations of £1.5 billion for TSB and nearly £1 billion for Abbey National. Excluding these issues the mean falls to £36 million.
12 Potential investors have to be convinced that they are likely to do better by buying the new shares than by simply buying existing shares on the market. Moreover the success of an issue depends on press comment,

which is much more likely to be favourable if there is a degree of under-pricing.

13 From 1987 to 1990 there was also a Third Market for companies with less than three years' trading experience, but this was abolished when the minimum for the USM was reduced to two years.

14 Counting purchases and sales as only one transaction.

15 The ability to sell stock in these conditions may be important for monetary management.

16 Provided that the interest rates were fixed for the same periods this would leave the bank with a short-term interest rate exposure – it would stand to lose if short-term interest rates fell unexpectedly – which could, however, be hedged in the interest-rate derivatives market.

17 Bank *acceptances*.

18 In practice the rates at which the Bank is prepared to deal in the bill markets sets the level of short-term rates. Only exceptionally does it have to compel the discount houses to borrow from it to enforce its wishes.

19 *Bank of England Quarterly Bulletin*, November 1989.

20 Though this may be an underestimate because certain institutions specializing in these contracts were not included in the survey.

21 Ignoring transactions costs, arbitrage will be profitable if the cash price of the stocks plus any carrying costs until settlement of the futures contract is less than the price in the futures market.

22 It is sometimes argued that the risk attached to a portfolio of securities can be *reduced* by writing options. If risk is measured by the variance of return on the portfolio, writing options which will be exercised if there are sharp changes in share prices can reduce the variance, with of course the added benefit of the premiums for the writer. However, if risk is interpreted as the probability of loss – either actual loss or the loss of an opportunity for gain – writing options cannot reduce risk, because the options will be exercised only if it is in the interest of the purchaser of the option to do so. From this perspective, the writing of options may be a worthwhile activity if the premiums are sufficiently high to compensate for the potential losses, but this should not be allowed to disguise the reality that the exposure to opportunity losses is increased.

23 This virtually eliminates 'counterparty' risk – the risk that the other party to a deal will fail – because each side technically has a contract with the exchange, which ensures that traders have sufficient resources to meet their commitments (and closes out positions automatically if there is any doubt). Traders do not therefore have to limit their dealings by reference to the resources of the other party to their deals.

Part V

The control and efficiency of the system

All economic activity is conducted against a legislative background, including laws of property, contract, competitive behaviour etc. which determine what economic agents may and may not do. Financial institutions and practitioners in financial markets are no exceptions to this rule, but in addition to the laws affecting business generally they are subjected to controls for prudential and sometimes also economic reasons. In chapter 15 we examine the need for these controls, the structure of prudential regulation in the UK, and the costs which they impose. We also consider issues connected with deposit insurance and with the marketing of retail savings products.

In the final chapter we attempt to appraise the success of the UK financial system in meeting society's needs. Judged by microeconomic criteria its performance, on the whole, seems very satisfactory. Competition is strong, pricing is fair, savers have an immense range of products to choose from, and the great majority of investors have access to the funds they need and can afford. From a macroeconomic standpoint, however, the verdict is less favourable. There are doubts as the whether the system as a whole creates a climate which is conducive to risk-taking and investment by industry and commerce. And there is no doubt that in the second half of the 1980s the behaviour of the financial system exacerbated instability in the UK economy.

15

Regulation and control

Some of the reasons why governments control the activities of financial institutions and regulate the securities markets have already been indicated in chapter 1, notably the prevention of failure by institutions and of fraudulent dealing in markets. Governments try to ensure that financial institutions are able to honour their commitments, that savers have access to the information they need to form a proper judgement about the prospects and risks attached to the securities they buy, and that dealing in financial markets is fair. Controls imposed for these purposes are described as *prudential* controls.

Governments also control the financial system as part of their financial and economic policies. We saw in chapters 5 and 6 how monetary policy affects short and long-term rates of interest in the economy: through these and other channels monetary policy influences economic activity and prices. The methods which governments employ to conduct their monetary policies frequently involve restricting the activities of financial institutions, notably banks. Governments also often attempt to influence the allocation of resources in the economy, sometimes through taxes or subsidies, sometimes by requesting or obliging financial institutions to provide finance for certain categories of borrower on favourable terms, and sometimes through their policies with regard to competition, restrictive practices and mergers, which impinge on the financial institutions. Regulations and controls applied for these reasons come under the general heading of *economic* controls.

In this chapter we shall deal primarily with the need for prudential controls and regulations, and with the structure of prudential regulation in the UK, after which we shall look briefly at economic controls and their influence of the financial system. No attempt is made to give a detailed description or critique of the current system of monetary and other controls in the UK.

The need for prudential controls

Before considering the forms taken by prudential controls and regulations in the financial system it is worthwhile pausing to consider why prudential controls are required at all. Why can financial institutions not be permitted a free rein within a market system, with the users making their own assessments of the quality of the liabilities issued by the different institutions? Presumably then the institutions which built up a good reputation over a long period would be in a strong competitive position to attract business, while savers would turn away from shakier enterprises. As with many other things which are brought and sold, the obligation to satisfy himself on the quality of the product he was buying would lie with the user.

In the case of financial services there are several reasons why 'leaving it all to the market' may not be desirable. It is often not easy for customers to evaluate with any confidence the quality of the services they are buying. Services are sold by description, the commitments entered into may be for very long periods, the quality of the service frequently cannot be judged until long after payment has been made, and a high reputation gained through sound business practices in the past may no longer be fully justified. It is seldom practicable for private individuals to obtain the information needed to form a judgement about the strength of a financial institution, and even if the information was available the great majority of people lack the expertise to appraise it properly; the process of evaluating the soundness of financial institutions is highly technical. In any case, for each individual to have to carry out such an appraisal would be time-consuming and inefficient, and it is something which can be avoided by a degree of standardization in the financial instruments offered. If, for example, bank deposits were known to be safe, consumers would not have to spend time and trouble in making enquiries about the bank with which they deposited their funds. So long as the constraints placed upon banks to ensure that their deposits really were safe did not seriously impede the activities of sound institutions, there would be a substantial net cost saving to society from standardization.

Prudential controls on financial institutions must also be seen in the context of consumer protection. In the UK the doctrine that the buyer should beware does not generally apply, and producers are under an obligation to supply products which perform the functions claimed for them. Prudential controls on financial institutions attempt to ensure that the same conditions apply within the financial sector – for example, that bank deposits are actually repaid on demand, that insurance cover is provided, and that purchasers of shares obtain title to the shares they buy. There is also the practical consideration that when, in the last two decades, financial institutions have failed their liability holders have usually received some compensation – though not without considerable delay and effort in some cases. During the secondary banking crisis of 1973–5 depositors with banks that failed eventually got their money back; and the same was true of building society failures. Policyholders with failed insurance companies were not invariably so fortunate, though they too received some of the benefits they expected. Investors who lost money could usually point to negligence that lent support to their claim for compensation. Where society as a whole is biased towards protecting the consumer, and where sound institutions are compelled to bear the cost of compensating for losses, there is clearly a strong case for attempting to avoid failures in the first place.

It would, however, be a mistake to suppose that all the arguments are in favour of protecting the customer at the expense of inhibiting the freedom of action of financial institutions and other participants in financial markets. A balance has to be found between opposing interests. Controls and regulations on institutions and markets are by no means costless: they inevitably impede competition, which is the main spur to efficiency and innovation in the economy. Rigid controls are all too liable to lead to inefficiency and to stifle new developments. Moreover, while controls may make financial institutions' liabilities more attractive in some respects, they may simultaneously reduce their attractions in other ways – for example by reducing the rate of return on funds or raising the cost of insurance. Regulations designed to improve the efficiency of markets may also have damaging side-effects, and the costs of enforcing control must not be overlooked. How far society goes in controlling institutions and markets must depend then on the priority given to promoting efficiency and innovation – a priority which is best pursued by allowing the institutions freedom of action – as against protecting their customers, including the ignorant or foolish, from loss.

Structure of prudential regulation

Prudential regulation in the UK derives from four principal Acts of Parliament, with responsibility divided amongst a substantial number of regulatory bodies. Banking is covered by the Banking Act 1987 with the responsible body being the Bank of England; building societies' operations are governed by the Building Societies Act 1986 with the regulations being implemented by the Building Societies Commission; insurance business (with the exception of companies' marketing and investment management activities) comes under the Insurance Companies Act 1982 with responsibility lying with the Department of Trade and Industry (DTI); and the Financial Services Act 1986 (FSA) covers investment business generally, with responsibility vested ultimately in the DTI but with many functions delegated to the Securities and Investments Board (SIB) and through them to a number of Self-Regulating Organisations (SROs) and Recognised Professional Bodies (RPBs). In addition there is the Takeover Panel which sets out rules for the conduct of takeovers and adjudicates on issues between the parties involved. All of the UK legislation has, of course, to be consistent with EC law – for example, directives governing the listing requirements for securities, the solvency requirements for banks, and in due course the proposed Investment Services Directive which will govern investment business.

There are a number of common threads which run through the legislation. The first is a requirement for *authorization*: companies engaged in any of the businesses covered by the legislation have to be authorized by a responsible body, and it is a criminal offence to engage in business without authorization. Before granting authorization the responsible body has to be satisfied that the business has sufficient capital and that it will be properly managed – that the people involved have sufficient expertise and experience and that they are not disqualified in other respects, that is that they are 'fit and proper persons'.

Secondly there is usually on-going reporting, *supervision* and inspection to ensure that businesses remain sound and are abiding by the regulations. This takes the form of returns made by firms to their respective supervisory bodies and which are monitored by them, discussions between officials and managements, and if necessary the sending in of teams of inspectors and/or accountants to delve into the firm's affairs. Penalties for non-compliance range from fines, the imposition of more frequent and rigorous reporting requirements to the withdrawal of authorization (which puts the firm out of business).

Thirdly, there are arrangements for *compensation* for private individuals when firms fail. Compensation is by no means unlimited and may be for less than 100 per cent of the firm's liability to the customer. But there is a general practice that customers who cannot be expected to possess a high degree of financial sophistication should enjoy some protection against loss through the failure of the firm with which they deal. (There is, of course, no similar protection against losses resulting from the normal investment risks.)

In the case of the Financial Services Act much of the regulation is designed to ensure fair dealing and the protection of the customer's interest. Thus there are regulations governing the provision of information; both what must be provided by, for example, companies seeking a Stock Exchange listing or fund managers advertising their products such as unit trust units, and what must *not* be provided – for example purely subjective projections of the likely rate of return on investments. Insider dealing is prohibited – it is a criminal offence to deal on the basis of 'inside' information, that is information which is available only to those with privileged access to a company's affairs. Companies which engage in a variety of businesses have to erect 'Chinese walls' between them, through which information is not allowed to pass. Thus arrangements have to be made to keep the corporate finance teams in a bank, who have access to privileged information about companies' businesses and financing, separate from their investment management teams, whose decisions would be likely to be influenced by such knowledge. 'Compliance officers' have to be employed with the task of ensuring that the regulations are observed. Financial companies' interests have to be disclosed to their clients so that they may be aware of any conflicts of interest which could arise.

The interests of the less sophisticated private customers are protected in a variety of ways. Customers' funds must be segregated from those of the company itself. Firms offering financial advice have an obligation to know enough about their customers' affairs to be able to advise them responsibly, and the advice they give should be in the client's best interest – they are expected to subordinate their own interest to that of their client.[1] Relationships between firms and their clients have generally to be set out in customer agreement letters, describing the services the firm provides, its responsibilities and its charges or other sources of remuneration (e.g. commissions). Retail sales of investments are normally subject to a cooling-off period, during which the customer can withdraw without penalty. Fees and commissions must be disclosed (though not generally until after the deal has been agreed, even if before the end of any cooling-off period). Lastly, firms selling investments such as insurance policies and unit trusts have to choose between on the one hand selling their own or a designated range of products and on the other performing as fully independent intermediaries who advise customers and act as their agents. This is designed to avoid the most obvious danger of customers believing they were being given independent advice, while in fact they were being sold a firm's own products.

The SIB is an agency, funded by the financial services industry, to which most of the DTI's powers have been transferred. It comprises practitioners from a wide variety of investment activities with the addition of a number of independent members, and has a full-time executive chairman. The SIB has its own rule-book and can authorize investment businesses itself, but in practice most author-ization is carried out indirectly through the four recognized SROs, each dealing with different aspects of investment business, and the RPBs.

The SROs are *The Securities and Futures Authority Limited* (SFA), whose members are concerned primarily with dealing in securities, including derivatives, and in advising on corporate finance; *The Financial Intermediaries, Managers and Brokers Regulatory Association* (FIMBRA) whose members are mainly concerned with advising on and arranging deals in life assurance, pensions and collective investment schemes such as unit trusts; *The Investment Management Regulatory Organisation* (IMRO) for firms engaged in investment management and associated activities; and *The Life Assurance and Unit Trust Regulatory Organisation* (LAUTRO) whose members are engaged in the retail marketing of these and similar products. Each SRO has its own rule-book, which has to be approved by SIB and by which its members much abide. A firm which is a member of an SRO is automatically authorized to carry on investment business of the kind specified. Each SRO has of course to have its own arrangements for accepting members and for monitoring them subsequently. However, by having regulation carried out by practitioners, who can be expected to be fully in touch with developments in the market, it is hoped to achieve a degree of flexibility in response to change greater than would be expected from a more centralized system of regulation.

Authorization is also granted to individuals who are members of certain RPBs, provided that investment business is not the main part of their business activities. There are nine RPBs including *inter alia* the main professional bodies for accountants and lawyers.

The SIB also recognizes certain *Recognized Investment Exchanges* (RIEs), which satisfy its requirements regarding their resources and modes of working. Examples are the International Stock Exchange and LIFFE. Business conducted through such exchanges is subject to less onerous reporting and disclosure requirements than business conducted elsewhere.

Regulatory costs

The structure of regulation in the UK imposes significant costs on financial services companies, which have to be borne ultimately by the users of the system. These costs are of four kinds: the administrative costs of the SROs and SIB, the administrative costs associated with firms' own compliance activities, the cost of dedicated capital to comply with SIB and SRO requirements, and contributions to funds needed to compensate the clients of other firms which have failed. All are controversial, and it is sometimes argued that the burden of these costs in the UK puts the City at a disadvantage in international competition – high costs of operation and/or restrictive regulations in the UK may encourage international firms to locate their activities in other countries.

The running costs of SIB and the SROs are a relatively small part of the total and are not a major issue for large firms. Nevertheless, for small firms engaged in financial advisory business the subscriptions to FIMBRA are a material cost and have been a cause of concern – particularly when associated with the possibility that members may be called upon to make significant contributions to the compensation fund.

Internal compliance costs are another matter, which many large firms find burdensome. For example, in the large banks the costs run to several million pounds a year and cannot readily be reduced. What was taken on trust prior to the FSA has now to be monitored systematically, and only specialists can hope to be fully *au fait* with the details of the rule-books. The need to consult compliance officers adds to the cost of doing business generally.

Capital costs are a thorny issue. We saw in chapter 11 how the solvency regulations for banks have been agreed internationally, so that banks from different countries can compete on level terms. Capital requirements under these regulations have been geared primarily to the bank's exposure to *credit* risk – the risk of loss because a borrower cannot repay a loan.[2]

For securities houses the main component of risk is *position* risk – the risk that the price realized for a security will differ from its value in the house's books. Measuring the position risk on an individual security depends on an assessment of the likely volatility of prices in the securities markets – that is, on a combination of objective analysis of past price behaviour and subjective judgement regarding the period over which data should be analysed and the likelihood of the future mirroring the past. Measuring the position risk for a portfolio is much more complex, because price changes in some elements of a portfolio are likely to compensate for movements in other parts – indeed, as we saw in chapter 14, securities houses use hedging instruments in the derivatives markets for this precise purpose. Nevertheless, some residual element of position risk remains, the *basis* risk that the price of a security will not move exactly in line with that of the hedging instrument. Moreover, there is also an element of *counterpart*[3] risk, namely the risk that the counterparty in a transaction will not honour his obligations, leaving the securities house exposed to much more position risk than it had anticipated. Lastly, particularly in equity markets, account has to be taken of portfolio diversification which reduces risk, as demonstrated in chapter 4.

It is hardly surprising that the capital requirements for securities houses have been the subject of considerable debate, with the regulators who had to confront these problems for the first time working in virtually uncharted territory. There is no international agreement on the capital support required for securities business, and with capital costs an important consideration decisions on the location of securities businesses could well be influenced by differences in regulatory requirements. The issue remains live, with agreement not yet having been reached on the content of the relevant EC Directive to ensure that firms throughout the EC are subject to similar rules.

It is not only securities houses for whom capital requirements are a concern. The minimum capital requirements for brokers, whose funds are not at risk in the securities markets, has also been an issue, in that capital requirements may act as a barrier to entry to this part of the financial services business. It has been suggested, for example, that capital requirements for some brokers could be dispensed with altogether, and that insurance policies, under which clients would be compensated for the non-performance of a broker, would serve clients' interests better.

The issues surrounding compensation will be discussed below, but in the meantime it is necessary to consider whether the benefits of regulation exceed the costs. It is not possible to give a definitive answer. Clearly some regulation is required, and effective regulation has the merit of ensuring high standards of conduct in the financial services markets, which should in itself help to attract business. The regulators and participants in the financial services industry have worked together to reach practical solutions to problems, which may be seen as one of the benefits of engaging the participants through SROs. There has been some simplification of the rules to ease the burden of regulation. Nevertheless, while there is no evidence yet of the regulatory regime in the UK having driven any significant business to other countries,[4] the costs of compliance remain high.

Compensation for loss

No matter how good the regulation, institutions will sometimes fail owing to unusually adverse economic conditions, incompetence which is detected too late, or fraud. No system is completely watertight. When failure occurs should the institution's customers be compensated, and if so by whom?

Consider first the case of bank and building society depositors. The great majority are not very expert in financial affairs and cannot reasonably be expected to assess the solvency of banks or building societies themselves. Unless there is some particular feature to put them on warning, such as the payment of interest rates much higher than are available elsewhere in the market, they have to take the deposit-takers' solvency on trust, in effect relying on the regulatory system to protect them. For this reason most countries have deposit protection schemes which compensate depositors up to prescribed limits when deposit-taking institutions fail. The compensation is usually for 100 per cent of their deposits up to the limit, though in Britain it is 75 per cent for banks and 90 per cent for building societies – the difference seems to be an accident of history rather than the result of rational argument. The limit in both cases is £20 000.

The provision of compensation of less than 100 per cent of deposits is, however, deliberate.[5] Full compensation removes any incentive to depositors to exercise prudence in deciding where to deposit their money. Since one deposit is rather like another they could simply deposit with whichever institution pays the highest interest. Full compensation thus gives rise to a problem of 'moral hazard' in that it removes the need for caution by depositors and makes it easier for institutions which offer high interest rates to attract funds.

Moral hazard increases the risk of failures in two ways. First it makes it easier for dishonest or fraudulent managers to enter deposit-taking business and to survive. Secondly, it encourages institutions to take risks with their funds in order to increase their earnings and thus their ability to attract deposits. Worse, it may even *compel* them to do so, because if other institutions are paying higher rates of interest the cautious manager who earns less on his funds will be unable to compete and is liable to be driven out of business. There may therefore be a generally high level of risk-taking from which even those managers who are predisposed to greater caution are unable to stand aside. Both these phenomena were present in the USA in the mid-eighties and led to widespread failures amongst Savings and Loan Associations, at a cost to the US taxpayer which will run eventually into hundreds of billions of dollars.

The moral hazard associated with full compensation of depositors adds to the regulators' tasks, because it means that they are working against the pressures of the market. One of their functions is to *prevent* excessive risk-taking, and depositors whose funds are at risk are normally on their side. Remove the risk to depositors and they have to try to restrain institutions who can argue legitimately that they have to take risks in order to remain competitive – putting the regulators in an almost impossible position. For this reason, deposit protection is only rarely extended to all depositors and deposits of more than a prescribed amount are at risk if an institution fails. Company treasurers, professional managers of funds, and wealthy individuals with substantial deposits are still expected to exercise their own judgement as to the security of their funds.

In practice, however, there are some banks at the core of the financial system for whom failure is virtually unthinkable, because the risk that failure would trigger a crisis in the whole financial system is too great. The payments system would be disrupted, and the consequence of a loss of confidence extending to the most important banks would be a sharp contraction of credit in the economy, damaging investment and economic activity. The implication is that the regulatory authorities have an added responsibility to ensure that these banks are well managed and that any action needed to avoid failure (such as a change of management) is taken in good time.

In the UK compensation to depositors is paid out of compensation funds to which the banks (or building societies) are compelled to subscribe, the amount subscribed by any institution being governed by the size of its deposit base. This is not popular with the banks, particularly the most reputable institutions who see no reason why they should bail out people who have chosen to deposit funds with less reputable competitors – particularly when any failures can be attributed to defective regulation, for which they are not responsible. However, the cost will in general be passed on eventually to their customers, and the alternative source of compensation would be the taxpayer. The choice over who should provide the protection for inexpert depositors therefore lies between bank depositors generally and the taxpayer.

Similar considerations apply to compensation for other investors as a result of the failure of the business with which they have dealt. Thus there are compensation arrangements for insurance policy holders and each of the SROs has its own compensation scheme, financed by its members. Again, there is usually an upper limit on the extent of any compensation, so that the protection is provided for the private individual rather than the professional investor. Where, as in the case of FIMBRA, losses have arisen as a result of fraud and the members of the SRO are not generally large organizations, the cost of providing this protection is significant.

Regulation and retail savings

Some of the regulations brought into force under the FSA have had a significant impact on the marketing of retail financial products, such as life assurance policies, unit trusts and other investment products (for example, PEPs). Not all of the regulations are unambiguously beneficial to the consumer.

First there are the regulations governing information. Firms supplying investment products are free to quote figures of their past performance, but are bound to point out that this may not be a guide to future performance and that the value of investments can go up or down – all of which is certainly true, but does tend to detract from the force of a superior record. Any projections of the value of investments in the\future, as for example with life assurance and pension policies, have to be made on standard assumptions, with no allowance for the supplier's past investment record or even for its costs (which are reflected in the proportions of the monies received from the customer and of investment income which are invested on their behalf). Thus suppliers with low marketing and other administrative costs are not permitted to reflect this in their projections. The result is that while customers are protected from misleading information, the information they do receive is not actually very helpful, particularly as the arrangements employed for deducting costs from insurance premiums and personal pension contributions are so complex as to be virtually unintelligible to the layman.

In this situation there is clearly a need for expert independent advisers to guide customers to the best companies. This is the role of the insurance broker or other adviser, whose remuneration has traditionally taken the form of commission on the business placed with each company. Prior to the FSA, informal arrangements amongst the insurance companies had set an upper limit on the commission payable, so that, at least between the major companies, the broker's advice was not likely to be biased by the amount of commission he would receive.

Under the FSA the regulations for marketing life assurance and other retail investment products included a provision for *polarization* – organizations selling these products had to decide whether they were going to act as *independent intermediaries*, which were precluded from selling any of their own products or the products of any company with which they were associated, or *company or appointed representatives*, which sold only the products of the company concerned. The intention was to ensure that customers would know when they were being given objective, independent advice and when they were being sold the products of a particular company – something which had previously been blurred when, for example, a bank manager might act both as adviser and salesman for his own bank's investment products (and be under pressure to maximize the sales of the latter).

The result was a substantial reduction in the number of independent advisers. Most of the major banks chose to have their branch staff act as company representatives, with independent advice available, if at all, only through specialized subsidiaries. Previously the business placed for their customers had been spread amongst a number of insurance companies and other suppliers. The same had been true of building societies, which had been the principal source of endowment business for many insurance companies. These sought to protect their position by arranging for particular societies to become appointed representatives of their insurance company. The arrangements to limit commission broke down, and commission levels climbed generally as the insurance companies competed to retain their flow of new business.

The end-result is that the consumers are having to pay considerably more for retail investments, the higher commission and marketing costs resulting eventually in lower returns on insurance policies, unit trusts etc. For a company to attempt to compete by cutting commissions would not be a sensible strategy because it could not *demonstrate* that its products would provide a higher return than those of its competitors with higher commission costs, and independent intermediaries would be only human if they placed their business elsewhere.

It is difficult to argue that consumers have actually benefited from these regulations; and it is not easy to see how the damage can be reversed.

Economic controls

In addition to prudential controls governments also sometimes impose controls on financial institutions for reasons of general economic policy. These include policies to maintain overall macroeconomic balance in the economy, to influence the allocation of resources between activities or sectors, and to sustain effective competition. Regulations for these purposes may affect the size and composition of balance sheets, as well as the terms on which particular types of business may be transacted. They may also prohibit restrictive agreements or mergers between institutions in the context of competition policy generally.

In almost every country banks are subject to regulation in the context of monetary control. They may have to observe lending or deposit ceilings, ceilings on the interest paid to depositors or charged to borrowers, or regulations governing their holdings of specified categories of assets. Until the 1980s banks in the UK were no exception. They were subjected to ceilings on their private lending for much of the 1960s, restrictions on their ability to compete for sterling deposits for most of the 1970s, and they had an obligation to conform to minimum balance sheet ratios throughout this period. They were also at times subject to guidance on the scale of lending for particular purposes, with high priority being given to manufacturing industry and exports and correspondingly low priority to lending to persons and for property development. From time to time consumer instalment lending was affected directly by regulations governing minimum down-payments and maximum repayment periods.

Since the early 1980s banks (and other financial institutions) in Britain have been free of these kinds of control. They still have to maintain compulsory non-interest bearing deposits with the Bank of England, of an amount equal to 0.45 per cent of their non-bank sterling deposits,[6] but the purpose of these deposits is to provide the Bank of England with income rather than to have a role in monetary control. Clearing banks also have to maintain operational balances with the Bank of England, which do play a part in the monetary control mechanism, but they are not fixed and are very small. Since the early 1980s monetary control in Britain has been conducted through interest rates rather than by trying to influence the banks' behaviour directly. The trend away from direct controls can also be observed in other European countries, though not generally to nearly the same extent as in the UK.

In many countries there are also controls on the operations of non-bank financial institutions, such as insurance companies and pension funds, whose freedom to invest is often severely restricted. For example, they may be obliged to invest a prescribed proportion of their assets in government securities, their freedom to invest in equities may be constrained, and upper limits may be placed on investment in foreign securities. Again, in the context of the EC's 1992 programme and the freedom of capital movements, such restrictions are gradually diminishing, but it is likely to be some time before they disappear altogether. In the UK no restrictions of these kinds are imposed for economic reasons.

Economic controls are frequently damaging to the institutions concerned and, if maintained for lengthy periods, to the economy at large. Controls on institutions weaken competition and stifle initiatives for new developments. Moreover, unless subsidies are paid in compensation, the institutions subject to control are placed at a competitive disadvantage relative to others which escape the net. For example, lending ceilings affect the earning capacity of the controlled institutions, making them less able to compete for funds with those outside.

Economic controls which affect the competitive strength of the controlled institutions are of only temporary value to the authorities, because the financial system adapts in ways which circumvent the controls. Examples of such adaptation abound from many countries. In the UK, lending ceilings on banks encouraged the development of the inter-company loan market, and the growth of the non-clearing banks in the 1960s was due, in part, to the fact that the clearing banks were subject to limits on their lending; in the consumer credit field, controls on hire purchase gave a boost to television rental – the banks lent to the rental companies rather than to the finance companies which would have undertaken the hire-purchase business. In the past, when economic controls on institutions have been introduced, some time has elapsed before financial arrangements avoiding the controls have evolved, with the result that the controls have had an impact on economic activity. However, as the system becomes more competitive, open and sophisticated any such time lags are likely to shorten.

The mortgage and consumer credit boom of the second part of the 1980s led to suggestions that controls on consumer and mortgage lending should be employed again in the UK. There were several reasons: some consumers were clearly borrowing more than they could afford, ready access to credit was contributing to overheating in the housing market, and the increases in interest rates required to bring this process to an end bore equally heavily on industrial investment.

It is clearly desirable to avoid the adverse social consequences of over-borrowing, and there is no doubt that credit was easily obtainable for some purposes in the late 1980s, without in-depth enquiries of the borrower being made. Subsequently some of the lenders experienced very high loss ratios. In the long run, they learned to their cost, more responsible lending would have proved more profitable. Whether controls on consumer credit could have curtailed this lending at the time is doubtful. Most consumers have access to credit from many sources, so that if credit from one source is rationed they simply turn to another. Controls on the terms of lending invite evasion, as has occurred in the past.[7] The widespread use of credit cards means that many consumers have automatic access to funds up to their credit limits, even if changed circumstances (of which the lender is unaware) mean that the limit is no longer appropriate. Lastly, a very high proportion of the people who got into difficulties through over-borrowing had borrowed from more than one source, usually without revealing their debts when taking out subsequent loans. It is not easy to devise controls which will compel borrowers to disclose their positions fully.

Competition between mortgage lenders during the housing boom led to a gradual increase in the amounts lent to individual borrowers and an easing of the repayment terms. For example, the multiples of income which institutions were prepared to lend increased, 'second' incomes were accorded more favourable treatment, and 'low-start' mortgages meant that the full servicing costs could be deferred.

While only a comparatively small proportion of borrowers took advantage of these facilities, if their access to funds had been restricted market prices would have risen more slowly and the boom would have been brought under control more easily.

It would not be impossible to devise regulations which achieved this objective. In particular, the repayment of loans secured by a first mortgage on a private dwelling could be made enforceable only if certain conditions were satisfied, regarding the relationship between the loan, the value of the property and the circumstances of the borrower. It would then seldom be in the interests of the lender to go beyond the specified terms. However, it must be recognized that any controls of this kind would bear particularly heavily on first-time buyers in the housing market, which would be regarded as inequitable, and would also reduce mobility in the housing and therefore the labour markets. There may be a case for controlling mortgage borrowing in this way in order to promote thrift and prudence in the consumer sector, but as a means of controlling a consumer and housing boom it seems inferior to the timely use of interest rate policy.[8]

The third argument for regulating consumer lending (including mortgages) is that it would help to keep down the cost of borrowing to industry and commerce – this would be desirable because there is a public interest in promoting investment. If the consumer and housing booms in the late 1980s had been controlled successfully by other means it is unlikely that interest rates would have risen so far (or that the subsequent recession would have been so deep). But the same could have been achieved by earlier increases in interest rates without the addition of credit controls, or by fiscal means. The problems arose through a failure to act in time rather than through the authorities having inappropriate instruments at their disposal. Moreover, as a permanent means of reducing the cost of industrial funding, credit controls on the consumer sector are unlikely to be successful, because in the long run the cost of capital in the UK is determined mainly by worldwide capital market conditions (see chapter 6) and the impact of a reduction in consumer borrowing in the UK on these conditions is minimal.

Competition policy is another source of economic controls which affect the financial system, in particular controls which inhibit mergers and the exercise of monopoly power. Such controls are regarded as particularly important in some countries, owing to the pervasive influence of banks within the economy, and links between banks and other industrial or commercial companies are also sometimes prohibited, lest the failure of the latter should undermine the financial position of the former. In other respects, competition policy is applied with the same objectives and by the same means to banks and other financial institutions as to companies in general. Within Europe competition in domestic markets will be enhanced as the provisions of the 1992 programme gradually come into effect.

Notes

1 This is extraordinarily difficult to police, and performance in this regard may not always match up with expectations.
2 Credit risks also arise in other parts of a bank's business.
3 Credit risk may be regarded as a particular kind of counterparty risk.
4 Though there are examples of fraudulent business, such as BCCI in banking, making use of less stringent regulatory climates elsewhere.
5 Though whether it is fair to people, who cannot possibly be expected to know that an institution (which is, after all, authorized to take deposits) is likely to fail, is another matter.
6 Strictly, their 'eligible liabilities'.
7 For example, the trade-in price of a used car can be inflated in order to increase the apparent down-payment on another car (whose price is inflated by the same amount).
8 Within a monetary union the use of interest rate policy for this purpose would, of course, be ruled out. Should any intervention in the housing market be necessary it would then have to take the form of controls on borrowing, fiscal or other (e.g. planning) measures.

16

The efficiency of the financial system

Before beginning an examination of the efficiency of the financial system it may be helpful to review its objectives briefly. The most basic function of any financial system, which we have virtually taken as read throughout this book, is the provision of payments facilities. The responsibility for this function lies with the monetary system, the note-issuing authority and the banks, and is the concern therefore of only one part of the system. The broader objective of the system as a whole is to meet the needs of society with regard to saving and investment. The financial system must provide savers and investors with financial instruments which have characteristics suited to their diverse needs. It must ensure that the terms available to individual savers are 'fair', in the sense that no group should be exploited or denied favourable opportunities which are open to others. The resources made available for investment should be allocated to those projects where they are likely to be most productive, i.e. where the return to society is highest, and without any undue bias against risk. Finally, it is a function of the financial system to maintain the balance between total saving and investment, and it is important that this balance should be achieved at a high level of economic activity.

We can classify these objectives into two categories. First, there are objectives concerned with microeconomic efficiency. Questions of *microeconomic efficiency* include the range of financial instruments available, the choices open to savers and investors, the ability of the system to cater for their needs, the allocation of funds between large-scale and small-scale borrowers and between projects with differing time-scales and risk-profiles, the prices which prevail in the financial system, intermediation costs and the capacity of the system to innovate and adapt to changing needs. The pricing of funds is a crucial element which involves not only the efficiency with which pricing takes place in the organized markets, but also the effects of market structure, regulations, taxes and subsidies on the cost of funds, and the question of divergences between social and private returns. The second category, *macroeconomic efficiency*, is concerned with aggregate saving and investment. Questions here concern the extent to which the financial system helps to meet society's objectives regarding the levels of saving and investment in the economy, which may be influenced by general social considerations as well as private preferences; the stability of both the volumes of saving and investment and the rates of interest which prevail; and how far the financial system can be relied upon to balance saving and investment at a high level of economic activity.

Range of financial instruments

Our first criterion for judging the microeconomic efficiency of the financial system relates to the range of financial instruments which are available to savers and investors. Does the range of instruments available meet the needs of the ultimate users of the system?

The British financial system performs well on the whole when judged by this criterion. Savers have a wide range of assets to choose from, ranging from deposits which are highly liquid, through index-linked gilts and national savings which are completely safe in real terms, to ordinary shares which allow those who seek a higher return at the cost of greater exposure to risk to achieve their aims. The quality of the organized securities market and the activities of specialized institutions ensure that savers who wish to avoid undue risk through diversification are able to do so. Borrowers too have access to a very wide range of financial instruments, including ordinary shares, long- or short-term loans, hire-purchase facilities, and the ability to lease or rent property. The most significant weaknesses are the lack of complete security against loss for bank and building society depositors, and the very limited availability of risk capital for small and high-risk enterprises.

Elasticity and choice

Next we consider a set of criteria, all of which have to do with the *allocative efficiency* of the financial system, that is the extent to which its function will lead to resources for investment being applied where their return to society is likely to be highest. A market economy relies heavily on competition to bring this about: for any given degree of risk savers will place their funds with those who offer the highest price for them, and those potential borrowers with the highest yielding investments in prospect will bid the highest prices. There may be difficulties in evaluating returns and assessing risks, particularly for much of the investment in infrastructure carried out by the government, and in some cases the return to the investor may differ from that to society. Clearly there must be some mechanism for ensuring that socially desirable investment is properly assessed and that the appropriate amount of funds is made available, matters which cannot be left entirely to a market system. But throughout the private sector it is generally left to the price system (often operating through financial intermediaries) to determine the allocation of funds, and the efficiency of this system depends on competition.

An adequate degree of competition within the financial system implies that the range of choice amongst similar financial instruments open to savers and borrowers must be satisfactory. Savers in Britain can make use of a variety of outlets for their saving – banks, building societies, unit trusts, insurance companies, and the stock market to name only some of those available. There is intense competition in the retail deposit market, and even in rural areas where there are few banks and building society branches depositors benefit from nationally-determined terms and conditions. The variety of other savings instruments on offer is bewildering, and they are tailored to meet almost every conceivable taste. Savers in the retail market do not suffer from any lack of choice. Those with large amounts of funds at their disposal can, of course, place them in highly competitive wholesale markets.

Borrowers seeking large amounts of funds are also well placed, because they too have access to the securities markets and have a large number of banks competing for their business. They can be fairly sure of obtaining funds at the going rate of interest, taking account of the risk characteristics of the financial instruments they wish to issue. In the new-issue market competition by issuing houses for their business is also keen. The breadth of choice available to small companies is much more limited, and when economic conditions generally are difficult they may have little option but to turn to the bank with which they customarily deal. But in normal circumstances most small companies could obtain finance from competitor banks if they wished to do so, and they also have access to financing in other forms, such as hire purchase or leasing. The position of the consumer is easier than that of the small firm, which may have difficulty in establishing its ability to repay debt. Provided the consumer's credit status is satisfactory he or she should have no difficulty in obtaining a mortgage loan, consumer instalment loan, or credit card from a number of competing banks or finance houses; and the standards by which credit status is judged are not invariably stringent.

Choice is one aspect of elasticity in the financial system. In an elastic system, if funds are more readily available from one source than from another borrowers can readily switch their business. For savers, elasticity implies that, if one group of borrowers is seeking funds more actively than another, they can easily direct their savings to those who wish to take them without the inconvenience of accepting an unsuitable financial instrument. An elastic financial system has the ability to direct funds from wherever financial surpluses arise to those economic agents with financial deficits, regardless of the sectors in which the deficit units are found.

The UK financial system is extremely elastic in this respect, due partly to the absence of any strong sector preferences on the part of the banks, partly to the willingness of the life assurance and pension funds to alter the *sector* composition of their asset portfolios, and partly to the existence of the sterling money markets (see chapters 11–14). In bank or institutional portfolios, and in the money markets, a small change in relative interest rates is sufficient to cause a substantial redirection in the flow of funds. For example, insurance companies are just as willing to hold company loan stocks as gilt-edged securities provided that the yield margin compensates them for the additional risk and inferior marketability, so that an increase in the demand by companies needs only to raise this margin slightly in order to attract funds. Similarly, in the sterling money markets, if building societies are short of finance at a time when, for example, company borrowing is slack, they have only to bid up rates slightly to obtain the money they need.

There is one respect in which the UK financial system may not in fact be very elastic – that of the maturity and structural preferences of the different financial institutions. Banks have traditionally preferred to make short- or medium-term loans at variable rates of interest, whereas the institutional investors wish to hold long-term fixed-rate loans or equity assets. This does not cause problems so long as the preferences of borrowers broadly coincide with the relative availability of funds from the different categories of institution. But if borrowers' preferences change it may not be easy to shift savings flowing through one category of institutions (e.g. the investing institutions) into the financial instruments normally provided by the other (e.g. the banks).

There was in fact a problem throughout the first half of the 1980s when nominal rates of interest were high and private sector borrowers were reluctant to enter into commitments to pay these rates for long periods. This led to a concentration on bank financing, while the flow of funds to the long-term institutions substantially exceeded the demands on them from domestic borrowers. The government solved this potential mismatch by 'overfunding'; i.e. issuing gilts which satisfied the institutions' preferences in amounts more than were required to meet the public sector's own borrowing needs, and using the surplus to buy commercial bills issued by industrial and commercial companies. Interest rate swaps in the international bond markets now carry out a similar function of reconciling borrowers' and investors' preferences.

International transactions have also helped to reconcile UK domestic institutions' preference for equity at a time when UK borrowers were issuing debt: the institutions built up their holdings of overseas ordinary shares, whilst the UK banks obtained some of the funds for domestic lending by drawing on deposits from overseas.

Scale

Resources will be allocated where their prospective return is highest only if finance is available irrespective of the scale of the investment and with due account being taken of the risk that investments will prove unsuccessful. One aspect of the efficiency of a financial system is therefore its ability to mobilize saving for large-scale investments. In this respect the UK financial system appears to be very satisfactory, so long as the risks entailed fall within the usual range. The size of the investing institutions and the large volume of funds available for long-term investment makes it possible to raise very large sums in the securities markets. Rights issues and other sales of ordinary shares amounting to several hundred million pounds are quite common, and issues of government long-term debt often exceed £1 billion. Through international syndication the banking system too is capable of providing extremely large loans when required, as for example to finance the Channel Tunnel.

If scale causes problems in the UK financial system it is at the other end of the range. Provided (and it is a big proviso) that banks are satisfied about the risks involved there is no problem for borrowers in obtaining small amounts of loan finance. The problem lies in obtaining equity finance for small companies, even when the risks involved are no more than average, and without sufficient equity, bank finance may not be available either. This is a topic which we have already discussed in chapter 8; the specialist institutions and other measures considered there have gone some way towards ameliorating the situation for small firms, but they have not remedied it altogether.

Risk

From society's point of view it is generally the expected return from an investment which matters, rather than the risk attached to it. An efficient financial system would therefore be characterized by the absence of any bias against risky investment projects. The only exceptions are *very* large projects, so large that the future welfare of the country as a whole is affected by the outcome of the project. Examples are the Channel Tunnel and nuclear power. For other projects, including projects which are very large by the standards of the firms which carry them out, diversification across the economy as a whole virtually eliminates all the specific risks. Thus while it is desirable for the financial system to impart a bias against risky projects which are likely to yield only a low rate of return, there should be no bias against risk *per se*.

The risk to which an investor is exposed depends both on the project itself and on who is carrying it out. A large project need not be unduly risky if it is carried out by a large enterprise, which has sufficient management and financial resources to see it through even if unexpected problems arise. Similar unexpected problems might be well beyond the capacity of a small firm to deal with. Most investment projects are in fact carried out by existing firms, using finance which is not specifically tied to the project in question. For the lender or equity shareholder it is the profitability of the firm overall, including the new risky project, that counts. It is only when the success of a particular project is likely to affect the viability of the enterprise as a whole that the financial investor is concerned with the specific risks.

Where individual projects, or individual high-risk firms, are concerned, equity finance can normally be obtained in the UK capital market, so long as the risks can be assessed reasonably objectively and the prospective returns are thought to be adequate. In the equity market as a whole there is no evidence that high specific risks (as opposed to a strong correlation with market-risk) lead to investors demanding a higher rate of return. Difficulties may, however, arise at both ends of the size range. Projects may be too large, or the return too conjectural, for existing firms to embark on, and a brand new company set up for the purpose would face enhanced risks of failure. The development of a new aircraft is an example. In these conditions most countries find it necessary to give some government assistance, possibly in the form of research and development contracts or other launch aid, and Britain is no exception.

At the other end of the scale, start-up capital for small companies is usually difficult to raise because the risk of total failure is very high. Also, the costs of investigation weigh heavily in relation to any potential reward, and for sums less than £250 000 the venture-capital companies are unlikely to be interested.

Whether the financial system as a whole in Britain displays an undue bias against risk is a much-debated question, to which we return below.

Security prices and rates of interest

The next condition which the financial system must satisfy in order to allocate funds efficiently is that the prices, or rates of interest, on financial instruments must be equal after allowing for differences in risk and transactions costs. Notice that by and large the financial system sets a price for funds, rather than allocating funds directly to selected users. Anybody can approach a bank for a loan and, provided they satisfy the bank's criteria regarding capacity to repay, are eligible for a loan at the going rate of interest. In the securities market, prospective borrowers or issuers of equity can come to the market and raise funds at the going price. The question for efficiency is whether there are any systematic biases in pricing, which lead to some borrowers obtaining funds too cheaply and others having to pay too much.

The first part of the system in which biases of this kind might conceivably exist is the stock market. Certain categories of share might be under-priced in relation to others; or new information might not be fully reflected in stock market prices. If information is reflected fully in prices, so that (after allowing for risk) the expected rate of return on the shares of different companies is the same, the market is said to be *technically efficient*.

Prima facie the British stock market, with substantial numbers of professional investors continually scrutinizing share prices and assessing the effects of new information on the value of shares, might be expected to be technically efficient, since otherwise investors would be able to detect opportunities for buying under-priced shares and selling them subsequently, and their activities would quickly eliminate under- or over-pricing in the system. In fact, studies that have been carried out suggest that new information is rapidly absorbed into share prices, and without any bias. This does not mean that the response is necessarily accurate initially; it implies only that when new information is received the response of share prices is as likely to be too little as too much; the behaviour of a share price in future cannot be deduced from its recent history.[1]

One would, however, hope for more than this from a stock market that purported to allocate funds efficiently. If the expected total return from shareholdings in different companies was the same (after allowing for market risk) shares with a low dividend yield could be expected to have greater future earnings growth, and consequently higher future dividends, than shares with a high dividend yield. In fact neither dividend yields nor price/earnings ratios, have proved to be good predictors of future earnings growth. But that does not necessarily condemn the pricing process as technically inefficient, because a company's future earnings are inherently uncertain and a very wide margin for error around the best estimate may be unavoidable. What matters for fair pricing of funds is that the average earnings growth of companies with high price/earnings ratios should be above those with low price/earnings ratios, and by an appropriate amount.

The allocative function of the prices for funds prevailing in the financial markets applies directly only to projects for which firms require external finance. However, much of industry's new equity capital does not in fact pass through the capital market at all, since it is accumulated out of each firm's own retained profits. We saw in chapter 8 that the proportion financed in this way declined in the second half of the eighties, but for 1983–7 as a whole it still represented nearly 60 per cent. Most large firms take account of the cost of capital in their investment decision procedures and, in principle, if firms judged investment proposals consistently by reference to an external cost of capital, the fact that part or all was financed from retained profits would have no influence on the allocation of resources. Nevertheless, in practice, many firms will demand higher prospective returns from investment which has to be financed by raising external equity capital, particularly if they think that their share price under-values the company, so the fact that so much of new equity does not pass through the market may have a distorting effect on resource allocation.[2]

The rules governing public sector investment may also introduce distortions. Social capital can seldom be appraised in these terms, and investment by public corporations is subject to different rules. Target rates of return on public sector investment may not equal those in the private sector, and ceilings may be imposed on borrowing by public corporations; it is certainly the case that privatization freed public corporations from restraints of this kind and enabled them to step up their investment programmes.

Market structure, taxes and subsidies

The prices which prevail in the securities markets are seldom subject to distortions as a result of restrictive practices, and are comparatively little affected by regulations, taxes or subsidies. Holders of securities are concerned with the after-tax return on their funds, and since many of the major institutions pay neither income nor capital gains tax the gross and net returns for them are the same.[3] By contrast, the terms on which financial institutions do business are sometimes significantly affected by these considerations.

In the first place rates of interest may be affected by market structure. At one time, the small number of clearing banks resulted in them paying less for retail deposits and charging more for retail loans than would have been expected in a more competitive situation, and the recommended rate system for building societies had a similar effect. These distortions probably had only minor effects on resource allocation, but are in any case now past history. Segments of the market where competition is relatively weak, such as small business, may be charged *slightly* more (in relation to the costs incurred) than other borrowers but the margin is not large.

Secondly, government regulations, taxes or subsidies may have significant effects on resource allocation. Prudential regulations often increase the costs or reduce the earnings of the regulated institutions, to the detriment[4] of those who use their services. If the effect is substantial the regulated institutions are likely to find their role in the financial system reduced, as credit flows pass through unregulated channels. Economic controls may have similar effects. Distortions of this kind interfere with 'competitive neutrality' – a condition in which the actions of the state do not affect the relative prices prevailing in the market. The UK financial system is comparatively free of such distortions at present, though in the past controls on the banks had a considerable effect on credit flows – which consequently by-passed the controlled banks – even if the effect on rates of interest was rather small.

The effects of taxes and subsidies are much more substantial. Sometimes the government deliberately sets out to create 'privileged circuits', to alter the prices prevailing in the market in order to favour certain categories of borrower, the most notable in the UK being house purchasers. This is a particular example of a more general case, the possibility of divergences between social and private returns. Circumstances may arise in which the benefit to society from allocating resources in a particular way differs from the benefit received by the private economic agent – investment which creates jobs in an area of high unemployment is an example. Or, social preferences may differ from the preferences of private individuals – for example, the government may decide that it is desirable to raise the level of saving and investment in the economy, for the benefit of future generations, even if left to their own devices the present generation would prefer to have a higher level of consumption now. By giving relief from taxes or making grants the government alters the cost to borrowers, so that the outcome of individual decisions accords more closely with what the government sees as social needs.

Departures from neutrality for reasons of this kind must be regarded as enhancing the efficiency of the financial system if they lead to an outcome which accords with social objectives. But many of the effects of taxes are less easy to justify, being the unintended side-effects of policies pursued for quite different reasons or the result of measures which, while possibly justified in the past, have outlived their usefulness. When this occurs the distortions in the financial system which result can only detract from its efficiency.

Apart from mortgage interest relief on owner-occupied housing, tax reliefs are not now employed widely in the UK as a means of influencing investment. Within the corporation tax structure the aim has been to achieve neutrality, rather than to deliberately distort the system in favour of certain categories of investment. Schemes such as the Business Expansion Scheme, under which private individuals who invest in certain kinds of investment can claim relief from income tax, do have this intent, though it is doubtful whether their impact has been large.[5]

As already noted in chapter 7, tax reliefs and other arrangements have had a considerable effect on the pattern of personal saving in Britain. Contributions to pension funds and personal pensions policies are free of tax, as is the income on their assets, and this undoubtedly encourages saving for retirement through pension schemes. The tax treatment can be justified as a form of income spreading – tax is not charged on contributions at the time they are earned, but the pension which is received subsequently is taxable. Nevertheless, this form of tax treatment is not open to people who choose to provide for their own retirement in other ways; and there is a clear anomaly in the fact that, in place of part of their pensions, lump sum payments are often made to employees at the time they retire, and these payments escape tax altogether.

Tax relief on deposit interest has been allowed on TESSAs and on investment income and capital gains within PEPs, the ostensible objective being to encourage saving through deposits and individual investment in the stock market respectively. In neither case is the tax benefit nearly as large as for pension contributions, and in both cases the main effect appears to have been to shift existing savings into forms where the income was free of tax rather than to stimulate new saving.

The government grants a variety of tax privileges to holders of its own securities. Gains on gilt-edged securities are free of capital gains tax, and the interest on national savings certificates is free of all taxes – to name only two concessions. These privileges allow the government to borrow more cheaply than would otherwise be the case, and while this probably does not affect the total sum raised by the government in the financial markets, it does conceal the true cost of government borrowing.

It seems unlikely that all these tax reliefs accord with current social or economic needs, and there is no doubt that the existing patterns of saving and investment are materially affected. While proposals to remove or reduce reliefs invariably arouse strong political resistance, these political costs must be weighed against the damage to the system in the longer-run from allowing distortions to continue unchecked.

Operational efficiency

The next aspect of microeconomic efficiency in the financial system is the question of its operational efficiency, the intermediation costs which have to be borne by the system's users. Competition is the chief weapon for cutting intermediation costs, since the more efficient institutions will be able to undercut their less efficient rivals and so attract business from them. Competition in most market segments is now keen, with institutions having little opportunity to take advantage of monopoly positions; and while it is difficult to devise objective standards by which to measure their efficiency, there is no evidence that intermediation costs of financial institutions in the UK are generally excessive by international standards.

The effect of lack of competition in the past on margins in the banking and building society sectors was clear. Prior to 1971 the clearing banks operated a cartel on interest rates, and not until the late eighties did competition, originating from the building societies, compel them to pay interest on current account deposits. This gave rise to a considerable narrowing of their margins between the average rate of interest earned on loans and the average cost of sterling deposits. The wider margins available previously had encouraged the banks to compete for deposits in other ways, for example through branch expansion, thus raising their operating costs. In the building society sector, recommended rates for mortgages, combined with restrictions on the ability of the banks to enter the field, protected the building societies from competitive pressures, with exactly the same results – over-branching and a proliferation of societies. In both cases more intense competition has cut intermediation costs – indeed it was the principal cause of the rapid decline in building society numbers in the eighties.

Nevertheless there are still two areas of the financial system where competition does not seem to operate effectively and where the level of intermediation costs gives cause for concern. The first is retail savings products, where commission or equivalent new business costs have risen sharply in recent years. As noted in chapter 15, it is not easy to see how competition will drive these costs down again. And the concern extends to personal pension policies where, by comparison with occupational pension schemes, the costs seem remarkably high.

The second is the securities market where the spreads for the less heavily traded stocks have also increased sharply and competition amongst market makers in these stocks is very weak. It seems likely that an alternative trading system for these stocks, such as matching buy and sell orders, would cut costs, though there would of course be less certainty of being able to carry out transactions without delay.

Dynamic efficiency

The final aspect of microeconomic efficiency to consider is the dynamic efficiency of the financial system – its ability to innovate and adapt to changing needs.

After a decade of such rapid change as occurred in the 1980s it would be difficult to argue that the financial system is not efficient in this sense. Novel instruments were devised, the new markets in derivatives created, a new structure for the capital markets put in place, new activities for the institutions taken on as the barriers between them were broken down. It was not a painless process – firms that could not adapt died and many others experienced heavy losses. But the system as a whole displayed great adaptability in response to the demands made on it, and maintained its standing in international markets.

Corporate governance

It is often suggested that the British financial system is biased against the long-term investment and risk-taking needed to develop strong businesses. There are several strands in the argument: first, that the banks and long-term investing institutions are unduly biased against risk; secondly, that they are too concerned with short-term performance and profitability at the expense of long-term growth; thirdly, that the prevalence of takeovers creates a climate of uncertainty which discourages long-term risk-taking and investment. A common factor in these complaints is that all are connected with the separation of ownership from managerial control, which is a feature of the British financial system. In reality the shareholders, who own companies and nominally control them by appointing the Boards of Directors, have little influence on company managements in normal circumstances. The structure through which the various interest groups in a company, including its shareholders, influence its management is known as *corporate governance*, and it is possible that the system of corporate governance in Britain leads to some economic inefficiency.

There is a natural tension between businessmen seeking additional resources for their businesses and financiers who have to decide whether to provide the funds. The businessmen tend to be enthusiastic and optimistic, even confident, about the success of their investment proposals. The financiers' caution and scepticism are necessary safeguards against unrealistic expectations – long experience tells them that there are more optimistic than successful businessmen. Moreover, businessmen can afford to take risks with other people's money (as well, perhaps, as their own), whereas financiers are seldom providing the funds themselves and have a duty of due diligence to those whose funds are in their charge.

It is suggested, however, that the problem goes deeper than this, and that financiers tend to have an exaggerated view of risks because they lack the expertise to assess them properly. It is certainly true that the businessman seeking a loan or an equity investment usually is, or ought to be, more expert in the business in question than the financier to whom he turns for funds, though the latter can, if he wishes, engage a consultant to supplement his own limited knowledge. For large projects financiers will automatically seek external advice, but it is a costly process which can be justified only by a sufficiently large return. When a request for funds is comparatively small and on preliminary examination the financier is not convinced by the proposal, rather than spend more on further investigation the financier may simply turn the proposal down.

Other than for very large projects British banks do not generally seek external advice, and nor do they retain permanent specialist advisers on their staffs. To justify employing specialist advisers the bank has to expect a continuing flow of new business in the relevant field, or at the very least a continuing requirement for monitoring the technical aspects of customers' businesses in connection with outstanding loans. Agriculture and property/construction are two industries where these conditions often apply, but elsewhere bankers rely on their training in assessing the financial aspects of proposals to see them through. Thus for the banker it is generally financial issues, together with the perceived quality and commitment of the management, which are crucial.[6] Unlike the equity investor, the banker gains no additional reward if the project is successful, so he is not particularly concerned with the chances of earning a high profit: what matters is the risk of loss if the venture does not succeed.

The alleged bias against risk may reflect no more than the fact that the risks genuinely are higher for external financiers. If we compare the situation of a subsidiary in a large company seeking finance for a risky project with that of an independent company attempting to raise money for the same purpose, we can pinpoint two important differences. First, the financiers providing external finance are likely to be less expert and less well-informed about the business than their internal financing counterparts. That ignorance translates into uncertainty about the outcome, which can only be reduced by incurring additional costs. Secondly, the internal financiers exert a much higher degree of control than their external counterparts after the investment has been made, which also contributes to a reduction in risk. Remedies for the higher risks involved in external finance may therefore lie in enhancing financiers' expertise, improving information, and giving financiers greater power to exercise control.

The second charge is that financiers in Britain have too much regard for short-term profits at the expense of long-term growth. In particular, it is argued that while the UK stock market does appear to be efficient in the sense that share prices react swiftly to new information, it is much less efficient in valuing likely future profit flows. Share price valuations give too much weight to current profits and dividends and too little to future profitability and growth.

It is extremely difficult to test this proposition because future profits are inherently uncertain. But it certainly reflects the conventional wisdom among both company managers and, more tellingly, their merchant bank advisers, who believe that share prices will be higher if profits are supported by curbing 'revenue' investment and if dividends are maintained at the expense of retentions, even if this makes the business less competitive in the long-run. The emphasis on short-term profitability and dividends affects companies' reactions to pressure on profits, because it encourages managers to cut back investment activity, particularly investment which is conventionally charged to revenue, such as investment in training and market development.

It is not immediately obvious why current profits and dividends should have an exaggerated weight in share price valuations. One possible explanation is that recent profits are a fact (even if imperfectly recorded) whereas future profits are mere conjecture. Attempts by company directors to justify apparently poor profits by reference to development expenditure are not accepted at face value because the managers are not entirely disinterested parties. In the UK, dividends attract special attention because they are usually regarded as an indication of the future profitability expected by a company's directors, and may therefore be acting as a proxy for these profits in valuation models.

Another possible explanation for the stress on profits and dividends is that, at least in the eyes of some businessmen, the average quality of the investment analysis emanating from securities houses is not thought to be very high.[7] If the analysts do not really understand the business, to the extent of being able to make informed judgements of future prospects, the stress on current profitability and dividends is hardly surprising. In any event, for whatever reason, share prices are thought to give undue weight to short-term performance.

Another factor contributing to short-termism in the system is said to be a bias on the part of the investing institutions towards focusing on short-term portfolio investment performance. These institutions are competing for savers' funds in the retail market as well as for other portfolio management business. Portfolio performance figures are published regularly in the financial press, with the position of individual funds and investment houses in the league tables identified, and to attract and retain business, managers have to be able to demonstrate a successful investment record. Of course long-term as well as short-term performance is publicized, and a consistently good long-term performance is an important selling point. But a poor short-term performance, even over periods as short as a year, puts a fund management group at a severe competitive disadvantage.

Fund managers are bound therefore to be concerned about their short-term record. However much they may believe that a company will perform well in the long run, an expectation of short-term difficulties makes a shareholding less attractive, and institutional investors are often distinctly unhappy when companies try to preserve their long-term competitiveness at the expense of a lower share price in the short-term.

The pressure to produce good short-run performance figures also influences portfolio managers' responses to takeover bids. If they believe that the share price will fall should the bid be allowed to lapse, they are tempted to accept the bid or sell the shares in the market, even when they have confidence in the company's existing management.[8] As a result, company managers cannot rely on the support of institutional investors.

The threat of a takeover makes company managers feel vulnerable. No matter that it may increase the value of the shareholders' investments, it usually does little for the career prospects of the incumbent executive management. The risk of a hostile takeover, and the consequential threat to careers, is greater in the UK (and in other Anglo-Saxon countries) than in most other western European countries or Japan; and it is, of course, heightened by any temporary share price weakness.

This is not necessarily undesirable because a financial system in which takeovers are comparatively common does have some advantages. Inferior management teams can be replaced relatively easily by others who, presumably, will use the company's resources more effectively and so add to the efficiency of the economy. The threat of takeover also provides a discipline and incentive to managements to employ their company's resources as profitably as possible, rather than diverting them for their own benefit.

There is some merit in both of these arguments, and there are many examples of companies whose performance has improved dramatically after they were taken over. However, studies of the effects of takeovers on companies' performance suggest that this is the exception rather than the rule – on average takeovers do not seem to have led to an improvement in the performance overall of the merged companies. Moreover, while considered in isolation the discipline on managements can be expected to have a positive effect on company performance, other aspects of the takeover phenomenon may have a number of negative effects. In well-managed as well as poorly-managed companies the risk of a takeover bid creates a climate of uncertainty, and with share price weakness increasing the risk, discourages policies which, though likely to be beneficial in the long-run, would impinge on short-term profits. Even at the best of times companies employ advisers to consider how to avoid the threat of a takeover, diverting management attention from other more productive tasks. Furthermore, far from providing an incentive to better management, the threat of a takeover may prove debilitating, in that it lowers staff morale and makes it harder to retain and recruit able members of staff without paying over the odds.

It is difficult to sustain the argument that the system of corporate governance in the UK and other Anglo-Saxon countries – which is characterized by arms-length relationships between financiers and industrial and commercial companies, and in which contested takeovers are common – is conducive to either long-term investment and risk-taking in industry or strong economic performance. At the very least it is obvious that the closer relations which exist in countries such as France, Germany and Japan have not prevented higher levels of investment and, in most respects, superior economic performance.

Macroeconomic efficiency

The levels of *saving and investment* are aspects of macroeconomic efficiency in the economy, and they are aspects on which the financial system clearly has some influence. But it is important to recognize that the financial system is not the sole, or even the main, determinant of the levels of saving and investment. For example, saving is affected by the demographic characteristics of the population, investment by the opportunities for profitable investment in industry and commerce; both are affected by government policies on public sector investment and the size of the public sector surplus or deficit; and the cost of capital generally in Britain is strongly affected by worldwide economic and financial conditions, on which the UK system has only a minor impact.

Nevertheless, the financial system does have a significant influence, and there is no doubt that the financial institutions in Britain have been a powerful force in encouraging and mobilizing personal saving. This can certainly be said of both insurance companies and financial advisers who market savings actively and who have lobbied successfully in favour of funded occupational and personal pensions, which generate much more saving than the unfunded government pension schemes in this and many other countries. It has also been true of institutions, such as building societies, which promoted private home ownership and the saving that went with it. Weighing against this, however, the financial system has also encouraged a high level of borrowing by the personal sector, for general consumption as well as for investment in housing, which tends to reduce the level of aggregate personal saving.

On the investment side the financial system usually has a facilitating rather than a promotional role. Funds are made available to (some of) those who seek them, on terms which reflect prevailing market conditions, and many of the financial institutions respond to the demands made on them rather than actively encourage clients to invest more. This is true of the investing institutions which acquire their assets in the capital markets, and also for the great bulk of bank and building society lending business. On the corporate side, however, bank officers seeking lending opportunities do encourage customers to develop their businesses, provided always that the risk of loss to the bank is small.

Whether banks and others (for example, VCCs) should facilitate more investment than they do is a moot point. At a time (1991) when the banks are experiencing levels of losses on business lending which are clearly unacceptable, it is difficult to argue that this is so. Nevertheless, we should not lose sight of the possibility that the system of corporate governance in the UK may impart a bias against risk-taking and long-term investment.

The second criterion for judging the macroeconomic efficiency of the financial system is *market stability*. In terms of the volume of long-term funds passing through the system the UK performs well. There is a large and steady flow of funds through the contractual saving institutions, which is available for investment in the capital market. In terms of the funds available from the deposit-taking institutions the verdict is less clear. There is no doubt that the deregulation affecting this sector led to excess capacity and a surge of lending on terms which became ever easier in the middle and late 1980s, followed by a rather abrupt return to more conventional standards subsequently. Fluctuations in the volume of lending were therefore not simply a reflection of changes in the demand for loans, but were also caused by varying supply conditions.

With regard to stability in the price of funds the performance of the UK financial system has not been satisfactory. Fluctuations in stock market prices have been associated to a considerable degree with worldwide stock market behaviour – the lack of stability is hardly a UK phenomenon. But fluctuations in nominal interest rates on deposits and loans (including home mortgages) have reflected conditions in the UK. It would be a mistake to blame the financial system for these conditions – the primary causes were failures of government policy – but the financial institutions cannot escape some responsibility for the strength of the boom in credit generally, for the property boom and for the excessive level of corporate financial activity in the late eighties. The high interest rates required at the end of the eighties were a response to this speculative fever.

It follows that the contribution of the financial system to *macroeconomic stability* must be called in question. Speculative booms and slumps disrupt economic stability. Again it is the government that has the main task of ensuring that financial conditions contribute to economic stability and growth, with its control of short-term interest rates the principal weapon. But that task is not made any easier either by swings in confidence in the financial sector, which have to be countered by interest rate movements, or by sharp changes in the disposition of institutional investment portfolios between, for example, UK and overseas equity investments, which affect the value of the pound. Thus the very flexibility that enhances the financial sector's performance at the micro-level is liable to create difficulties for macroeconomic policy.

While fads and fashions in the financial system cause difficulties of one kind, a failure to react quickly enough to changing circumstances causes problems of another. Experience shows that nominal interest rates adjust too slowly to inflation, so that when inflation is rising real rates of interest are low and when inflation is falling real interest rates are high. This suggests that savers are slow to believe (possibly wisely) that any trend towards higher or lower inflation will continue. Since rising inflation normally means that there is excess demand which should be discouraged by high real rates, and falling inflation is usually associated with slack demand warranting lower rates, this is exactly the opposite of what is required for macro-economic stability. It is not something which can be cured readily – people are entitled to be sceptical of government pledges to reduce inflation until they have actually delivered – though it can of course be met by a countercyclical fiscal policy.

Conclusion

When its efficiency is judged by reference to microeconomic criteria the UK financial system scores very well. Savers and borrowers usually have plenty of choice, it is a flexible system, large-scale funding seldom presents problems, pricing is fair, and there is a good supply of equity capital for normal purposes. Moreover, in most areas costs are kept down by keen competition, though the marketing of some retail financial products appears to be an exception.

In terms of macroeconomic efficiency the performance of the financial system leaves more to be desired. The system of corporate governance in the UK and its effects on investment and growth are, to say the least, controversial. While the speculative boom of the late eighties can be attributed partly to the accompanying deregula-tion and structural change, as well as to worldwide financial conditions at the time, it was also a symptom of a market-oriented system subject to swings of confidence and fashion. When the latest episode has receded in financiers' memories there is a danger that they, or their successors, will behave in the same way again. The conflict between a competitive system, substantially free of economic controls, which promotes microeconomic efficiency, and a more controlled system, likely to deliver greater macroeconomic stability, has not been resolved.

Notes

1 A systematic tendency to underestimate the final effect of new information would mean that investors could expect shares which fell after some news to fall further subsequently, and those that rose to rise further subsequently; this does not in fact occur.
2 Against this, it can be argued that firms may be more willing to undertake *risky* investment projects with retained funds, whose use they do not have to justify publicly, than with external finance, and this may help to counter any bias against risk-taking in the system.

3 Taxes do affect yields if the market is segmented, so that securities of a particular kind are held by groups with one tax status, while other securities are held by groups with a different tax status. The most important instances are preference shares, which are typically held by taxable funds, and low-coupon gilt-edged stocks, which are also attractive to tax-paying private investors.
4 Of course, prudential regulations are intended to provide other benefits to users to set against these costs.
5 Much of the funding in 1989 to 1991 went into assured letting schemes, with the clear intention that the properties should revert to private owner-occupation after five years had elapsed.
6 In this respect British banks differ from those in France, where technical experts are employed more widely, and in Germany, where there appears to be greater career mobility between banking and other industries. However, in many other countries the practice is similar to that in the UK.
7 For most industries there are notable exceptions to this general rule, in the form of individual analysts whose work is highly regarded by practitioners in the industry.
8 It can be argued that this is in their liability-holders' interest, because the proceeds can be invested elsewhere in the market, in principle on terms no less favourable than those previously available on their existing investment if the market was efficient in valuing shares. They should therefore decline a bid only if they believe that the shares were under-valued previously by at least as much as the bid premium.

Select bibliography and further reading

General references

Van Horne, James, C. (1990), *Financial Market Rates and Flows*, 3rd edn, Prentice-Hall International.
Goacher, D.J. and Curwen, P.J. (1987), *British Non-Bank Financial Intermediaries*, Allen and Unwin.
Green, Christopher J. and Llewellyn, David T. (1991), *Surveys in Monetary Economics Volume 2: Financial Markets and Institutions*, Basil Blackwell.
Bank of England, *Quarterly Bulletin* (*BEQB*).
National Westminster Bank, *Quarterly Review* (*NWBR*).
Financial Statistics, HMSO, monthly.
United Kingdom National Accounts (The CSO Blue Book), HMSO, monthly.

Specific topics

Flow of funds system (chapter 2)

Van Horne, ch. 2.
Bain, A.D. (1977), 'Flow of funds analysis', in Royal Economic Society, *Surveys of Applied Economics*, vol. 2, Macmillan Press, pp. 73–111.

Theory of financial intermediation (chapters 3, 4)

Van Horne, ch. 3.
Hirshleifer, J. (1970), *Investment, Interest and Capital*, Prentice-Hall International.

Loanable funds approach to interest rates (chapter 5)

Goodhart, C.A.E. (1984), 'Disequilibrium money – a note', in *Monetary Theory and Practice: the UK Experience*, Macmillan, ch. X.
Bain, A.D. and McGregor, Peter G. (1985), 'Buffer-stock monetarism and the theory of financial buffers', *The Manchester School*, pp. 385–403.

Structure of interest rates (chapter 5)

Van Horne, chs 4, 5.
Lutz, Friedrich A. (1967), *The Theory of Interest*, D. Reidel Publishing Company, chs 17–19.

Personal sector financing (chapter 7)

BEQB (1987), 'The financial behaviour of the UK personal sector 1976–85', pp. 223–33.

Company sector financing (chapter 8)

BEQB (1988), 'The financial behaviour of industrial and commercial companies 1970–86', pp. 75–82.

Deposit-taking institutions (chapter 11)

Goacher and Curwen, ch. 5.
Lewis, Mervyn K. (1991), 'Theory and practice of the banking firm', in Green and Llewellyn, pp. 116–65.
BEQB (1990), 'The development of the building societies sector in the 1980s', pp. 503–10.
Lomax, David F. (1987), 'Risk–asset ratios – a new departure in supervisory policy', in *NWBR*, August 1987, pp. 14–25.
Boleat, Mark (1987), 'Building societies: the new supervisory framework', in *NWBR*, August 1987, pp. 26–34.

Long-term savings institutions (chapter 12)

Goacher and Curwen, chs 7–10.
BEQB (1991), 'The development of pension funds – an international comparison', pp. 380–90.

Terry, Nick (1988), 'The changing UK pension system', in *NWBR*, May 1988, pp. 2–13.

Specialized financial institutions (chapter 13)

Goacher and Curwen, ch. 5.
BEQB (1990), 'Venture capital in the United Kingdom', pp. 78–83.

Financial markets (chapter 14)

Thomas, W.A. (1989), *The Securities Market*, Philip Allan.
Harrington, Richard (1991), 'The London financial markets', in Green and Llewellyn, pp. 260–302.
BEQB (1985), 'Change in the Stock Exchange and regulation in the City', pp. 544–50.
BEQB (1990), 'New equity issues in the United Kingdom', pp. 243–52.
BEQB (1989), 'The gilt-edged market since Big Bang', pp. 49–58.
BEQB (1989), 'The market in foreign exchange in London', pp. 531–5.
BEQB (1989), 'Bank of England operations in the sterling money markets', pp. 92–103.
BEQB (1990), 'The role of brokers in the London money markets', pp. 221–7.
BEQB (1989), 'The market in currency options', pp. 235–41.
BEQB (1989), 'A survey of interest rate futures', pp. 388–98.

Regulation in the financial system (chapter 15)

Thomas, W.A. (1989), *The Securities Market*, Philip Allan, ch. 10.
Goacher and Curwen, ch. 12.
Hall, Maximilian B. (1991), 'Financial regulation in the UK: deregulation or regulation?', in Green and Llewellyn, pp. 166–209.

Efficiency of the financial system (chapter 16)

Llewellyn, David T. (1991), 'Structural change in the British financial system', in Green and Llewellyn, pp. 210–59.

Index

Abbey National Bank 19, 189, 198
accelerated depreciation
    allowances 139–40
advances *see* loans
allocation of funds 84–6
arbitrage 263
asset transformation 51–71, 219
Assisted Areas 140

balancing item 30
bank bills *see* commercial bills
Banking Act 1987 180, 272
bank lending *see* loans
Bank of England 65, 88
banks 18, 63, 180, 193–8, 282
    British merchant 197
    clearing 64, 65, 282
    other British 197–8
    overseas 198
    regulation of 181–4, 186–7
    retail 195–6
    sterling lending 194–5
    see also deposit-taking institutions
banks and building societies
        sector 179–202
    deposits and lending 190–3
    see also deposit-taking institutions
Basle agreement 181
Big Bang 18, 246–8, 253–4
bought deals 247, 256
brokers and advisers 4, 5, 254–5, 260,
        276
    in stock market 240, 246–8, 249
buffer assets 88
building societies 18, 63, 64, 180, 198–
        201

regulatory requirements 183–4, 187
Building Societies Act 1986 183, 272
Building Societies Commission 187,
        272
Business Expansion Scheme
        (BES) 149–50, 234–5, 295

capital issues by UK companies
        243–4, 248–53
central government 22–5, 152, 160–4
centralized mortgage lenders 236–7
certificates of deposit (CDs) 256–8
Chinese walls 273
commercial bills 80, 88, 127, 137, 163–
        4, 256–60
commercial paper 127, 256–8
*Committee to Review the Functioning of
        Financial Institutions* 4, 15, 146,
        148, 217
company representatives 280
company sector 124–51
    balance sheet 124–8
    sources and uses of funds 140–6
compensation for loss 273, 277–9
competition
    between financial institutions 83–5,
        183–4, 188–90, 288, 297
    and regulation 282, 284–5
compliance 273, 275
consumer credit 49, 50, 230–1, 283–4
contract hire 229, 230
contractual saving 115
controls *see* regulation
corporate governance 298–302
corporate venturing 235
cost of funds 72–3

council house sales 24, 33, 153–4, 156
credit *see* loans
credit cards 117, 119–20

debentures 126
debt *see* loans
debt capital/finance 128–34, 136–8, 147
debt/equity ratio *see* gearing, primary
default risk 53, 88
  and charge for loans 57, 79–80, 84,
    132
  control 54–8, 131
  and institutions' capital 57
deposits 6, 7, 179–80
  banks and building societies 18, 19,
    73, 88, 106–7, 122
  foreign currency 29, 31, 32
  money-market 256–9
  retail and wholesale 19, 65, 185
  sterling 29, 30, 31, 32
  see also banks; building societies
deposit-taking institutions 18, 63–5,
    179–202
  capital 181–4
  liquidity 184–7
  sources of income 187–8
  see also banks and building societies
    sector; banks; building societies
deregulation 17, 18, 49, 189, 190
derivatives 6, 21, 239, 254, 262–5
development capital companies *see*
  venture capital companies
discount houses/market 13, 20, 88, 256,
    258–60
distribution function 241–2, 243, 249
diversification 60, 61, 81, 82, 276

efficiency of the system 286–306
  dynamic 297–8
  macroeconomic 84, 302–5
  operational 296–7
  in resource allocation 14, 84–6, 204,
    287–302
  and taxes and subsidies 294–6
  technical 292–3
elasticity 287–90
end-users *see* ultimate savers and
  borrowers
enterprise zones 139
equity assets 7
equity capital/finance 10, 52–3, 128,
  133, 134–5, 145–6, 147

equity risk 53, 58–62, 80–2, 129–34,
  135
equity withdrawal 49, 112
Eurobonds 242–4, 245
European Monetary System 87
European monetary union 87, 100
Exchange Rate Mechanism (ERM) 83,
  87, 94, 97–100, 261
exchange rate policy 170
expectations effects 79
export credit 138
Export Credits Guarantee
  Department 138
external finance 144–6, 147

factoring 21, 147, 180, 236
fees and commissions 187, 189, 274
FIMBRA 274, 275, 279
finance houses 227–31
financial assets, net acquisition of 27–8,
  30
financial companies and institutions
  sector 22–32
financial institutions/intermediaries 3,
  4, 5, 10–13, 18–21
financial instruments 6–8, 287
  characteristics of 7–8
  derivatives *see* derivatives
financial markets 3, 4, 10–13, 18–21,
  239–66
  organized 5, 7, 12, 62–3, 262–4
  retail and wholesale 19, 64, 65,
    288–9
financial services 12, 180, 270
Financial Services Act 1986
  (FSA) 272–5, 279–81
financial surplus (deficit) 25–32
flow-of-funds table 27–32
foreign exchange market 3, 239, 260–2
foreign exchange reserves 160, 162–4,
  170–1, 174–5
foreign securities *see* overseas securities
forward contracts 262, 264
fund management 203–6
futures contracts 262–3

gearing 128–34
  income 130
  primary 129
  secondary 136
general government sector 22–32, 153,
  166

general insurance funds 203, 204, 219–21
Gilt-Edged Market Makers (GEMMs) 253–6
gilt-edged securities 88, 153, 155, 164
   index-linked 20
government grants 139–40

hedging 263
high-risk investment 81, 225, 232–3, 291–2
hire purchase 227, 229, 230–1
house prices 17, 108, 112, 118–19
housing boom 24, 119, 283–4

IMRO 274
independence 59
independent intermediaries 280
index-linked securities 211, 253
industrial and commercial companies sector 22–32
information 10, 11–12
   costs *see* transactions costs
inheritance tax 122
insurance companies 10, 19; *see also* general insurance funds; life assurance funds
Insurance Companies Act 1982 272
Inter-Dealer Brokers (IDBs) 254
interest rates *see* rate of interest
intermediation effects 48
internal finance 144–5, 147
International Stock Exchange (ISE) 13, 20, 239, 243–56, 275
investing institutions 19, 203–26, 300–1
   and the capital market 224–6
investment 4, 10, 22–5, 52
   abroad *see* overseas finance/investment
   and asset transformation 68–70
   in Britain 21–5
   and financial system 38–42, 48–50, 302–3
   and rate of interest 74–8
investment trust companies 19, 203, 204, 221–3
invoice discounting *see* factoring
issuing house 249–50

jobbers 240, 246

LAUTRO 274
leasing 24, 125, 138–9, 147, 180, 227–30
legislative factors 115–17, 217–18
life assurance and pension funds 19, 30, 31, 106–7, 109, 122, 123, 155, 203–14, 217–19
life assurance and pension policies 116, 206–9
liquid assets 142–3, 185–7
liquidity 7, 9, 12, 51, 62–6, 184–7, 246
liquidity premia 79, 84
loanable funds 73–8
Loan Guarantee Scheme (LGS) 148–9
loans 6, 7, 52, 73, 127, 179–80
   bridging 120
   consumer 117, 119, 227, 230–1, 283–4
   house purchase/mortgage 17, 30, 31, 49, 108, 116, 118, 120, 121–2, 157–8, 207, 209, 236–7, 283–4
   long-term 9, 126, 128, 136–8
   medium-term 120, 127, 137, 138
   overdrafts 117, 137
   project 79, 127, 137–8
   and rate of interest 74–8
   rationing 17, 73, 108
   retail and wholesale 83
   short-term 120, 137–8
   sterling bank 18, 19, 29, 30, 31, 32
local authorities 22–5, 152, 157–9
   debt 155
London International Financial Futures Exchange (LIFFE) 239, 262, 264, 275
London Traded Options Market (LTOM) 262–3, 264
long-term assets 87–8

Macmillan Committee/gap 147, 234
management buy-out/buy-in 232–3
margin 187
marketability 7, 184, 225
market factors 116–17, 218
market makers 6, 20, 63, 240–1, 242–3, 246–8, 258–60; *see also* financial markets, organized
market stability 303–4
matching 204–5, 210–11, 220
maturity 7, 78–9, 184
maturity transformation 10, 11, 64, 69; *see also* liquidity

mergers *see* takeovers
mezzanine finance 138
monetary policy 73, 159, 162–4, 258–60, 281–4
money 73, 87
  demand for 89
  and long-term assets 87–9
  and rate of interest 74–8
money market 3, 13, 19–20, 239, 256–8
money market brokers 13, 256, 258
mortgages *see* loans

National Loans Fund (NLF) 158, 160
national savings 88, 106, 122, 163–4
new issue market 13
nominal value 7
non-marketable tenancy rights 106, 107, 108
notes and coin 30, 88, 106–7, 163, 164

offer for sale 250
options contracts 262–4
organized markets *see* financial markets, organized
origination function 239–40, 241, 242–3, 249
overdrafts *see* loans
overseas finance/investment 31–2, 128, 143, 145, 170–5, 212, 213–14
overseas sector 26, 32, 170–5
  bank deposits, loans etc. 174
  direct investment 172–3
  portfolio investment 173–4
owner-occupied housing 108, 112, 116

payments facilities 3, 179, 286
pension funds *see* life assurance and pension funds
pension schemes 112–13, 115–16, 122, 208, 209–10, 214–17, 297
perpetuity 84, 86
Personal Equity Plan (PEP) 116, 296
personal pensions 116, 122, 297
personal sector 22–32, 106
  borrowing 117–20
  choice of assets 115–17
  financial transactions 120–3
  liquid assets 113–14, 122
  saving and investment 22–5, 105–23
  wealth 106–9
placing 135, 250
polarization 280

position-taking 187–8, 276
primary market 239, 242–4, 248–53, 255–6; *see* also gilt-edged market
privatization 24, 31, 152, 153, 156, 165, 219, 251–2
privileged circuit 123, 295
profits 83–4, 85
property 8, 24, 77, 139, 145, 146, 172, 211, 212, 214
public corporations 22–32, 152, 159–60
  debt 155
public sector 152–69
  balance sheet 154–7
  debt 29, 156–7, 166–8
  saving and investment 153–4, 294
  stocks 20
  see also gilt-edged securities
public sector borrowing 17–18, 164–9
  financial deficit (PSFD) 164–5
  requirement (PSBR) 164–6
Public Works Loan Board 158–9

rate of interest 13–15
  determinants of 65, 72–84, 87–99, 153
  and ERM 97–100
  and exchange rates 93–5, 170
  and fiscal and regulatory barriers 93, 95
  and inflation 82–3, 96–7, 304
  and investment 45–8
  and monetary policy 90–3, 94, 260
  nominal and real 82, 84, 96–7
  and political risks 93, 95–6
  and resource allocation 292–6
  retail and wholesale 88
  and saving 42–5, 112
  structure of 78–84
  transformation 65–6
  see also yield
real value certainty 7, 9
Recognised Investment Exchanges (RIEs) 275
Recognised Professional Bodies (RPBs) 272, 274–5
Regional Selective Assistance 140
regulation 6, 83, 84, 260, 269–85, 294–5
  economic 281–5
  prudential 270–81
regulators 4, 6, 66
residual error 26

Retirement Pensions Scheme 115
rights issue 135, 251
risk 7, 85, 276, 291–2, 298–302
    transformation 10, 11, 52–3, 69, 219
    see also default risk; diversification;
        equity risk
risk assets ratio 181–4

safety 9, 10, 51, 219
savers and investors 4, 8–10, 51
saving 4
    and asset transformation 68–70
    in Britain 21–5
    and financial system 38–42, 216–19,
        302–3
    and inflation 113–14
    mobilizing 10, 12, 37–50
    motives for 109–10
    and rate of interest 74–8, 112, 217
    and regulation 279–81
    theories of 110–14
Savings and Loan Associations 65
savings ratio 108, 110, 111, 112, 114
Scottish Enterprise 150, 234
secondary banking crisis 65
secondary market 240–1, 244–8, 253–5
Securities and Investments Board
    (SIB) 272, 274–5
securities markets 19–20, 239–56, 297
    gilt-edged 253–6
    international 242–4
    UK 244–52
    unlisted 20, 150, 252–3
    see also primary market; secondary
        market
security 132; *see also* safety
Self-Regulating Organisations
    (SROs) 272, 274, 275, 277
senior debt 138
SFA 274
shares
    building society *see* deposits; building
        societies
    ordinary and preference 6, 7, 88, 126
short-term assets *see* liquid assets
short-termism 300–2
single capacity 246
small firms 20, 135, 146–50, 225–6,
    235, 288–9, 291, 292
SMEs 140, 150; *see also* small firms
Social Security Act 1986 207, 208
specialized financial institutions 227–38

speculation 263
State Earnings-Related Pension
    Scheme (SERPS) 215
Stock Exchange *see* International Stock
    Exchange
Stock Exchange automated quotation
    system (SEAQ) 247–8
Stock Exchange Money Brokers
    (SEMBs) 254
stock market *see* securities markets
    crash 18, 77, 122–3
structural factors 115, 117, 217
swaps 242, 261, 262

Takeover Panel 272
takeovers 143, 144–5, 146, 172, 180,
    251, 301–2
Tax Exempt Special Savings Account
    (TESSA) 116, 296
term *see* maturity
touch 248
trade credit 127
transactions costs 10, 12, 13, 62, 66–8,
    83–4, 246
transactions in financial assets *see* flow-
    of-funds table
Treasury bills 88, 155, 163–4, 175, 256–
    60
turnover 244–6, 253–5, 258–9, 261–2

ultimate savers and borrowers 4
unit trusts 19, 180, 203, 204, 223–4
UK company securities 30, 31, 32, 106–
    7, 122, 123, 212–13, 220–1; *see also*
    shares, ordinary and preference
Unlisted Securities Market (USM) *see*
    securities markets, unlisted

vendor placing 251
venture capital companies (VCCs) 21,
    148, 149, 150, 180, 232–35

Welsh Development Agency 150, 234
Wilson Committee *see Committee to
    Review the Functioning of Financial
    Institutions*

yield 9, 13, 84
    and asset prices 90
    dividend 81, 84, 135
    equity 80–1, 135
    on long-term assets 87, 89–90